GCE **AS Level**

AS Level for Edexcel

Applied ICT

Series editor:
K. Mary Reid

www.heinemann.co.uk
✓ Free online support
✓ Useful weblinks
✓ 24 hour online ordering

01865 888058

Heinemann

Inspiring generations

Heinemann Educational Publishers
Halley Court, Jordan Hill, Oxford OX2 8EJ
Part of Harcourt Education

Heinemann is a registered trademark of
Harcourt Education Limited

© Alan Jarvis, Jenny Lawson, Andrew Smith, Sharon Yull, 2005

First published 2005

10 09 08 07 06
10 9 8 7 6 5 4 3 2

British Library Cataloguing in Publication Data is available
from the British Library on request.

10-digit ISBN: 0 435462 01 6
13-digit ISBN: 978 0 435462 01 7

Edited by David Kelshaw, Fiona Mcdonald
Designed by Lorraine Inglis
Typeset by Thomson Digital, India

Original illustrations © Harcourt Education Limited, 2005

Cover design by Wooden Ark Studios

Printed by Bath Colourbooks

Cover photo: © Photonica

Acknowledgements
Every effort has been made to contact copyright holders of material reproduced in this book.
Any omissions will be rectified in subsequent printings if notice is given to the publishers.

Websites
There are links to relevant websites in this book. In order to ensure that the links are up to date,
that the links work, and that the sites are not inadvertently linked to sites that could be
considered offensive, we have made the links available on the Heinemann website at
www.heinemann.co.uk/hotlinks. When you access the site the express code is 2016P.

Please note that the examples of websites suggested in this book were up to date at the time of
writing. It is essential for tutors to preview each site before using it to ensure that the URL is still
accurate and the content is appropriate. We suggest that tutors bookmark useful sites and consider
enabling students to access them through the school or college intranet.

Contents

Acknowledgements

The authors and publisher would like to thank all those who have granted permission to reproduce copyright material.

Microsoft product screen shots reprinted with permission of Microsoft Corporation.

Pipex screengrab/with permission from PIPEX
Choice Point article by Paul Roberts/TheStandard.com
Bill Gates gets 4 million emails a day/Copyright Guardian Newspapers Limited 2004
Yahoo! Messenger screengrab reproduced with permission of Yahoo! Inc. © Yahoo! Inc. and the Yahoo! Logo are trademarks of Yahoo! Inc.
DVLA/Crown copyright material is reproduced with the permission of the Controller of HMSO
Interactive online game/Weboggle.shackworks.com
eBay screengrab/eBay
The Digital Divide/BT
flybmi material pages 14, 15, 17/Images reproduced with kind permission of bmi
Gerry Baptist
Macromedia
Edexcel
redhouse
writersdock.co.uk
Yahoo! geocities reproduced with permission of Yahoo! Inc. © Yahoo! Inc. YAHOO! and the YAHOO! logo are trademarks of Yahoo! Inc.
Winzip is a registered trademark of Winzip International LLC. All rights reserved.
McAfee security center

The extract from the Computer Misuse Act is reproduced under the terms of Crown Copyright Policy Guidance issued by HMSO

The authors and publisher would like to thank the following for permission to reproduce photographs:

Alamy/page 20
Corbis/page 24
Getty Images/photodisc/page 40
Courtesy of Apple/page 48
Harcourt Education Ltd/Gareth Boden/pages 136, 141 (2), 142, 143, 144, 147, 148, 154 (2), 155, 158, 232, 236 (3)
Harcourt Education Ltd/Peter Morris/page 144
Getty Images/Photodisc/page 150

Every effort has been made to contact copyright holders of material produced in this book. Any omissions will be rectified in subsequent printings if notice is given to the publishers.

Introduction

This is one in a series of four volumes that covers the Edexcel qualifications in Applied Information and Communication Technology for GCE. The books are organised like this:

* AS (Single Award), which covers units 1 to 3

* AS (Double Award), which covers units 1 to 6

* A2 (Single Award), which covers units 7, 8, 10, 11, 12

* A2 (Double Award), which covers units 7 to 14.

The two AS Level (Single and Double Award) qualifications are covered by one book each. The two A Level (Single and Double Award) qualifications are covered by two books each, one at AS and one at A2 level.

This book covers the six units that are offered in the AS (Double Award):

* Unit 1: The information age

* Unit 2: The digital economy

* Unit 3: The knowledge worker

* Unit 4: System design and installation

* Unit 5: Web development

* Unit 6: Technical support.

To complete the AS (Double Award) you should study all six units. To complete the AS (Single Award) you should study Units 1 to 3 only.

In addition, 'Standard Ways of Working' runs as a common theme through all the units and is covered separately. Students are advised to read this (pages IX–XVIII) before starting on the units.

Assessment

Your achievements on this qualification will be assessed through portfolios of evidence and an examination. Portfolios will be assessed internally and the examination will be assessed externally.

All the AS units except Unit 3 will be assessed internally. You will be expected to construct an e-portfolio for each unit. Further guidance on this is given in Standard Ways of Working. Unit 3 will be assessed externally, through a 2 hour examination. In preparation for the examination you will be given a scenario to study. The examination itself will be taken at a computer where you will be presented with additional e-resources, such as a spreadsheet model, to help you solve a problem. Your solution will be submitted online.

Further information

You can find further information about this qualification at www.edexcel.org.uk. Remember to search for GCE Applied ICT. You can download the complete specification, which gives full details of all the units, both AS and A2, and how they are assessed. This document is nearly 300 pages long. Edexcel also provide a one page Student Guide, which could help you if you are trying to decide whether to study for this qualification.

A Tutor Resource File will provide additional material for these units.

We hope you enjoy your studies and wish you every success.

K Mary Reid
April 2005

Standard ways of working

Introduction

As an experienced ICT user, you already know a great deal about how to get the best out of your ICT equipment. But you can probably learn some new tricks.

In this chapter you will be comparing the way that you work with the standard ways of working which ICT professionals use. This should help you to act responsibly and legally, to watch out for your own safety, and to save time. Mastering these ways of working will definitely impress a future employer.

File management

There are a number of questions to ask yourself to ensure that you employ standard ways of managing your files. Do you:

* save your work regularly
* use sensible filenames
* organise your files into directories/folders
* make backup copies
* choose appropriate file formats
* limit access to confidential or sensitive files
* use effective virus protection
* use 'readme' files where appropriate to provide technical information, e.g. system requirements?

Saving work regularly

It is important to save your work regularly to avoid losing it if your computer crashes. Some people learn this lesson the hard way - as a result of their computer crashing. To avoid it happening:

* save any new file as soon as you start it
* if you can, configure the software to autosave your work at regular intervals.

Using sensible filenames

Which of these is a sensible file name:

* myfile.doc

* janejones.jpg

* Doom.pdf

* Unit 3 Project v1.doc?

Of course, what counts as 'sensible' depends on what you are going to do with the file. At work, you would probably have to pass a file to someone else to use or to read and comment on. The filename should clearly identify:

* what the file contains

* the version number (where appropriate).

Setting up directory/folder structures

You can very quickly build up a large collection of working files, such as word processing documents, databases, spreadsheet workbooks, etc. If you are using Microsoft Window® then these will be normally be placed in the My Documents folder (also known as a directory). You can create as many extra folders as you like within My Documents.

You might think it a good idea to place all your word processing documents in one folder, all your desk top publishing publications in another folder and so on. But many people prefer to organise their work by subject matter instead.

Think about the sorts of activities you will use your computer for, and how you can most usefully organise related files to suit your needs.

When you are working on a networked PC at your centre or at work, then you will only be able to save files in My Documents or possibly in a folder that you share with a group. On a home computer you will find that you can create folders anywhere you like, and you may want to set up new folders elsewhere on the hard disk system.

Making backups

It is very reassuring to know that your files are backed up. If the system does malfunction then you will be able to retrieve the work that you have spent so much time over.

On a network, the complete system will be backed up at least once a day. This will happen automatically. You might like to ask the network administrator at your centre about the backup procedures that are followed.

On your home computer, you are responsible for making sure that backups are created. You can do this in several ways:

* You can set up some software applications to make a backup of each file as you create it. Whenever you save the file the previously saved version is renamed as the backup copy. Look out for **Options** or **Preferences** in the main menus.

* Copy important files to an external medium such as a CD or external hard disk. You should do this on a regular basis. Important files could include your email address book or key documents that you are working on for assessment.

* Use the Backup utility that is provided with some versions of operating system software.

Choosing appropriate file formats

Did you know that you can save a word processing file in half a dozen different formats?

For example, Figure 1 shows the different options offered in Microsoft Word. If you go to the **File** menu and select **Save As**, you will see all these options under **Save As Type**.

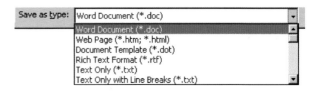

FIGURE 1 *Format options*

The last part of the filename, such as .doc or .txt, indicates which format was used for the file. Do you know what each format can be used for?

* *word document (*.doc):* a normal word processed document

* *web page (*.htm; *.html):* for converting into a format suitable for uploading to the web. This is useful for quick conversions of word processed documents for web use, but should not be used for general web design

* *document template (*.doc):* a document that can be used at any time as a basis for other

documents. It will be stored with other templates and available when you create a new page

* *rich text format* (*.rtf*): a simplified word processed format which can be read by many software applications, including older word processing packages. The formatting of the text is preserved, but some of the more specific features, such as footnotes and macros, will be lost

* *text only* (*.txt*), and *text only with line breaks* (*.txt*): the simplest possible text files, containing ASCII characters, with or without the line break character. These files can be read by any program that handles text.

> **Key term**
>
> ASCII (American Standard Code for Information Interchange) is a set of binary codes that are used to represent text characters in computer systems and communications.

Similarly, images can be saved in a variety of formats including:

* *bitmap* (*.bmp*): stores a colour value for each pixel in the image

* *JPEG* (*.jpg*): a method of compressing bitmaps so they use less memory. This is widely used for photographs and is one of the standard formats used on the World Wide Web

* *graphics interchange format* (*.gif*): another compressed bitmap format used on the Web. It is limited to 256 colour values, so is often used for simple diagrams and icons that do not require finely graduated colour

* *portable network graphics image* (*.png*): a compressed bitmap format that is replacing gifs on the Web

* *tagged image file format* (*.tif*): a widely used bitmap format for storing images on PCs

* *flash movie* (*.swf*): a vector graphic animation format used to develop animations and interactive applications for websites.

There are also a number of specialist formats that are only used by specific graphics applications, as well as audio and video formats. You do need to understand the differences between all these formats, and others, in order to use them effectively.

When you prepare work for publication you should consider using formats that are 'read only' (i.e. people can access but cannot make changes to). For example, if you allow people to download a word processed file from a website, they will be able to change it without your knowledge. A common 'read only' format is pdf (portable document format) format. You can convert a word processed file into a pdf before you make it available to the general public. You will need to use pdf converter software to do this (e.g. Adobe Acrobat).

Limiting access to confidential or sensitive files

If you want to protect your work from other people, you can create a password for it. You may have to read the Help files for your application to find out how to do this.

However, beware of creating password-protected documents if you want to share them with a teacher, assessor or work colleague.

Using effective virus protection

Virus protection is not an optional extra these days. You should refuse to work on any PC that is not adequately protected.

Not only should the right kind of software be installed, but the virus definition files should be updated regularly. In many systems, virus definitions are updated every few hours. This is because new viruses can be transmitted via e-mail to many thousands of computers within minutes.

Networks normally have high levels of virus protection. Check the level of protection that has been installed on the network that you use.

On a home computer, you should download virus protection software if it is not already installed. You will have to pay a modest annual subscription to keep your virus definition files up to date, but this should not be neglected.

Using 'readme' files where appropriate

A ReadMe file contains basic information and advice for a software application. It is supplied as part of the application, ensuring that important information about the application will always be available to the user, even if supporting printed documentation is subsequently lost. It is usually created in a simple text editor, such as Notepad, although you can use a word processing package, then save it in *.txt format.

Personal effectiveness

There are a number of questions to ask yourself to ensure that you employ standard ways of maximising your personal effectiveness. Do you:

* customise settings in applications
* create and use shortcuts
* use available sources of help
* use a plan to help you organise your work and meet deadlines?

Selecting appropriate ICT tools and techniques

One mark of your effectiveness as a student or employee is whether you use the right tools for the job. For example, you may be asked to produce a simple name and address list for an organisation. You can create this in a word processing package, a spreadsheet or in a database. To decide which to use you need to be able to ask relevant questions, do you want to:

* be able to print out mailing labels
* sort the addresses in different ways
* search the data
* mailmerge the data with letters
* add other types of data?

You will use the answers to such questions to help you determine the ICT tools and techniques appropriate to the task at hand.

Customising settings in applications

It is always helpful and more efficient if you customise the software applications and operating system to match your own needs and preferences. Some examples include:

* create your own document templates, e.g. to standardise the appearance of your documents
* create macros for commonly performed tasks, so that you can click a single button or combination of keystrokes instead of a series of clicks to perform the same command
* add and remove menu items from the standard toolbars, and create your own toolbars.

Most applications have menu items called **Options**, **Customise** or **Preferences**. Look at these to see the possibilities for customising the settings on your computer to suit your needs better.

Creating and using shortcuts

A shortcut can be placed on your desktop or in a menu. It helps you to go straight to a file, a folder or an application that you use frequently, instead of having to drill down through layers of folders.

In Windows, you can create a shortcut to almost anything by right-clicking on its icon and selecting **Create Shortcut**. The shortcut will be placed in the same folder as the original. You can then move the shortcut to where you want it to go. You can place a shortcut in any of these locations:

* on the desktop
* in the **Start** menu or one of its submenus
* in any folder on your computer.

If you delete a shortcut, it does not delete the original file or application.

Using available sources of help

A smart employee does not know everything, but does know where to find things out. This is particularly true of ICT skills. Most people only use about 10 per cent of the facilities in a software application, but when they do need to use a new feature they learn how to use it through the Help resources.

You probably use some sources of help, but you may not be aware of all there are. Some sources are listed below:

* the CD used to install the software often contains a manual. This is meant to replace, or add to, a printed manual

* the Help menu in software applications may direct you towards:
  – tutorials
  – an index of help topics
  – an answer tool – this may be in the form of a guide like the Office Assistant
  – resources on the Web

* you should be able to find an online community, or other helpful websites, dedicated to getting the most out of your chosen software. Type the software name in your usual search engine.

Using a plan

When you begin a piece of work you should always decide when you are going to finish it. You may be set a deadline by your employer or teacher, but you would be wise to aim to finish before the deadline. Because life can sometimes get in the way of the best plans (e.g. falling sick, 'losing' work time due to unexpected events, etc.), it is a good idea to build in some buffer time, so that despite the unexpected, you can still meet the deadline.

If it is a substantial project that will take many days or weeks, you can work backwards from the deadline to decide what you need to achieve at key dates. Draw this up as a plan at the beginning, and monitor your progress during the project against the plan. The earlier you establish you are falling behind, the easier it will be to make up the time, or change the plan accordingly.

You may need to provide several different types of documents and files. Again, list what you need to do and fit them into the plan. If you do all this at the beginning you will not be in danger of getting to the end and finding that key components are missing.

Quality assurance

There are a number of questions to ask yourself to ensure that you employ standard ways of assuring the quality of your work. Do you:

* use spell check
* use grammar check
* use print preview
* proofread
* seek the views of others
* authenticate your work?

Using spell check

Unless your spelling and typing skills are perfect, you should always use check your spelling in a text document. The spell check can usually be configured through **Options** or **Preferences**, as in the Microsoft Office® example in Figure 2. You can choose to have your spelling checked as you enter it. The software will highlight the incorrect word in some way; if you right-click on the word you will be given a list of alternative spellings to choose from. For example, if you mean to type 'thorough' but accidentally type 'torough' you are offered these alternative spellings: 'thorough', 'trough', 'through', and others. If you are unsure of the correct spelling for the word you want to use, you may need to look up the alternative spellings in a traditional dictionary to find one

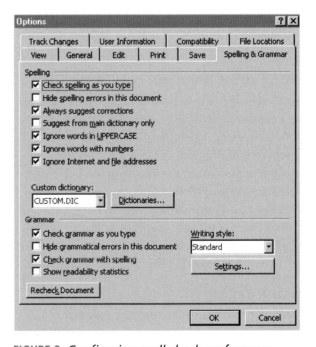

FIGURE 2 *Configuring spell check preferences*

which means the same as the one you want to use.

You can also choose to have the spellings of words corrected automatically. To do this, the spell checker draws on its huge bank of regular words. But you need to read your work carefully afterwards, because sometimes the software will 'autocorrect' a word incorrectly and your text may not make sense.

Make sure that the software is using a dictionary that is set for your language. Many software applications are pre-set for US English, and you will probably want to change this to UK English, as spellings do differ, e.g. whether words end in –ise or –ize, or –our or –or (the first in each pair being UK, the second being US spelling).

Using grammar check

The grammar check is another very useful tool, but again can produce very odd results if you do not use it intelligently and carefully check your text at the end.

It is useful to have this set up so that it checks your grammar as you write. It will then highlight errors and offer you alternatives when you right-click. Always read the corrected sentence again to yourself and ask whether it still means what you intended.

Some applications let you select the style of writing that you wish to use, e.g. formal, technical or casual.

Using print preview

You have probably wasted several sheets of paper and considerable time by printing a document before checking what it looks like, only to discover that things don't look right on the printed pages. To avoid this, go to the **File** menu and select **Print Preview** first.

Most applications allow you to change the layout, such as moving margins, in Print Preview mode. This is useful, because you can see the effect on a complete page as you make the changes.

Proofreading

Everyone makes errors when they create documents, and some of these are not detected by spell and grammar checks. Examples include:

* getting your facts wrong
* explaining things in a confusing way
* mistyping names of people and places
* writing ideas in the wrong order
* omitting sentences or paragraphs as you type, or putting them in the wrong places.

These errors can only be identified and corrected by humans, not computers.

The process of reading what you have written very carefully is known as proofreading. If a document is going to be published, like a book or leaflet, then at least two people should proofread it – the author and a second person (whose judgement can be trusted). It is very easy for the original author to overlook errors they have made, but someone else will read it with a fresh eye. Having your material read by an independent eye will not guarantee it will be error-free, but it should help.

A book, such as this one, is checked by a professional proofreader who marks up errors on the printout. These errors are corrected and then checked on subsequent sets of proofs until, ideally, the work is error-free.

Seeking views of others

Colleagues at work and fellow students can all help you to improve your documents. If you ask them to look over your work, then be prepared to do the same for them at some time. You can ask others to:

* proofread your document
* comment on the style and readability
* comment on the design and layout
* comment on the contents
* work with you to improve your work.

You need to be careful asking others to be involved with any of these aspects if the material they are looking at is to be presented as your own work. See the section on plagiarism below. If you are in any doubt about the type of help you can have, then check with your teacher or employer.

Authenticate work

On any document you should always supply, as a header/footer or at some appropriate point in the text, the following information:

* your name
* any other essential details about you, e.g. your department at work or your centre number
* the date on which you completed this version of the document.

These features identify you as the author of the document.

For assessment purposes you will have to produce further evidence to authenticate the work. This can be in the form of a monitoring checklist kept by a teacher, or witness statements. You will also be required to sign a statement that you have completed the work yourself.

Legislation and codes of practice

There are a number of questions to ask yourself to ensure that you conform to the requirements of legislation and codes of practice. Do you:

* acknowledge your sources
* respect copyright
* avoid plagiarism
* protect confidentiality?

Acknowledging sources

If you use or refer to work that someone else has done, then it is only fair to mention them. In fact, in certain circumstances, you could be breaking the law if you do not do so. There are several ways in which you can acknowledge a source:

* use a direct quote, in quotation marks, e.g.

  'Be nice to nerds. Chances are you'll end up working for one.' Bill Gates: *Business @ The Speed of Thought*

* refer to it in the text, e.g.

  Bill Gates once wrote in his book *Business @ The Speed of Thought* that you should be nice to nerds. He said that the chances are you'll end up working for one.

* use a footnote or endnote, e.g.

  It has been said that you should be nice to nerds, because the chances are you'll end up working for one.[14]

At the bottom of the page, or at end of the document, you will see this:

---

[14] Bill Gates: *Business @ The Speed of Thought*

What you should not do is to write something like this, without acknowledging that Bill Gates originally wrote it:

  I think you should be nice to nerds. After all, the chances are you'll end up working for one.

Respect copyright

You will learn about the laws on copyright in detail in Unit 1. If someone writes anything, develops software, designs an image or creates an art object, they have the copyright for that item. That means that only they have the right to copy the material, unless they have given permission to someone else to do so. Copyright lasts throughout the lifetime, and for 70 years afterwards (when it is handled by the person's executors).

You can usually use quotes (as we did above) from an item that is under copyright, or use extracts, for educational purposes. The copyright laws are one reason for always acknowledging sources. (If you inadvertently infringe a copyright law but have acknowledged your source(s), it will imply 'good faith' on your part.)

Wholesale copying of material, especially when it is then sold by the copier, is illegal. This is often known as piracy, especially in relation to software.

Avoiding plagiarism

Plagiarism occurs when someone passes off someone else's work as his or her own. It can happen in novels, in songwriting and in academic work. The most serious form of plagiarism is when students submit coursework as their own, although it has been written by someone else. Examination boards and universities disqualify students who are found doing this. In some cases the student copies coursework that has been previously submitted successfully; in other cases the student asks someone to write the coursework for them.

You should, of course, not submit work under false pretences. You should also protect your own good work to make sure that noone else tries to pass it off as their own.

One difficulty that some students have is in deciding how much help they should ask for with their work. The best advice is to discuss this with the teacher, who will know exactly how much support they and other people can give you.

Protecting confidentiality

It is good practice not to use the names of living people in anything you write, unless you have their permission. For example, if you are asked, as a student, to write a report on the IT systems within an organisation, you should explain to the member of staff what you are writing and ask permission to refer to them. You may like to send them a copy before you submit it.

If you have data about the customers or clients of an organisation, and you need to refer to them, then it is usual to 'anonymise' their names, addresses and any other identifying information. You can do this either by removing the data altogether, for example, by obscuring any handwritten information (perhaps by using a 'white out' of some sort, or a heavy felt pen). Alternatively, you can use pseudonyms instead of real names, in which case you should mention that you have done so (e.g. writing at the end of the piece of work, 'Names have been changed to protect confidentiality.').

If you are working for an employer and your report is for internal use only, then it is acceptable to use real names in many instances.

You will learn more about the laws that govern information about people in Unit 2.

Safe working

There are a number of questions to ask yourself to ensure that you employ standard ways of working safely. Do you:

* ensure that hardware, cables, seating, etc. are positioned correctly

* ensure that lighting is appropriate
* take regular breaks
* handle and store media correctly?

Ensuring that hardware, cables, seating, etc. are positioned correctly

You probably expect to use a computer regularly over many years, both for your studies and for work. You need to protect yourself from the risks of accidents or long-term health problems. You will learn about Health and Safety regulations in Unit 1, and safe working and ergonomic workspaces are covered in Unit 4. But most aspects of health and safety are commonsense. Here are some questions to ask about all the PCs you use regularly, whether at your place of study, at home, at work or at a library:

* Are the cables fastened out of reach, so I can't trip on them or pull them accidentally?

* Is the desk the correct height? (When seated, your desk is at the right height if your elbows make an angle of 90° or slightly greater when you reach the keyboard.) Are the feet planted horizontally on the floor? Is there a footrest if it is too high? (Old telephone directories make a cheap footrest.)

* Can I adjust the seat to view the monitor comfortably? Have I done so? (You should be looking horizontally at or slightly down to the screen.) Does the seat provide appropriate back support? (When you are seated your knees should be at 90°, and the angle between your back and thighs should also be around 90°.)

* Am I at a distance from the screen so I can read it comfortably?

Ensuring that lighting is appropriate

Employers are required to install suitable lighting in rooms where computers are used. The lights should be strong enough and should not flicker. You should also avoid glare on the screens by positioning them so that they do not catch bright sunlight or badly placed desk lights.

You should check the lighting at your place of study and in any room where you use a PC at home. You can also adjust the brightness and contrast on your screen so that it is comfortable to use.

Your eyesight is precious, so do not risk damaging it by using a computer in poor light.

Taking regular breaks

Most computer users are tempted to miss breaks and carry on working for several hours, especially when they are absorbed in an activity. You should aim to take a brief break every hour or so. For five minutes or so get up, walk around, have a drink, do another task. Your eyes will benefit from focusing on something other than the screen, and your work on the computer will actually be more productive as a result of the few minutes break.

Handling and storing media correctly

All storage media (disks and tape) have to be treated with some care. Avoid placing them near heat or in very cold places, and keep them well away from liquids and dirt. Magnetic media, like floppy disks and standalone hard disks, can be damaged when placed next to strong magnetic forces or motors. Optical media, like CDs and DVDs, may seem more robust but can still deteriorate if kept in poor conditions.

When you pick up a CD or DVD hold it by the edges so that finger marks are not placed on the surface. Never touch the surface of magnetic media.

E-portfolio

For all but one of the units in this AS qualification you will be assessed by an e-portfolio. The exception is Unit 3, which is externally assessed. The e-portfolio will contain all your assessment work for a particular unit. You should design it to be viewed onscreen, using a standard web browser. There are five steps to consider when planning your portfolio and putting it together:

* *Step 1*: create an appropriate structure for the e-portfolio
* *Step 2*: collect together all the required information, converting files to an appropriate format if necessary
* *Step 3*: authenticate your work

* *Step 4*: provide a table of contents, using hyperlinks to locate information easily
* *Step 5*: test for size, compatibility and ease of use, ensuring that it conforms to the technical specification.

Step 1 Creating an appropriate structure

In the specification for each unit, check the assessment requirements. If you do not have a paper copy of the specification, you can download it from the Edexcel website. Read carefully the section headed 'Assessment Evidence'. You will also be able to see how your work will be judged in the section headed 'Assessment Criteria'. (Also, refer to the introductory section to each unit in this book.)

List all the evidence that you have to produce for the unit. These could be documents, websites, e-books, presentations, databases, videos, etc. You could make this into a checklist, and tick off each item as you produce it.

Decide on the order in which you would like to present the evidence, and create a folder structure for your e-portfolio accordingly.

Step 2 Collect together all the required information, converting files to an appropriate format

Check that you have covered all the assessment objectives for the unit.

You may have to convert your working files into appropriate formats. These would normally be:

* pdf format for documents that would normally be printed
* swf (Flash movie) format for animations
* jpg or png format for images
* html for onscreen presentations.

If your PowerPoint® presentations include animations, you should convert them to Flash format. If not, then convert them to html. You may include audio and video as well.

New suitable formats may become available during the course of your work, and you should check with your teacher whether they can be used.

Step 3 Authenticate your work

Teachers are expected to give you guidance as you are putting your e-portfolios together. They are required to note down any help they have given you that goes beyond the general help they have given to everyone in your teaching group. The level of their help is taken into account when assessing your work. Discuss with your teacher if you are at all unclear about the appropriate level of help that you should be receiving.

Your teacher should also monitor your work as it develops so that he or she can be sure that it is your own work. They will keep a checklist and/or witness statements to authenticate your work. You will need to include these in your e-portfolio. You could ask your teacher what he or she is doing to monitor and record this evidence.

Step 4 Provide a table of contents, using hyperlinks

You will present your e-portfolio with an introductory page in web format. The web page should be clear and businesslike. It should be viewable at 1024 × 768 pixels resolution. The introductory page should give:

* your name, candidate number and centre number

* an index of links to all the work contained in the e-portfolio. Each link can take the viewer to another web page or alternatively to any page or document in a suitable read-only format.

Step 5 Test for size, compatibility and ease of use

There are some important checks you need to carry out before submitting your e-portfolio for assessment. Check:

* how much memory the complete e-portfolio requires. You will be expected to use compression techniques to reduce the memory size of images and sounds

* that your e-portfolio displays correctly in a number of browsers, and on different types and sizes of screen

* that a viewer will find it easy to use and navigate – ask a fellow student to comment on this

* you have complied with the technical requirements for the relevant unit.

UNIT 1

The information age

Introduction

Information communication technology (ICT) is advancing at such a rate it now impacts upon the majority of households and organisations in the developed world. This unit focuses on how ICT can enable users to access, exchange and use the information ICT is able to provide for social, economic and commercial purposes.

In particular, this unit investigates the Internet, the Internet's contribution to the 'information age' and the services it provides. Because ICT has had an enormous influence on personal, social and professional users in terms of working styles, employment opportunities, education, banking, shopping, entertainment, leisure, crime and legislation, the positive and negative aspects of ICT are also discussed in this unit. Finally, the unit will help you to develop your practical ICT skills as you conduct Internet-based research and use multimedia to develop an e-book.

What you need to learn

In completing this unit, you should achieve these learning outcomes:

* Know about the opportunities and issues of the 'information age'
* Understand the advantages and disadvantages of online services
* Have investigated e-books
* Be able to use a range of ICT tools and techniques such as e-books, website navigation and browser software
* Know how to create, develop and use an e-book.

Resource toolkit

To complete this unit, you need these essential resources:

* access to computer hardware including a printer, digital camera and scanner

* access to computer software, in particular Microsoft Word, Powerpoint and graphics and web authoring software

* access to the Internet and sufficient storage space.

How you will be assessed

This unit is internally assessed. Page vii explains what this means.

There are three assessment objectives:

AO1 Investigate aspects of the information age in which you live

AO2 Design and create an e-book to present your evidence and provide a snapshot of life in today's information age

AO3 Evaluate your e-book and your own performance.

To demonstrate your coverage of these assessment objectives, you will produce an e-portfolio of evidence, showing what you have learnt and what you can do:

(a) You will write a description and evaluation of at least five different types of online service, drawn together to give a picture of the current scope and limitations of the Internet as a whole.

(b) You will write a description of how ICT is affecting at least five different aspects of people's lives, considering the benefits and of life overall in the information age.

(c) You will include a description of at least three factors contributing to the digital divide and some of the measures being taken to bridge the gap, with an evaluation of the impact/extent of the digital divide, drawn together to give a picture of the current situation.

(d)/(e) Your e-book should include:

* your work for (a), (b), and (c)

* evidence that demonstrates your understanding of multimedia design principles and your ability to use software tools appropriately.

* some ready-made and some original multimedia components

(f) You should also include in your portfolio an evaluation of your e-book and your own performance on this unit.

How high can you aim?

The information age has provided a wealth of opportunities to almost all sectors of society. Through this unit, you will explore a range of issues associated with the benefits, issues and challenges of living in this information age. This unit will also identify some of the boundaries that the information age has generated to the extent of creating a digital divide between communities and countries. You will also be expected to embrace the information age and develop your own e-book and evaluate your own performance throughout this process.

This unit will be assessed internally and some of the **Assessment activities** provided can be used towards your e-portfolio. These contain **Assessment hints** on what you need to do to pass (✓), gain a better mark (✓✓) or get top marks (✓✓✓). For example, when identifying different online services available to home and business users, higher grades can be achieved by providing an in-depth evaluation of at least five different types of online service.

The assessment that covers ICT and how it affects your daily life, can feed into your e-portfolio evidence where at least five different aspects of people's lives need to be analysed in conjunction with how ICT has impacted upon them. Higher grades can be achieved by analysing the benefits and drawbacks of each to give a clear and balanced picture of life in the information age.

The research assessment into factors contributing to the digital divide will contribute to your evidence for your e-portfolio with the aim of describing at least three aspects of the digital divide (two global and one local). Higher grades can be achieved through analysis of the causes and effects of each and the measures taken to bridge the gap.

The creation of an e-book will allow you to use a range of multimedia tools and techniques and appropriate software tools. Higher grades can be achieved through originality in the selection and use of these tools in your e-book design.

Finally higher grades on the evaluation of the e-book assessment evidence can be achieved through the incorporation of user feedback, instead of just evaluative comments based on the key features.

Ready to start?

Why not keep a log of the time you take to complete this unit? Devise a blank form that you could use to record the time that you spend on this course.

1.1 The information age

Digital technologies are having a profound effect on the way individuals and businesses operate, and they are all part and parcel of this new, ever advancing information age. Information can be exchanged globally in milliseconds, shared between millions of users simultaneously and stored in devices no bigger than a pen.

Some of the benefits of, and opportunities created by, the information age are shown in Figure 1.1.

These opportunities exist because of a range of new technologies:

* the Internet
* multimedia
* broadband
* wireless
* digital and mobile technologies (for example, TV, video and telephones).

The Internet

The Internet is a network that links computers globally, thus enabling them to store and to transfer vast amounts of data. In order to access the Internet, a number of factors have to be considered, and these fall into three broad categories:

* hardware
* software
* services.

Initially, the hardware you needed to enable you to connect to the Internet included a computer and a modem, and access to a telephone line. However, the need for faster, more reliable connections has created more efficient ways of accessing the Internet (Figure 1.2).

Each method brings a host of benefits:

* you can use your landline to make telephone calls whilst you are surfing on the Internet
* faster connection speeds
* better reliability in terms of connecting and instant connection
* there is a permanent connection – you do not need continually to dial up.

Key term

The term *landline* is often used to describe a fixed telephone connection at home or work, a connection that travels over terrestrial circuits.

FIGURE 1.1 *The benefits and opportunities of the information age*

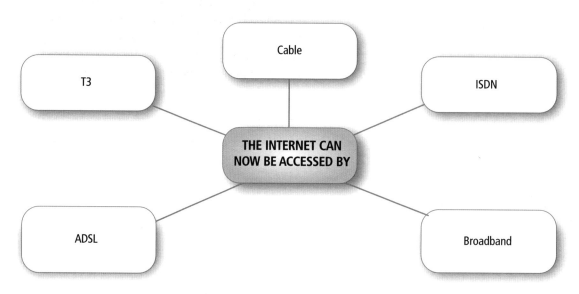

FIGURE 1.2 *Modern ways to access the Internet*

For some people, however, especially occasional users of the Internet, the additional costs associated with upgrading to a faster medium of connection do not make this a viable option and, for others, there is no alternative but to use a landline if these newer services are not provided in the area where they live. In recent years, however, newer and more accessible systems have become widely available, which means that users now do not even need a computer to connect with the Internet. In this advanced information age, users who cannot access the Internet via a traditional PC can use alternative technologies (Figure 1.3).

In terms of software, most operating systems today have integrated Internet access software that includes dial-up networking and browsers. Once access to the Internet has been gained via an ISP (internet service provider), a number of services are available to users:

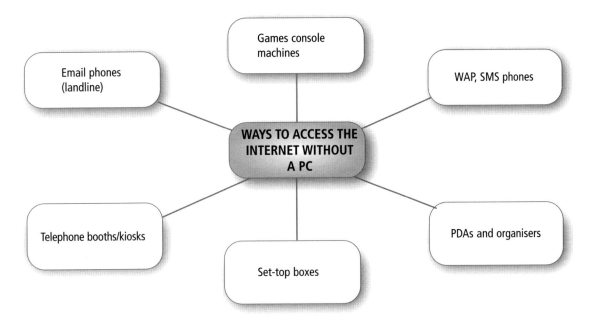

FIGURE 1.3 *Alternative ways to access the Internet*

* e-mail
* web browsing
* file transfer protocol (FTP)
* newsgroups
* internet relay chat (IRC).

Key term

File transfer protocol (FTP) is the protocol (set of rules) used for exchanging files over the Internet.

In addition, other services may be available from an ISP, including web space, web hosting and helpdesk support.

Multimedia

Multimedia tools can be used to generate sounds, moving images, pictures and graphics. Multimedia can enhance documents, presentations, web pages and e-books, etc. The ability to download sounds, pictures and clips and use scanning and photographic facilities has played a major role in the creation of e-books and other dynamic documents.

Broadband

Broadband is a very high-speed connection to the Internet that is always active (i.e. on). It has a

much larger capacity than a traditional landline to receive and send data (up to 10 or 20 times faster than a 56 K modem, thus allowing you to view web content and download files more quickly). A number of providers offer broadband services – PIPEX (Figure 1.4) being just one of these.

FIGURE 1.4 *PIPEX home page*

Wireless, digital and mobile technologies

Key term

Wireless technology operates without the use of cables (i.e. wires) needing to be attached to a hardware device, thus making the use of the device more flexible.

There is a wide range of wireless technologies available. Some of these are designed to meet the needs of businesses, such as:

* local wireless
* wireless networks (WLAN)
* mobile phone networks.

Local wireless incorporates cordless products, such as keyboards and mice that use infrared or radio technologies. This provides a certain element of flexibility, providing connectivity within range of the desktop. One of the more versatile types of radio technology is 'Bluetooth'. Bluetooth technology facilitates communication between mobile phones, PDAs, PCs and other PC-related devices within a range of 10 metres.

Mobile phone networks are used for much more than voice calls. The capability and sophistication of handsets and networks' increased data transfer speeds has enabled the development of more dynamic, innovative devices.

Wireless networks operate without the need for cables; they offer the same benefits as traditional cabled networks, but without the restrictions and confinements for users. Devices that are WLAN-enabled, such as laptops, can be connected at anytime, providing they are within range. Wireless networks are more advanced than local wireless in terms of the range available.

The growth of wireless, digital and mobile technologies is evident in the range of ICT devices now available. Wireless and mobile technologies (such as laptops, PDAs and wireless networks) mean you are not restricted to working in a conventional environment, such as an office. These technologies enable people to work from home, on the move or in another branch of the same organisation.

Digital television and video

Digital television (DTV) is the transmission of television signals using digital rather than conventional analog methods. The advantages of DTV over analog TV include:

* superior image resolution (detail) for a given bandwidth

* smaller bandwidth for a given image resolution
* compatibility with computers and the Internet
* interactivity
* superior audio quality
* consistency of reception over varying distances.

Digital video is part of digital versatile disc (DVD), a new optical disc technology. The DVD holds 4.7 gigabytes of information on one of its two sides, or enough for a 133-minute movie. With two layers on each of its two sides, it will hold up to 17 gigabytes of video, audio or other information.

The opportunities of the information age

The information age has provided many opportunities, some of which are described below.

The presentation of information

Businesses and other organisations can create templates that can be used on a national or even global basis, and multimedia tools offer the ability to produce designs that are more creative and visual (for example, on websites or in presentations at conferences or meetings).

> **Key term**
>
> A *template* is a master document that can be used again and again. For example, a company may create templates of letters, reports and other documents all employees must use in their communications with clients or customers. Each template will contain basic information that can be changed for the particular circumstances. Templates are designed carefully so that the company presents the same image to all its customers and, in this way, it can control how it appears to the outside world.

Sharing information quickly

Rapid information sharing has been enabled through such technologies as webcams, email, video conferencing and the emergence of virtual communities set up on the Internet that offer newsgroups and chat rooms, etc. The facilities of mobile phone technology to send and receive pictures or text have also contributed to the speed at which data and information are communicated.

Greater interaction with others and organisations

This has again been achieved through technologies that have enabled effective and speedy interactions. The emphasis on 'collaborative' working environments and work spaces, where people share ideas and data, has had an impact of the types of software that are being marketed to organisations – for example, e-mail, intranets, extranets and the Internet now make more dynamic interaction across organisations, and even across communities, possible. Such devices as laptops, PDAs and mobile phones permit people to be more flexible in the places where they choose to work: indeed, more and more workers are now home rather than office based. ICT has thus helped to overcome the barriers of geographical distance: colleagues can communicate with each other instantly from almost all parts of the world.

Business opportunities large and small

The information age has created a more flexible and open marketplace for businesses. Many small companies that could not possibly afford to set up and trade conventionally have been given the opportunity to trade online. For example, specialist suppliers of such goods as cheese, chocolate and wines can advertise their range of goods on their websites, and customers may browse and order online. These suppliers no longer need to be located near their customers and can operate with the minimum number of staff.

Virtual communities

These have been created as a result of the Internet bringing people together – people who share the same interests, hobbies, views and opinions. Virtual communities are held together by a sense of purpose and belonging (for example, communities that have been set up on the Internet to provide help and support for school children or to give them homework advice).

Mobile technologies

These range from PDAs to laptops and mobile phones. The capabilities of mobile technologies have enabled people to work and socialise on the move.

A self-service environment is what online consumers expect

With the growth in online shopping, banking and learning, in many cases it has become the 'norm' to click a button to carry out a transaction or to download information. Now you can store your personal details on websites, consumers do not even have to key in delivery or payment details, thus enabling them to be completely self-sufficient in their purchases.

Think it over...

We now expect things to be available wherever and whenever we want them. Think about what life would be like without computers, without Internet access, without mobile phones, without digital television and access to Sky, etc.

Issues and challenges arising from the information age

The information age has made people more aware of the implications of living and working within a society driven by communication technologies. The challenges people who live in this community face include:

* the need to be lifelong learners
* privacy rights
* copyright and legislation
* impacts on employment
* the digital divide.

Lifelong learners

'Lifelong learners' is a concept that has become a reality in this new information age. Learners from all generations can now gain access to learning resources, training opportunities, online courses and educational materials. The ability to download materials and to use the support of online tutors has given many people who were possibly prevented from studying via conventional methods new opportunities. The expectations of employers with regards to the skills base of their employees has also increased, resulting in a demand for more flexible 'knowledge workers'. This demand has driven many people into a continuous cycle of studying so that they become more 'marketable'.

Privacy rights

As more and more information is passed quickly between users and, in some cases, stored permanently on PCs, we all need to be aware of the legal issues surrounding the protection of data, privacy and the security of information, copyright and other legislative measures.

The Data Protection Act 1998

The Data Protection Act applies to the processing of personal information by any means, electronic or paper-based. The Act places obligations on people (data controllers) who collect, process and store personal records about consumers or customers

Key terms

Data controllers are those who control the contents of and use of, a collection of personal data. They can be any type of company or organisation, large or small, within the public or private sector. A data controller need not necessarily own a computer.

Data subjects are the individuals to whom the personal data relates.

CASE STUDY

ChoicePoint stops selling some personal data
By Paul Roberts

Embattled personal data vendor ChoicePoint Inc. said on Friday that it will stop selling sensitive consumer data to many of its customers, except when that data helps complete a consumer transaction or helps government or law enforcement, the company said in a statement.

The company decided to stop selling sensitive data, such as Social Security numbers and driver's license numbers after being tricked into divulging personal information on about 145,000 people to identity thieves who posed as customers, according to a statement attributed to ChoicePoint Chairman and Chief Executive Officer (CEO) Derek V. Smith.

"These changes are a direct result of the recent fraud activity, our review . . . of our experience and products, and the response of consumers who have made it clear to us that they do not approve of sensitive personal data being used without direct benefit to them,"

Smith said in the statement, which was posted on ChoicePoint's Web site.

From now on, ChoicePoint will only sell sensitive personal information to customers when the data is necessary to complete a transaction, to accredited corporate customers that will use the data for user authentication or fraud prevention, or to help federal, state and local government and criminal justice agencies, ChoicePoint said.

The move, which should be complete within 90 days, will eliminate a number of "information products" that the company now sells to its customers, especially small businesses, the company said.

ChoicePoint also said it is creating an independent office of credentialing compliance and privacy. The office will oversee ChoicePoint's overhaul of the company's customer credentialing process, which was blamed for allowing identity thieves to register as legitimate customers and order personal information, the company said in its statement.

The Industry Standard

(data subjects). It also gives individuals certain rights regarding the information held about them.

Principles of good practice for data controllers

The Act sets out eight principles of good practice for data controllers. These are that data must be:

* fairly and lawfully processed
* processed for limited purposes
* adequate, relevant and not excessive
* accurate and up to date
* not kept longer than necessary
* processed in accordance with the individual's rights
* secure
* not transferred to countries outside the European Economic area unless the country has adequate protection for the individual.

Rights for individuals

The Act gives rights to individuals in respect of personal data held about them by data controllers. These include the rights to:

* *Subject access*: this allows people to find out what information is held about them on computer and within some manual records.
* *Prevent processing*: anyone can ask a data controller not to process information relating to him or her that causes substantial unwarranted damage or distress to them or anyone else.
* *Prevent processing for direct marketing*: anyone can ask a data controller not to process information relating to him or her for direct marketing purposes.
* *Automated decision-taking*: individuals have a right to object to decisions made only by automatic means, i.e. where there is no human involvement.
* *Compensation*: an individual can claim compensation from a data controller for damage and distress caused by any breach of the Act. Compensation for distress alone can only be claimed in limited circumstances.
* *Rectification, blocking, erasure and destruction*: individuals can apply to the court to order a

data controller to rectify, block or destroy personal details if they are inaccurate or contain expressions of opinion based on inaccurate information.

* *Ask the Commissioner to assess whether the Act has been contravened*: if someone believes their personal information has not been processed in accordance with the Act, they can ask the Commissioner to make an assessment. If the Act is found to have been breached and the matter cannot be settled informally, an enforcement notice may be served on the data controller in question.

The Act does provide wide exemptions for journalistic, artistic, or literary purposes that would otherwise be in breach of the law.

Key terms

Personal data refers to information about living, identifiable individuals. Personal data does not have to be particularly sensitive information and can be as little as name and address.

Automatically processed means processed by computer or other technology such as documents image-processing systems.

The role of the Information Commissioner

The Information Commissioner is an independent supervisory authority which has both national and international roles. Primarily the Commissioner is responsible for ensuring that the Data Protection Act and the Freedom of Information Act are enforced.

In the UK, the Commissioner's duties include:

* promoting good information handling
* encouraging codes of practice for data controllers
* serving information notices which require data controllers to provide information in order to assess their compliance with the Act
* enforcing the Act where a breach of the law occurs

In order to carry out these duties, the Commissioner maintains a public register of data controllers, which includes information about the controller such as their name, address and a description of the processing of the personal data to be carried out.

Register of data controllers

Anyone processing personal information, with a few exceptions, must notify the Commissioner's Office that they are doing so, giving their name, address and broad descriptions of:

* those about whom personal data are held

* the items of data held

* the purposes for which the data are used

* the sources from which the information may be disclosed i.e. shown or passed to

* any overseas countries or territories to which the data may be transferred.

For more information about the Data Protection Act, see Unit 2 and the Information Commissioner's website (a link to the site is available at www.heinemann.co.uk/hotlinks (express code 2016P).

Computer Misuse Act 1990

The Computer Misuse Act was enforced to address the increased threat of hackers trying to gain unauthorised access to computer systems. Prior to this Act there was minimal protection, and there were difficulties in prosecuting hackers because theft of data in this way was not considered to be a deprivation to the owner. There a number of offences and penalties under this Act.

Offences

* *Unauthorised access*: an attempt by a hacker to gain unauthorised access to a computer system

* *Unauthorised access with the intention of committing another offence*: on gaining access a hacker will then continue with the intent of committing a further crime

* *Unauthorised modification of data or programs*: introducing viruses to a computer system is a criminal offence. Guilt is assessed by the level of intent to cause disruption, or to impair the processes of a computer system.

Penalties

* *Unauthorised access*: imprisonment for up to six months and/or a fine of up to £2,000

* *Unauthorised access with the intention of committing another offence*: imprisonment for up to five years and/or an unlimited fine

* *Unauthorised modification*: imprisonment for up to five years and/or an unlimited fine.

Copyright and legislation

Copyright is awarded automatically to a product (be it a book, a painting or a piece of software) immediately it is completed; no further action is required in order to activate copyright. Copyright is transferable if the originator/author grants it and it can exist for up to fifty years following the death of the originator/author.

The are a number of copyright issues concerning software. First is software piracy – the copying of software to be used on more machines than the individual licences allow for. Secondly is ownership – if a piece of software has been developed for a specific organisation, the copyright remains with the developer unless conditions to the contrary have been written into a contract. Finally is transference – can an employee who has developed a piece of software for his or her organisation take the ownership and copyright with him or her to another organisation? Again, unless this is addressed in the employee's contract, the organisation will have no right to any software the employee has developed.

Copyright, Designs and Patent Act

The Copyright, Designs and Patent Act provides protection to software developers and organisations against unauthorised copying of their software, designs, printed material and any other products. Under copyright legislation, an organisation or developer can ensure that its intellectual property (IP) has been safeguarded against those who wish to exploit and make gains from the originator's research and developments.

> ### Key terms
>
> A person's or organisation's *intellectual property (IP)* is their ideas, inventions or 'creativity' (for example, the work of writers or artists). It is protected, for example, by patents, trade marks and copyright, which give the owner *intellectual property rights (IPR)* to protect their 'property' under the Copyright, Designs and Patents Act.

Software piracy can be broken down into a number of key areas:

* *Recordable CD-ROMs*: Pirates copy large amounts of software on to one recordable CD-ROM and make multiple copies of this CD-ROM.

* *Professional counterfeits*: These are professionally made copies of software, including media packages, licences and even security holograms. They are made to resemble the genuine article.

* *Internet piracy*: The downloading or distribution of software on the Internet that infringes any copyright laws.

* *Corporate overuse*: This occurs when organisations install software package(s) on to more machines than they have licences for.

* *Hard disk loaders*: Unscrupulous retail outlets or dealers load illegal versions of software on to computer systems to encourage customers to buy their computer hardware. Customers will not have the appropriate licences or be entitled to other services, such as technical support or upgrades.

The Federation Against Software Theft (FAST) was set up in 1984 by the software industry with the aim of preventing software piracy. Anybody caught breaching the copyright law would be prosecuted under this federation.

Impact on employment

The information age has had a profound impact upon employment. The move towards automated jobs has led to a rise in the demand for 'knowledge workers' – employees who have the required level of skills to operate a computer, to input data, extract information, manipulate data sheets, and to design and develop applications, documents, programs and websites. For some workers, the information age has meant that a lack of these skills has hindered their promotion and has even forced some employees out of their jobs. For employers, the challenges that face them are costly, both financially and in terms of time and resources.

Investment in newer technologies has impacted upon the working environment, leading to more workplace legislation and health and safety requirements. In addition, more resources have had to be channelled into the training and development of staff so that full advantage can be taken of these technologies.

The digital divide

The 'digital divide' is the term used to describe how people can be excluded from the online world. People may not be able to go online because they do not have the money, the knowledge or the hardware or software. People may also be excluded because they fear the new technology, because they feel they are too old to learn new skills or because they have a physical or mental disability. For whatever reason people are prevented from going online, there is a divide between those who can and those who cannot. Those who can benefit from all those things ICT can offer (access to the Internet, online shopping and banking, etc.); those who cannot are prevented from enjoying these benefits.

This divide is very apparent all over the world, but in some countries it is compensated for to a certain extent by people having access to some forms of technology. An example of this can be seen in the rise in mobile phone ownership. In some households, even those in the most deprived areas of the world, mobile phone ownership is considered to be the 'norm'. In other parts of the world, most households also have access to digital or satellite television.

Think it over...

In some parts of the world, having fresh water each day would be considered to be a luxury, especially if you didn't have to walk miles and miles to get it. In other parts of the world, fresh water is taken for granted, and having a computer, Internet access and a mobile phone is also taken for granted. Having the luxury and choice to watch, shop, entertain, learn and develop using ICT is still unfortunately dictated by where you live and how much money you have.

Knowledge check

1 How has the Internet revolutionised the way in which we communicate?

2 What is meant by the term 'multimedia'?

3 What opportunities have been created by the 'information age'?

4 What are the benefits of using broadband?

1.2 Online services

A vast range of online services is available on the Internet (Figure 1.5), and these services have become very accessible. Because the Internet provides a global gateway that can be accessed by home and business users, the Internet presents many opportunities:

* more advanced, quicker and cheaper communication links for individuals, businesses and the government

* access to real-time information

* the ability to shop, bank, educate and entertain

* the ability to download and archive a range of multimedia products and services.

Communication

In the digital age, communication (and whom you communicate with) has no geographical boundaries.

The services provided by the Internet have enabled people to use a range of communication media:

* e-mail

* instant messaging and chat services

* newsgroups

* online conferencing

* blogs.

E-mail

E-mail has become one of the fastest and most widely accessible forms of communication in recent years. E-mail is no longer a matter of sitting

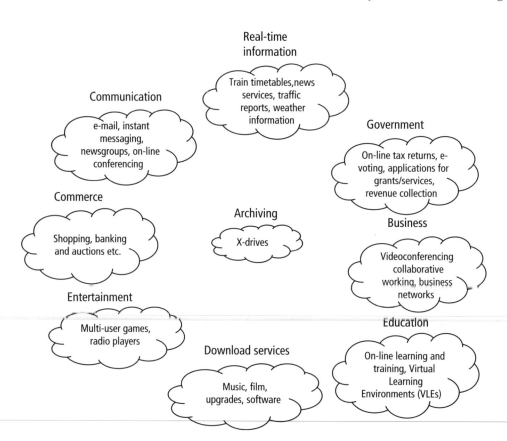

FIGURE 1.5 *The services available on the Internet*

down in front of a computer terminal and tapping commands into a keyboard. New and more portable tools are now available: games consoles, WAP phones, digital televisions and set-top boxes.

The advantages of using e-mail include:

✳ *Speed*: you can send messages immediately to anywhere in the world at the touch of the button.

✳ *Multiple sends and copies*: you can send the same message to many recipients.

✳ *Cost*: the costs are minimal and, in some instances, to e-mail may be free (for example, if you send e-mails from some educational establishments).

✳ *Convenience*: you can communicate 24 hours a day, 7 days a week.

✳ *Sharing data*: because the same information can be transferred to many users, these users have access to the same attached files, graphics and moving images, etc.

✳ *Ease of use*: once you are familiar with some of the basic functions of an e-mail package, it is very easy to send and receive e-mails because the system is icon driven.

There are a number of other benefits to e-mail. You can keep a historical record (audit) of the messages you have sent and received. Your messages can also be saved into different formats, updated and printed out if required. E-mail contains a range of multimedia elements that allow you to send messages containing graphics, sound, moving images and even hyperlinks to Internet pages.

The disadvantages of e-mail mainly concern technical and security issues, such as the following:

✳ *Spamming*: spam e-mails are unwanted messages you are sent by advertisers and unknown users who broadcast their messages universally to an entire address book.

✳ *Routing*: e-mail is not always sent direct from A to B; it can be routed to other destinations before it finally reaches the receiver(s). Routing can cause a number of problems. For example, it takes more time before the message reaches its destination, and there are more opportunities for the message to be intercepted. The message may also become distorted or lost.

✳ *Security*: an e-mail can be easily intercepted unless you have applied some form of encryption to the message.

Key term

Encryption software scrambles message transmissions. When a message is encrypted, a secret numerical code is applied – an 'encryption key' – and the message is transmitted or stored in indecipherable characters. The message can only be read after it has been reconstructed through the use of a 'matching key'. Some Internet-based companies use encryption software to protect sensitive user information and also to authenticate passwords that have been sent to a user to set-up new accounts, etc.

CASE STUDY

Bill Gates gets 4 million emails a day
David Teather in New York
Friday November 19, 2004

The Guardian

The next time you're sifting through the mortgage offers, cheap Rolex watches or dubious business proposals from Nigeria, spare a thought for Bill Gates. The Microsoft founder is the most spammed man in the world, with 4m emails arriving in his inbox each day.

Steve Ballmer, Microsoft's chief executive, told a conference in Singapore that being the world's best-known software billionaire has its down side: "Bill receives 4m pieces of email per day, most of it spam."

The upside of the Microsoft founder's bulging inbox is that it appears to have focused his mind on the problem.

Spam is regarded as perhaps the biggest threat to the internet, with some experts putting it as high as 80% of the world's online traffic.

* *Confidentiality*: because an e-mail can be lost, intercepted or distorted, it is not deemed appropriate to send confidential messages via e-mail.

Instant messaging and chat services

There is a wide range of messaging and chat services available to all types of business and home users. Some of these services are tailored to meet individual needs and requirements. For example, business community chat services are marketed at specific types of business organisations and educational messaging services provide updates on training and educational developments. These services are similar to forums in that they provide an environment where people can share and swap ideas.

For home users, the range of services is extensive. For example, facilities such as MSN and

Yahoo Messenger© (Figures 1.6 and 1.7) allow subscribers to join specialist user groups. Users are then able to monitor who is available online and can chat with individuals from their list.

Newsgroups

Newsgroups can be described as 'interactive discussion forums'. They allow users who share the same interests or research areas to communicate across the Internet, an intranet or an extranet system (Figure 1.8). Newsgroups are very interactive in that people respond, post facts and ideas, and view current articles that have been included on the site (Figure 1.9). Examples of different categories of newsgroups include:

* online games/gaming sites
* environmental protection
* fan-sites for pop singers or football clubs.

FIGURE 1.6 *MSN Messenger*

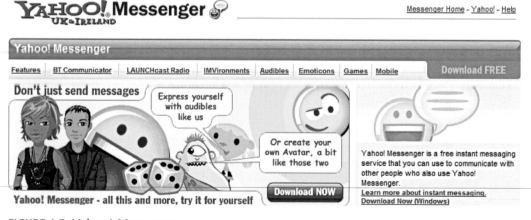

FIGURE 1.7 *Yahoo! Messenger*

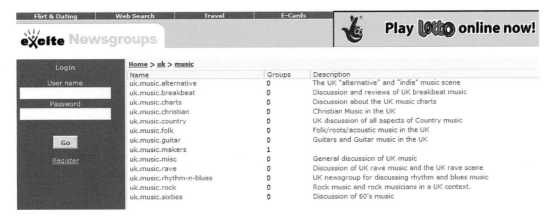

FIGURE1.8 *Excite newsgroups*

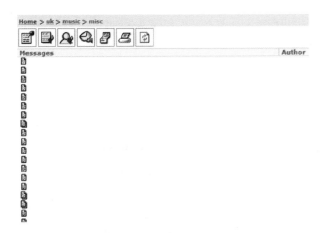

FIGURE 1.9 *Messages posted on a site*

Think it over...

There are a number of ways that people can communicate online, using chat rooms and messaging services, subscribing to newsgroups and forums.

Over a period of one week, track how many times you are invited to chat online with a friend, and note how long you actually spend chatting online. In addition, have a look at a forum that is of interest to you, for example, online games, a hobby, music or film topic. Over the course of a week, see how many postings are made and the types of questions that are presented to forum members.

At the end of the week report your findings to the rest of your class.

Online conferencing

Key term

Online conferencing allows people to share information with large audiences, interactively and cost effectively, thus eliminating the need to travel to meetings. For example it can bring employees together for training sessions, or it can bring suppliers and customers closer to the organisations they deal with.

Blogs

A blog is a web page that serves as a publicly accessible personal journal for an individual.

Key term

Blog is shortened form of 'weblog'.

Real-time information

The ability to view regularly updated news and train, bus and flight timetables, weather reports and sporting results online has improved the quality of information for people who are travelling or who require constantly updated information. People and organisations who want to be able to plan a journey online by viewing travel times have created a huge demand for sites that offer these facilities, such as ferryport.com (Figure 1.10).

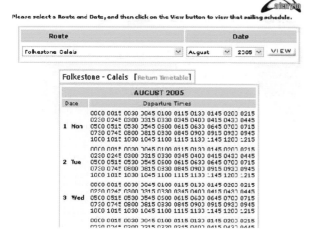

Please select a Route and Date, and then click on the View button to view that sailing schedule.

Route	Date
Folkestone Calais	August	2005	VIEW

Folkestone - Calais [Return Timetable]

AUGUST 2005	
Date	Departure Times
1 Mon	0000 0015 0030 0045 0100 0115 0130 0145 0200 0215 0230 0245 0300 0315 0330 0345 0400 0415 0430 0445 0500 0515 0530 0545 0600 0615 0630 0645 0700 0715 0730 0745 0800 0815 0830 0845 0900 0915 0930 0945 1000 1015 1030 1045 1100 1115 1130 1145 1200 1215
2 Tue	0000 0015 0030 0045 0100 0115 0130 0145 0200 0215 0230 0245 0300 0315 0330 0345 0400 0415 0430 0445 0500 0515 0530 0545 0600 0615 0630 0645 0700 0715 0730 0745 0800 0815 0830 0845 0900 0915 0930 0945 1000 1015 1030 1045 1100 1115 1130 1145 1200 1215
3 Wed	0000 0015 0030 0045 0100 0115 0130 0145 0200 0215 0230 0245 0300 0315 0330 0345 0400 0415 0430 0445 0500 0515 0530 0545 0600 0615 0630 0645 0700 0715 0730 0745 0800 0815 0830 0845 0900 0915 0930 0945 1000 1015 1030 1045 1100 1115 1130 1145 1200 1215
	0000 0015 0030 0045 0100 0115 0130 0145 0200 0215 0230 0245 0300 0315 0330 0345 0400 0415 0430 0445

FIGURE 1.10 *Eurotunnel Folkestone to Calais timetable*

It is also now possible to listen to radio programmes in real-time, as well as still being able to listen to recently recently aired programmes.

Commerce

E-commerce has had a profound effect on the way that we shop and bank. It has provided flexibility and in many cases cost-effectiveness to high-street shopping.

In shopping, e-commerce has created more choice. We can view a range of products in online stores, compare prices and make informed choices about our purchases. In addition payments can be made easily and securely online.

Auction sites, such as ebay.co.uk, have grown rapidly over the last few years. Almost anything and everything seems to be on sale, from film props, to food items, rare memorabilia to modern books, CDs, DVDs and other merchandise.

Banking has also adopted online service provision. Almost every bank has a website where information can be viewed and downloaded, personal accounts activated, loans arranged and transactions carried out.

Government

You can now carry out many interactions with government departments online. For example, you can:

* book your driving test (see Figure 1.11)
* apply for a passport
* claim Child Benefit
* fill in your Income Tax return and pay any tax you owe
* get health advice
* find out about your rights as an employee and many, many more things.

For some tasks, such as applying for an Educational Maintenance Grant, you do have to fill in a paper form and post it with supporting documents. In all these cases you can download the forms and read the information about them online.

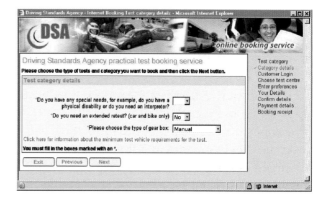

FIGURE 1.11 *Booking a driving test on the Driving Standards Agency website (a link to the site is available at www.heinemann.co.uk/hotlinks, express code 2008P)*

Each government service has its own website, but you can find your way to the right one from the Directgov site (www.directgov.gov.uk).

From Directgov you will also be able to locate your local council's website, where you should be able to:

* report graffiti
* book adult education classes
* raise a petition
* respond to a consultation
* express your views about local issues
* pay council tax

At election time you may be able to vote online, or to register your vote at a voting machine; this is known as e-voting.

You should be able to find out easily online who your elected representatives (Members of Parliament and councillors) are. Many have their own websites, and all can be contacted by email.

Education

There is a wide range of online services that have been set up to support education, training and development. The creation of VLEs (Virtual Learning Environments) and the growth in online organisations that promote courses and qualifications such as Learn Direct, CISCO and ECDL (European Computer Driving Licence) qualifications, have enabled wider participation for learners who cannot physically get to a place of learning. The ability to work through course materials and study online has also helped to support different types of learners who may have difficulties with keeping up in a class environment, or for those learners who do not feel challenged enough and can work through at a more advanced pace.

Business

Online services have improved the efficiency, cost-effectiveness, competitiveness and productivity of some businesses. Videoconferencing has enabled businesses from across the world to sit in on meetings and training events and to be able to take part in decision-making processes within a matter of seconds. Online services have also promoted a culture of collaborative working within departments and throughout all the branches of organisations that operate on a worldwide scale.

Business networks have been set up at various levels to support multinational corporations through to single business users. These networks offer support and advice on a range of business and financial issues to encourage the use and sharing of good practice as a business standard. For some business users, these networks provide a lifeline to what's actually happening in business communities, especially if they are constrained geographically and feel quite cut off from the city or other local businesses.

Entertainment

The ability to access radio, news, video clips and games (Figure 1.12) online has created more opportunities for people to interact socially with other people and to keep people up to date with developments in entertainment.

In addition, single or multi-user online gaming (from such things as role playing to chess) has united certain groups of people into cultures that are not geographically divided and that are driven by interactivity and social participation.

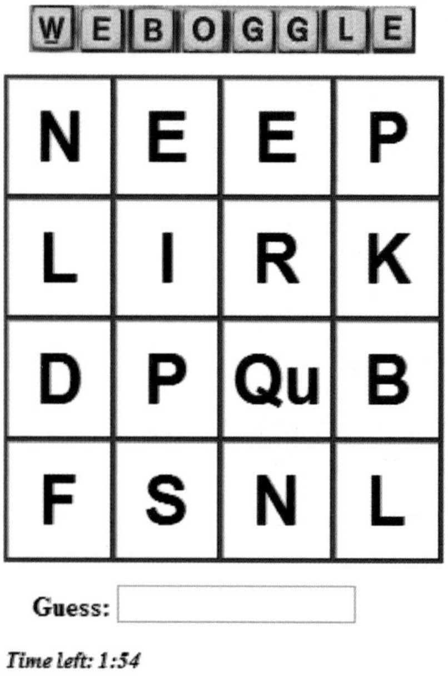

W E B O G G L E

N	E	E	P
L	I	R	K
D	P	Qu	B
F	S	N	L

Guess: [   ]

Time left: 1:54

FIGURE 1.12 *An interactive online game at Weboggle (a link to the site is available at www. heinemann.co.uk/hotlinks,express code 2016P)*

Download services and archiving

The ability to download information (such as upgrades, software and entertainment files) has enabled people to access resources at the touch of a button. Once this information has been downloaded, it can be archived for future use. Information can now also be accessed and shared on an x-drive, that enables information to be stored in a designated area on the Web allowing access at anytime.

You can archive information (for example, a link, a web address or web page, etc.) temporarily or permanently on removable storage media (DVDs, CD-ROMs, etc.) or in Favorites or on your hard disk drive. Archiving information allows you to keep track and register pages that you have viewed for future reference. This information can then be accessed easily, downloaded and used as and when required.

STUDENT	BUSINESS	RETIRED
Type of service 1 2 3	Type of service 1 2 3	Type of service 1 2 3
Benefits of service 1 2 3	Benefits of service 1 2 3	Benefits of service 1 2 3
Ease of use 1 2 3	Ease of use 1 2 3	Ease of use 1 2 3
Example of service (site) 1 2 3	Example of service (site) 1 2 3	Example of service (site) 1 2 3

TABLE 1.1 *Online services and different types of user*

 ## Signpost for e-portfolio evidence

Save this work in your e-portfolio. It could contribute towards covering evidence (a).

Knowledge check

1 List three online services.

2 What are the advantages and disadvantages of using e-mail?

1.3 Life in the information age

ICT has had an enormous impact on the way people do things in their personal, professional and social lives. The effects of the information age can now be felt in such areas of life as:

* working styles
* communication
* education
* entertainment and leisure
* banking and shopping
* decision-making
* employment opportunities
* crime and crime prevention
* civil rights
* legislation.

Working styles

ICT has had a tremendous effect on work styles and the way in which everyday tasks are carried out in organisations. ICT has also affected the way in which data is processed, information is transmitted and knowledge is applied. Similarly, ICT has influenced the physical environment of the workplace (for example, most offices are now designed to accommodate individual workstations), what workers do, where they are based, their job roles, their interaction with other people and their needs for skills updating (for example, they must be trained to operate computers and in the features of the software they use).

Most offices are now designed to accommodate individual workstations

Communication

ICT has affected not only the way people communicate and but also the means of communication. In today's society, the preferred method of communication is either e-mail or chat, messenger and text facilities. The emphasis now is on speed, interactivity and collaboration. For example, Word permits people to add comments to a document without changing the wording of the document. This document can then be sent as an attachment to other people who can similarly add their comments. When the changes to the document have been agreed by all concerned, the comments can either be incorporated into the document or disregarded.

Education

The effects of ICT on education have been felt at all levels of learning. For example, the National Curriculum requires that children can use computers from an early age and are proficient in applications software as they progress into secondary, further and higher education. Pupils are encouraged to use ICT in nearly all the subject areas they study, from English and maths to art and foreign languages.

To support the teaching of ICT in schools and colleges, a number of initiatives have been set up to provide them with the resources they need to deliver this teaching. For example, reduced-price computers for teachers and laptops for teaching purposes have been introduced in an attempt to promote wider access to ICT and, hopefully, to encourage new ways of delivering the knowledge the pupils need. Support from local county councils to get schools connected to the Internet and to provide them with hardware and software for classrooms has also contributed to widening participation in ICT.

The impact of ICT on education has been a positive one as children and students are taught practical ICT skills that are transferable to the workplace. ICT has also filtered into other academic and training organisations, providing opportunities for all levels and ages of learner. For example, e-learning has risen in popularity as more and more people have become aware of such online courses as ECDL (European Computer Driving Licence), Learn Direct and Webwise.

Entertainment and leisure

Entertainment and leisure pursuits have changed in terms of what we do and how we do it. These changes are primarily due to the Internet, which provides endless opportunities for people to communicate, play games and be involved in interactive pursuits. The Internet also allows people to plan their leisure activities online by enabling them to book tickets for flights, concerts, attractions and holidays. In addition, such technologies as mobile phones and games consoles have contributed to the changes in the way people are now entertained.

Banking and shopping

ICT has changed the way people bank and shop. Some of these changes can be considered to be part of an older technology (such as ATM machines (the 'holes in the wall') and electronic data capture at the point of sale in shops). However, recent changes and advances in ICT have opened up new opportunities for both commercial and retail organisations and their customers. These opportunities include:

* online banking
* online ordering
* online payments
* over-the-phone transactions and services, such as:
  - mortgages
  - setting up accounts
  - payments
  - orders
* automatic stock control and processing systems
* the introduction of loyalty schemes based on information gathered from bar-code products and customer data (for example, Tesco's and other supermarkets' loyalty cards).

Decision-making

To a certain extent, the decision-making process has become more automated in the information age. Certain decisions, especially within organisations, have been taken away from individuals and have become part of an electronic process based on data, statistics, forecasting and analysis. For example, loan companies will assess how much money someone may borrow based on data fed into a software program, and the designs for some new products are tested via computer simulations, which will highlight any modifications that need to be made to the product.

At a personal level, the decision-making process has also been changed. For example, a decision to book a holiday before the information age might have involved physically visiting a travel agent, searching through brochures, paying a deposit, going back to make the final payment, being sent your tickets, etc. – a process that could have taken months. In the information age, however, this process can be reduced to a matter of minutes, and it can save you hundreds if not thousands of pounds – all with the click of a button.

Employment opportunities

In terms of employment opportunities, the impact of ICT on the banking sector, for example, has been both positive and negative, as Table 1.2 shows.

The demands of e-commerce now require organisations to provide electronic and online facilities for payment methods, ordering and transaction services. Those organisations that fail to supply these facilities often suffer in terms of a shift in customer loyalty to more dynamic organisations that do provide these facilities.

At the end of the day, pension, financial and other specialist advisers are being replaced by intelligent systems and competent operators who can navigate their way through menu systems and decision tables.

POSITIVE	NEGATIVE
More streamlined and efficient service (people are available at the end of a phone or computer)	Loss of personal one-to-one service, no need to speak to somebody in person (e.g. bank manager)
Greater flexibility (e.g. wider payment options, able to shop around for the best deals and compare prices, etc.)	Could lead to a loss in jobs or unwanted changes in job roles
More choice in products and services available (online)	Not everybody feels comfortable with using ICT facilities to bank and would prefer a personal service
Convenience (you do not have to leave home for mortgage advice or to transfer funds, etc.)	Smaller branches may be forced to close, especially ones located in rural areas

TABLE 1.2 *The impact of ICT on banking*

Crime and crime prevention, civil rights and legislation

As has already been noted in this unit, ICT has impacted on almost every area of our lives. However, the rapid rate at which ICT is being embraced by almost everyone has caused some concerns about how we can ensure we are working within a secure environment. You learnt earlier in this unit that some legislation is already in place to protect users of ICT (for example, the Data Protection Act and the Computer Misuse Act). There are, however, other ways in which ICT may be misused, and it is these misuses that have resulted in calls for new legislative measures to be introduced.

Because the Internet can be accessed privately, people interact and behave differently online where they think their activities might go unnoticed. The issue of the Internet being 'unregulated', therefore, has, to an extent, created situations where the exchange of data and information is not welcomed by the community at large. The dangers of individuals asserting their rights to 'free speech' have been highlighted by sites that have been set up to promote criminal activities, or that encourage the dissemination of material that expresses extreme political views or is racial, pornographic or unethical in nature. Although there is only limited power to stop sites such as these being created, internet service providers have been encouraged to monitor sites that are considered to be controversial or indeed harmful to certain vulnerable sectors of the community. For example, some sites that promoted and glorified anorexia, where images of girls were displayed like trophies, have recently been closed down.

In the United States legislative procedures and the policing of sites have also led to 'raids' on individuals who have been involved with paedophilia and pornography. In addition, legislation has given the police powers to search through files and to seek out subscriber information to these sites and, if appropriate, to prosecute.

> **Think it over...**
>
> The Internet is almost like 'Jekyll and Hyde'. One part of it provides a wealth of knowledge and opportunity, freedom of expression, freedom of choice and the freedom to communicate whenever and with whom you wish. However, the other part promotes a more cynical aspect of society, a society that preys on the vulnerable and those that are easily targeted by propaganda, to be a part of racial, cultural, pornographic and illegal activities – activities that can be shared globally, with the Internet as the gateway.

The increasing power of mass lobbying will indeed bring about more changes in the legislation concerning the use of the Internet. Recently, a new law was passed in the UK to tackle the problem of 'Internet grooming' (where paedophiles surf the Web in order to lure vulnerable children into conversation). Under this new law, a paedophile was convicted in January 2005 to a four-year prison sentence. In the end, however, the Internet could be said to be about 'free speech' and the rights of individuals to 'choose', and about choices and decisions concerning what to buy, sell, view, download and whom to chat to, etc.

The information age has indeed created many opportunities for people at all levels – professionally and socially. Professionally, ICT has affected how jobs are carried out, workers' skill requirements, research and development, and the day-to-day activities of working life. Socially, ICT has enabled people to communicate better in terms of speed, interaction and creativity. People can use the Internet, messaging services, PDAs and mobile phone technology to send and receive instant text, picture and video messages. People can shop, bank and entertain from the comfort of their own home, or in transit using WAP technologies.

In terms of the impact ICT has had on social elements such as shopping, the growth in the popularity of buying online and trading through auction sites such as eBay is phenomenal (Figure 1.13).

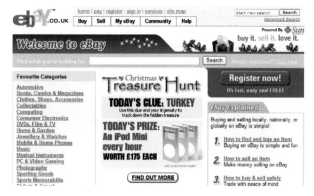

FIGURE 1.13 *Buying and trading through eBay*

Think it over...

What would happen if the Internet disappeared overnight? How would this affect our daily lives?

Assessment activity

How does ICT affect your daily life?
Choose one particular aspect (for example, education, travel or communication) and research the impact of ICT on it.
Include both the benefits and drawbacks of ICT. Present and compare your results with others to see the scope of the impact of ICT on our lives.

Assessment hint

✓ Provide a description of how ICT is affecting at least five different aspects of people's lives and identify some benefits and drawbacks.

✓✓ Provide a description with some analysis of the benefits and drawbacks giving a clear picture of life in the information age.

📁 **Signpost for e-portfolio evidence**

Save this work in your e-portfolio. It could contribute towards covering evidence (b).

Knowledge check

✳ How has the Internet affected everyday communication?

✳ What are the advantages and disadvantages of Internet banking?

All these elements have contributed to the growth of the digital society, a society that will continue to expand in the future.

1.4 The digital divide

Although access to ICT has transformed many people's lives in a positive way, there are also other considerations that must be addressed. As you have seen, there are people who cannot access these technologies for a variety of reasons and who therefore cannot share the digital experience.

Factors which create the digital divide

There are a number of factors that have lead to this digital divide:

✳ technological
✳ economic
✳ social
✳ geographical
✳ fear of technology
✳ lack of motivation, knowledge and skills.

Technological

Technology is advancing at an alarming rate: systems that were considered 'cutting edge' only a few years ago are now being replaced by faster, more robust systems (for example, broadband technology is rapidly replacing modems and landlines). It is no surprise, therefore, that users cannot keep up in terms of developments and costs, and so a divide has been created between those who understand and can afford these new developments and those who cannot. The digital divide has, to a large extent, been created by hardware and software manufacturers, who dictate the minimum system requirements. As new software is released, higher specification systems are needed to accommodate these.

Economic

In addition, changes in mobile phone technology and digital and satellite media mean that not only are people being forced into updating their existing provision to encompass the latest devices at a greater expense but, in some cases, the trends are also dictating what is considered to be acceptable in society. For example, peer group pressure amongst teenagers to have the latest camera or video phone has led teenagers to take drastic measures to ensure they acquire these, and thus the divide between those who can afford to keep up with the technology and those who cannot is widened even further.

There is peer group pressure amongst teenagers to have the latest mobile phone

Social

The gap is ever growing in today's society. A report commissioned by BT (see page 25) identifies how people could face social exclusion if the gap between those who have access to technology and those who do not continues to widen over the next twenty years.

This gap, however, will continue to increase if people cannot afford the costs associated with up-to-date technology. For some households, especially families, the absence of technology has in some cases made children 'social outcasts' as they cannot participate in the benefits of interactive socialising with their friends who do have access.

Geographical

Geographically, it is still impossible in some rural communities to obtain fast access to ICT – i.e. broadband connection is still not available in all parts of the country. Therefore the use of conventional dial-up methods excludes households in these areas from appreciating the full benefits of online services as the download time makes it almost impossible to tap into multimedia facilities.

Fear of technology

Some people are still wary of using technology. There are people who are happy to use a computer for the sole purpose of producing documents, etc., and nothing else, and there are others who refuse to embrace technology at all. Certain sectors of society who do not have the knowledge and, therefore, cannot access the benefits of technology remain excluded from this new information age. For more mature people, the impetus and motivation to learn about how computers work and the about the benefits they can bring are lacking. Boundaries are easily created, thus excluding them from participating in the growing digital economy.

A number of initiatives have been set up by various bodies that range from educating people about the information age to supplying low-income families with computers. However, the digital divide will only be addressed fully if there is equality in terms of every household having good access to the technology and possessing the knowledge to appreciate and engage in the services provided by the technology. This is a goal that may never be achieved because of people's differing circumstances.

Lack of motivation, knowledge and skills

The lack of skills, ability and knowledge is a reccuring issue that has contributed to the digital divide. There is a big difference in skills between those people who are competent in the use of ICT and those who are not. This has been recognised by software companies that have tried to market their software as being 'user friendly' (for example, by incorporating such features as graphical user interfaces, icons, menus and help facilities).

A user's ability or disability contributes to the digital divide. If a disabled user does not have access to the required specialist devices that can assist him or her in interfacing with a computer or other electronic device, he or she will be disadvantaged. Some of these devices include headsets and head pointers for physically disabled people or tactile keyboards that have been adapted for blind or partially sighted people.

Assessment activity

1 Research three factors contributing to the digital divide. What is being done to bridge the gap?

2 Go to **www.heinemann.co.uk/hotlinks** and use the link to Computer Aid International (express code 2008P). Learn about what the organisation does and discuss these questions:

  ✱ Is it right that developing countries should get our 'cast-offs'?

  ✱ What can they do with the equipment they are given?

  ✱ How is their access to ICT affected by power supply and telecommunications issues?

(See Assessment hint on page 26)

CASE STUDY

The Digital Divide 2025

New report to tackle 'digital divide'

A new BT commissioned report – The Digital Divide 2025 – which the company is launching today (Tuesday) has revealed that millions of Britons could face social exclusion if the gap between those with access to technology and those without continues without direct action over the next 20 years.

Launching today at the BT Tower in London, the report – conducted by The Future Foundation – predicts that while the number of digitally excluded people will fall from 27 million to 23 million by 2025, the people excluded risk losing access to fundamental services like medical information and education.

Currently one in two adults (51 per cent) are disadvantaged by not being online and the report warns that the gap between the 'have nets' and 'have nots' will widen if the government, commercial organisations and designers of new technology fail to engage people who have so far rejected the digital age.

(Continued)

BT's corporate responsibility director Adrian Hosford said: 'Britain could be facing grave consequences if the digital divide is not taken seriously. If we don't address this problem now, it will get a lot worse. People will find it more difficult to find jobs, education opportunities will be limited and they'll simply not be able to keep up with society.

'However the good news is that there is a lot that can be done to avoid this happening. Organisations such as BT can help to tackle the problem and we have a number of grass roots projects which are working to help people in disadvantaged communities overcome digital exclusion.'

Adrian added: 'We've been working with the government and other agencies for many years now on these community projects and have already seen some wonderful results. This is a good start but more needs to be done by all those involved if we are to tackle the scale of this issue.'

BT is also a founder member of the Alliance for Digital Inclusion – an independent industry body which encourages collaboration and partnerships between industry, government and the voluntary sector to promote the use of information communication technology for social benefit.

1 Does this BT-commissioned report estimate that, by 2025, the number of digitally excluded people will increase or decrease?
2 Currently, what percentage of people are disadvantaged by not being online?
3 What consequences may be faced by Britons if the digital divide is not addressed?

Assessment hint

✓ Provide a a description of the digital divide, with some indication of the causes and effects, plus a description of two measures being taken to bridge the gap.

✓✓ Provide a description of the digital divide, with some analysis of the causes and effects, plus a description of two measures being taken to bridge the gap.

Signpost for e-portfolio evidence

Save this work in your e-portfolio. It could contribute towards covering evidence (c).

Knowledge check

✳ Who may not benefit from access to ICT?
✳ What are the factors contributing to the digital divide?

1.5 What is an e-book?

E-books are an alternative form of publishing to paper-based books. They are viewed on screen, either on a desktop PC or on a handheld system.

The simplest e-books are versions of traditional books that are made available in an online format, such as pdf. These can be read from beginning to end like any other book, although the use of bookmarks can make it easier to find particular sections easily.

However, the real value of e-books is realised when they make full use of multi-media components that cannot be used in traditional books, such as video, animations and sound.

E-books also exploit hypertext, with links between related topics, so that readers can follow lines of interest. This is especially useful for non-fiction e-books, but even fiction can be made more exciting by following alternative story lines.

E-books can be downloaded from the Internet or can easily be distributed on optical media.

Hypertext is text which contains links to related material, allowing the reader to jump from one section to another instead of having to read through in sequence.

The concept of hypertext was invented in 1945, just as the first computers were being developed. It had only limited applications in, for example, computer games and paper based adventure books, until the Web was introduced in the 1990s.

Theory into practice

Search the Web for different examples of e-books (for example, novels, reference books, user guides, collaborative books (books written by more than one author), children's books, etc.).

Presentation of e-books

The way any written material is presented can affect the way in it is interpreted and understood. The factors that can influence an understanding of all written materials include:

* the content (i.e. the subject matter the writing discusses)

* the structure and layout (how the writing is organised into chapters, sections, etc., the number of words (or pages) it contains and the way the material is arranged on the page)

* the style of the language the author(s) have chosen to use

* its fitness for its purpose (i.e. has it been written in the most appropriate way for the intended readership?).

There are some factors, however, that apply specifically to e-books:

* their use of multimedia components

* the way the readers navigate through the e-book

* how easy or not it is to use or access.

Content

Almost any type of book can be designed and viewed as an e-book. However certain books do lend themselves more to being in an electronic format. These can include:

* encyclopaedias

* manuals and instruction books

* catalogues

* story books.

The content of an e-book is not very different to the content of a normal book. The layout may be more visually orientated with navigation aids, such as arrows, guiding you from one page to the next. Links can also be incorporated to take you to key sections within the text.

Structure and layout

There are many things that affect the way all books are structured and laid out. For example, if an organisation wanted to design an e-book that is to be used as a training manual for newly appointed staff, it might be necessary to include many different documents in this e-book that have been written by staff in all departments of that organisation. To make sure each section of the e-book covers the same points as the others (safe working practices, health and safety, etc.) and that each section is immediately recognisable, the compiler of the e-book would use templates and standard connections. This way not only would the readers understand the overall structure of the e-book but the compiler would also be able to ensure all facets of training were included.

The layout of an e-book can also be affected by the tools and techniques the author or compiler has chosen to use and by such things as the size and style of fonts:

Format, size and *style* of fonts

The layout will also be affected by the insertion of pictures, graphics, cartoons or photographs. These are used for a number of different purposes which range from providing a general understanding of such things as human anatomy to humour, through the insertion of cartoons and comic strips.

Pictures will enhance any e-book, providing they are used for a specific purpose. Graphs and charts can provide the readers with a visual interpretation of data shown in tables but, again, must be used for a purpose.

The number of pages in an e-book will have an impact on how easily the material is understood. For example, if all you need is a couple of pages outlining how to set up a spreadsheet, trying to master a thousand-page book on the uses and applications of software could be futile experience. Similarly, reading a few pages on surgery would not qualify you to perform surgery.

Language and style

The way in which any writing is expressed (in terms of the language it uses and its level of formality – i.e. whether it is informal and 'chatty' or formal and impersonal) will also influence the reader. Readers will have expectations that certain reading matter will be presented in a particular way. For example, you would have different expectations of:

* exam papers
* instruction manuals
* course textbooks
* letters
* legal documents.

If you picked up a romantic novel you would expect the language to be informal and familiar, and to suit the context of telling a story. A course textbook, however, would be more technical, outlining specific techniques or theories in a more formal way.

Fitness for its purpose

While all e-books should have a good balance between written and visual information, all should be written in a language and style that reflect their intended purpose and audience. The writer or compiler of an e-book must understand the needs and expectations of the readers and must arrange the material in such a way these needs and expectations are met.

Multimedia

Moving images have become one of the most important forms of visual communication, especially with the ever-increasing popularity of the Internet and mobile and digital technologies. The dynamics of an e-book allow for the use of multimedia tools and techniques, including moving images (video clips, etc.).

In an e-book, multimedia facilities can provide a more dynamic experience for the readers. Depending on its purpose, an e-book can use multimedia to:

* advertise and sell
* entertain
* instruct and educate.

The use of multimedia will transform a very static document into a dynamic, creative document that entices the readers into viewing the content.

Navigation

Navigating through an e-book is as easy as turning the pages of a normal book but with the added benefits of using links on certain key words to advance you further in the text. Similar to the navigation devices on a website, an e-book can be set up with tools to assist you in turning over the pages and advancing through the text.

> **Think it over...**
>
> When reading books printed on paper we move from one page to the next by physically turning the paper it's printed on (turning the page). How do e-books emulate this?

Ease of use and accessibility

Almost anybody can use and access an e-book; you do not need any specialist skills or software to download or view it. Once the e-book has been selected, it will download and be ready for you to navigate through, similar to a traditional textbook. The navigation buttons will guide you through each page and assist you with the selection of any command or information that you wish to view.

Evaluation of e-books

When you evaluate e-books, you should consider all those things discussed in the previous section that go to make an e-book successful or not. To do this, you should look at the layout, style, presentation and use of multimedia tools and techniques in a variety of e-books and assess these to see whether or not the e-books fulfil the purpose they set out to achieve. You should study a variety of e-books that have different purposes. For example:

* creative writing books
* reference materials (for example, encyclopaedias and historical manuscripts)
* collaborative projects (i.e. books written by more than one author)
* children's books.

Assessment activity

Design an e-book that conforms to a given technical specification.

Assessment hint

✓ Identify the content of an e-book and start to develop an e-book that demonstrates the use of suitable ready-made multimedia components, original creation, the use of appropriate software.

✓✓ Identify the content of an e-book and start to develop an e-book that demonstrates the selection and appropriate use of suitable ready-made multimedia components, creation and appropriate use of original multimedia components, the use of appropriate software and good use of testing and quality assurance procedures.

📁 Signpost for e-portfolio evidence

Save this work in your e-portfolio. It could contribute towards covering evidence (d) and (e).

Knowledge check

1 What is an e-book?

2 What are the different stages of creating an e-book?

1.6 Developing an e-book

There are a number of things you must consider when you develop your own e-book:

* the intended audience
* the purpose of the e-book
* any content that must be included
* the message you are trying to convey
* the technical specification you must adhere to
* the deadline for completion.

Storyboards

Key term

A *storyboard* (see Figure 1.14) is a panel or a series of panels of rough sketches that can outline a sequence of events or activities in a story, normally associated with a plot or film production. A storyboard can be used in the initial stages of developing an e-book where rough ideas and designs can be sketched to form the basis of each page.

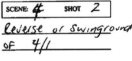

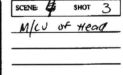

FIGURE 1.14 *An example of a storyboard*

* REMEMBER!

When creating a storyboard, check that the final product will meet the needs of the audience.

How to create an e-book

To start your e-book, you can draft some ideas in Word, identifying titles, content, suggested graphics, etc. Once you have generated your ideas, separate each topic onto a separate page in Word as it would appear in the order of the e-book. Each single page will form an HTML page of your e-book.

However you create your e-book, at some point you will need an e-book compiler. An e-book compiler is a program that takes the source files (the content of your e-book) and compiles them into an easy-to-distribute format.

Types of compilers

There are three main types of compilers that you could use:

* HTML compilers
* PDF compilers
* other compilers.

HTML compilers

HTML compilers convert HTML files (like those on a website) into an easy-to-distribute format, often self-contained Windows programs.

An HTML compiler may be a good choice for you if:

* you generally expect your e-book to be read on the computer screen (not all HTML e-books print well or easily).
* you want to take advantage of the 'special' features used on web pages, or that some HTML compilers allow to be used in e-books (for example: CGI forms)
* you have experience designing web pages. (Creating your e-book is likely to be a similar process to creating web pages.)

PDF compilers

PDF is a file format created by Adobe that can be used for e-books (and distributing other types of documents too).

A PDF compiler may be a good choice if any of the following apply:

* you want your e-book to be printed – PDFs print easily and well
* you want the e-book to always have an exact appearance as specified by you – PDFs look like the original document
* you do not have experience designing web pages
* you want to reach an audience who cannot read HTML compiled e-books – for example Apple Macintosh users.

If you are going to create PDF files, you will need the PDF authoring tools, the PDF file format and the software for publishing in this format.

Other compilers

There are also e-book compilers that convert other file formats such as plain text into e-books.

The template for your e-book can be pre-defined if you are using specialist design and template software, or you can create your own e-book template. If you are designing your own template, you should ensure that you include the following:

* an index page that will form the entry point to your e-book
* a contents page listing the chapters, etc.
* a link at the top of each page taking you back to the contents page
* a chapter title on the top of each page
* a set of links at the top of each page allowing you to navigate through your e-book
* forward and backward hyperlinked arrows allowing you to navigate between pages.

If you follow these steps you should find that you create a very functional and user-friendly e-book.

Development issues

When you are well on the way to developing your e-book, you should check it regularly:

* Proofread it to make sure the spelling,

punctuation and grammar are correct and that the language is appropriate for the subject matter and the readers (for example, technical language is appropriate for an e-book on computers but not for a children's story).

* Check the layout to ensure it meets the specified requirements and that it is functional (for example, can the users navigate through the pages easily?).

* Check all the links and pathways to ensure they work and that they have been integrated correctly.

* Try it out on 'test users' to ensure your e-book is functional and fit for its purpose.

To obtain constructive feedback on your e-book, you should test it on a range of end-users so that they can give you their comments. To collect this feedback, you could use a form such as that given in Table 1.3 so that all the feedback you receive covers the same areas.

> **✱ REMEMBER!**
>
> E-books must always fit their brief and the target audience. No matter how good a multimedia product is, there is always room for improvement!

> **Knowledge check**
>
> What factors should be considered when testing an e-book?

> **✱ REMEMBER!**
>
> Creating an e-book is part of your assessment for this unit. You will also need to evaluate your e-book.

Please rate this e-book by ticking a number from 1 to 5 for each of the criteria listed:

1 = excellent; 2 = very good; 3 = good; 4 = average; 5 = below average

		1	2	3	4	5
1	Content of the e-book (textual and visual)					
2	Overall structure					
3	Screen layout of the pages					
4	Use of multimedia components					
5	Presentation techniques					
6	Ease of navigation					
7	Consistency of information and layout					
8	Accessibility					
9	Suitability for the given audience					
10	Use of language/technical content					
Any other comments and recommendations:						

TABLE 1.3 *E-book feedback form*

Evaluating your e-book

When you evaluate your e-book, you should consider how its content is set out in terms of layout, style, format and structure.

If you have followed the stages involved in creating an e-book carefully, you should find that there are no issues concerning the design, how it looks and how it works. At the end of the design, you should feel that your e-book meets all of your original objectives in terms of the content, layout and functionality. Therefore, in the evaluation part, these are the areas that you need to concentrate on.

You should evaluate each stage of the e-book design, from the original draft designs and use of Word for setting out your initial ideas, through to the compiling and template structure. The types of questions that you should be addressing in this evaluation stage include:

* Has all of the topic and content been covered fully?

* Are there any areas that have been missed out, and if so why?

* Did you manage to work within your own deadlines?

* Did you feel that you had enough knowledge and skills to develop the e-book, and how was this reflected in your final design?

* Does the e-book look professional?

* Does the e-book have a mix of graphics and text, colour and multimedia?

* Do all of the links and navigation buttons work?

* Is the e-book easy to read?

By evaluating all of these areas, you should find that you have addressed the main, layout, style, format and structure issues.

Signpost for e-portfolio evidence

Save this work in your e-portfolio. It could contribute towards covering evidence (e).

1.7 ICT skills

The Internet is one of the most dynamic research tools available – it provides a bank of information on a multitude of topics, however obscure or diverse. One of the major advantages of using the Internet to carry out research is the fact that everything can be accessed from a single computer: there is no need physically to visit different places to gather information because this is what the Internet is doing on your behalf.

Advantages of using the Internet to research

There are many advantages in using the Internet as a research tool:

* A wide range of topics and interests can be found.

* It is a concentrated source of research – there is no need for you to collect information from elsewhere.

* It is relatively quick.

* It can be a cheaper method of data collection than some other research tools (for example, you do not incur travelling and photocopying costs).

* It can be easy to use.

* Online help is provided to assist you in gathering the information.

* You do not need to depend on others to delivery the information (for example, you do not have to wait for it to arrive in the post).

* The information is presented in a variety of formats which aids your understanding and learning.

* You can receive up-to-the-minute information.

* You can share information and ideas easily through online user groups.

There are, however, problems when using the Internet as a research tool:

* You may not be familiar with its use and how to search for information.

* It can be frustrating to use a search engine for information on a such a broad topic as 'universities' because anything with 'universities' in the title will be displayed from all over the world, bringing up perhaps thousands or more sites.

* It is vital you are familiar with the way search engines work, with advanced features, Boolean operators, links and with the basics of keying in a web address. If not, you may have problems searching for appropriate and meaningful information.

Research using the Internet

When you embark on your research using the Internet, there a number of tools and techniques you can use to help in the research process.

Browser software

Browser software (Figure 1.15) enables you to move from one site to another. For example, the **Forward** and **Backward** buttons permit you to go back to the previous page or to move forward to the next. **Home** returns you to your home page, and **History** to review the pages you have visited in the past few weeks.

FIGURE 1.15 *Internet Explorer toolbar*

Sites you find that you think will be useful to you later you can add to **Favorites** (click on **Favorites, Add to Favorites**). By clicking the **Favorites** button on the toolbar, you will be able to see a list of those sites already saved in Favorites. Clicking on the **Organize...** button brings up the **Organize Favorites** dialogue box (Figure 1.16), where you can create new folders, move stored sites to other folders and delete any unwanted sites.

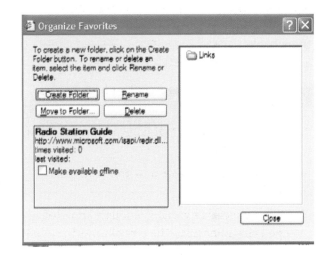

FIGURE 1.16 *Organize Favorites dialogue box*

Search engines

To use search engines effectively, you must be able to refine your searches, otherwise you may be presented with thousands of irrelevant sites. The search engine itself may offer you choices to limit your search (in Figure 1.17 you can limit your search to the UK only or Ireland only, instead of searching all the Web).

FIGURE 1.17 *Yahoo!'s search engine*

Other ways to refine your search include the use of logical operators (AND (or + or &), NOT (or -) and OR) between the words you enter in the search box. If you use AND (or + or &), your results should produce sites that contain all the words you joined together with AND. If you use NOT (or -), the sites shown should not contain the words that come after NOT, and if you use OR the sites should contain all or any of the words you separated with OR.

Navigation of websites

Most websites contain navigation buttons that take you to other pages on that website. In Figure 1.18, you could click on the navigation button 'IT & Office Technology', which would then bring up pages devoted to these books.

Theory into practice

Visit this website http://www.train-ed.co.uk and practise your navigation skills and your browser options.

Hyperlinks

Some sites have hyperlinks to other sites that may contain information that could be of value to you. In Figure 1.18, if you were to click on 'Heinemann Direct', you would be taken to the site shown in Figure 1.19.

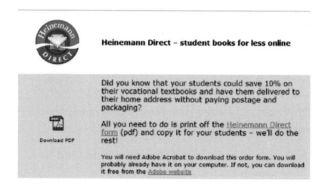

FIGURE 1.19 *Hyperlinks take you to related sites*

Judging the quality of the information found

Once you have found a site that seems to provide the information you need, you must make an informed judgement about its accuracy, reliability and currency.

FIGURE 1.18 *Navigation buttons*

Using the Internet as a research tool, carry out searches on the following subjects and record the information you obtain using a template such as the one provided in Table 1.4. You should use four search engines to undertake this activity.

Find out information on:

1 The five latest cinema film releases

2 An actor or actress who appears in two new film releases

3 What other films this actor or actress has appeared in.

When you have finished your searches, present a summary of the information you have obtained to the rest of your group. You should use an appropriate software tool to deliver this information, such as PowerPoint.

Acknowledgements

If you decide to use information you find on a website, you must acknowledge the fact that this was the source of the information – you must not attempt to masquerade the information as your own. This is plagiarism – passing information off as your own when you have in fact copied it from elsewhere.

There are a number of ways that people would expect you to acknowledge any information that you have used from their website. These can include:

* E-mailing or writing off for permissions.

* Acknowledging the author/company in your work or on your website.

* Providing a link on your website to their website (if appropriate).

Have a look at a range of websites, for example, media, forum sites, sporting sites, major companies, etc., and see whether or not you can use materials from their site, and what you need to do in order to download, copy and paste it.

Multimedia content for e-books

One of the most important features of all e-books is that they contain images and links. It is this that differentiates e-books from normal, static textbooks and makes them more dynamic to read. To make sure the e-books you create are dynamic, there are a number of steps you can follow:

1 Try to use ready-made multimedia components.

2 Use a digital camera and scanner to capture images.

3 Try to capture screen-based images.

4 Use word-processed documents.

5 Create links.

6 Use appropriate file formats.

7 Try to combine information created in one type of software with information created in a different type of software.

Search engine:	Web page address:
Links used:	
Summary of site information:	

TABLE 1.4 *Internet research template*

UNIT ASSESSMENT

1 Using your experience of creating an e-book, write up your report and include:

  * what design principles you followed and why

  * who was your intended audience and did your audience affect specific elements of your e-book (i.e. size of text, etc)?

2 From your evaluation of your e-book, what would you do to improve it?

UNIT 2

The digital economy

Introduction

This unit is about how the Internet has transformed the way business is done. ICT has always had an important role in supporting the information needs of organisations and, with the advent of the World Wide Web, transactions that are entirely electronic have become a reality. This unit builds on the material covered in Unit 1, so you should have completed that unit before you start this one.

What you need to learn

In completing this unit, you should achieve these learning outcomes:

* Know about the different information needs of organisations
* Understand the advantages and disadvantages of shopping online
* Have investigated the design of commercial transactional websites
* Be able to describe the back-office processes associated with making an online purchase
* Create and use a database to store a set of data and extract meaningful information from it, or order it to identify significant patterns and trends and make recommendations.

Resource toolkit

To complete this unit, you need these essential resources:

* access to computer hardware, including a printer
* access to computer software, in particular database software such as Microsoft Access®
* access to the Internet.

How you will be assessed

This unit is internally assessed. Page vii explains what this means.

There are four assessment objectives:

AO1 Investigate the design of a commercial transactional website.

AO2 Use diagrams to show what happens when someone purchases a product online.

AO3 Investigate potential threats to customer data collected via the Web and the measures taken to protect it.

AO4 Create a database to store a given set of data and extract useful information from it and evaluate it.

To demonstrate your coverage of these assessment objectives, you will produce an e-portfolio of evidence, showing what you have learnt and what you can do:

(a) You will write a description of the design of a commercial transactional website, including details of its structure, the goods offered, the way customer information is captured and payments are made, and the techniques used to engage and retain customers. This will also include an in-depth evaluation of the key features of the website design and some suggestions for improvements.

(b) You will include detailed diagrams illustrating the chain of events involved in an online purchase, showing information flows and the back-office processes.

(c) You will write a description and evaluation of the security and legislation issues relevant to online selling.

(d) You will create a customised database designed to store a given set of data, and provide recommendations based on the trends identified from the given data.

(e) You will provide an evaluation of your own performance on this unit.

How high can you aim?

Your e-portfolio will contain all the evidence on which your performance will be judged. Some **Assessment activities** can be used towards your e-portfolio. These contain **Assessment hints** on what you can do to pass (✓), gain a better mark (✓✓) or top marks (✓✓✓). For example, when describing the design of a commercial transactional website you can only obtain the higher marks if your description includes an in-depth evaluation of the techniques used to engage, retain and/or entice the customers, and an evaluation of the site as a whole and the 'customer experience' it provides. You should also make suggestions for improvements.

The diagrams you draw to explain the process of placing an online order should describe the back-office processes in detail (payment processing, stock control, despatch, etc.), as well as the processes involving direct interaction with the customer.

In the section on security threats, preventative measures and legislation, you need to provide in-depth evaluations as well as descriptions of these aspects of e-commerce to achieve the higher marks.

The database you create must include appropriate fields types, formats and validation checks and you need to carry out sorts and searches on the data you import into the database and present the results in a clear, easy-to-understand format. Finally, you must interpret the output from the sorts and searches you do on the given dataset, and the degree to which you can identify significant trends and make recommendations for future developments will determine your mark.

Ready to start?

Why not keep a log of the time you take to complete this unit? Devise a blank form that you could use to record the time that you spend on this course.

2.1 Information needs of organisations

Information is, in many ways, the life blood of most organisations. This is nothing new, but the use of ICT has revolutionised how information is gathered, communicated and analysed. Since the 1950s computers have been used by organisations to support their information processing needs, so that today all but the very smallest of businesses are heavily reliant on ICT. Since the 1980s another revolution has taken place – the phenomenal growth of the Internet – which has provided a completely new way for organisations to communicate with their customers and each other.

Not all organisations are the same, and different organisations have different information needs. There are a number of ways to categorise organisations. Dividing them into public and private sectors is one way to do this, which is useful because organisations in these different sectors have different priorities and therefore different information requirements:

* *Public sector* organisations are funded by the public through taxes and they provide some kind of service to the public. As such they are ultimately controlled by the government and are accountable to them and the public. Examples include schools, libraries, local councils, the police and the armed forces.

* *Private sector* organisations are owned by individuals or shareholders and range from self-employed people to large multinational corporations such as Ford, Sony and Tesco.

Another way organisations can be classified is by their type. Just as organisations in different sectors have different information requirements, so different types of organisations use ICT for different things. Companies generally fall into one of three categories, industrial, commercial and service:

* *Industrial* – companies that either manufacture things or produce the raw materials (such as oil, iron, copper) from which things are made. Examples in this sector are Shell, the Ford Motor Company and British Aerospace. The key uses for ICT in industrial organisations include the control of manufacturing processes, the research, design and development of new products, and the control of the stock of components from which finished goods are made.

Key terms

Stock is the goods that a company has in storage which, in the case of a commercial organisation, is waiting to be sold. The items on the shelves of a supermarket are also stock. *Stock control* refers to the methods an organisation uses to track and record the stock it has. Stock costs money to buy and so is a valuable asset. Keeping just the right amount of stock is also important: too much stock is a waste of money, too little may leave customers dissatisfied.

* *Commercial* – companies sell the goods that the industrial organisations make. Examples include Sainsbury's, Argos and your local corner shop. Commercial companies use ICT systems for the control of purchasing, stock control and the recording of sales transactions.

* *Service* – companies provide a service, either to other businesses or to people like you. Banks and insurance companies are examples of these types of organisations. Most public sector organisations fall into this category. The key uses for ICT include keeping track of customer accounts and transactions.

The vast majority of the organisations you come into contact with on a day-to-day basis are in the commercial or service sector. The customers for many commercial organisations such as shops and supermarkets are people like you and I. However, these commercial organisations are customers in their own right. The goods they sell have to be made by other organisations, so an electrical store such as Comet is a customer of an industrial organisations such as Sony or Hotpoint. These industrial companies are in turn customers of the companies that make components such as electric motors or switches from which their finished goods are made. Most businesses therefore have a complex series of customer and supplier relationships.

In what ways do these different organisations use ICT to communicate and do business? The following examples briefly explain how ICT can be used to support key business processes.

Capturing and processing data

Many organisations – from schools and colleges to banks, utility companies and supermarkets – need to capture and process large quantities of data. This data capture was originally done via the computer's keyboard. Organisations such as banks and utility companies (gas, electricity, water and other service suppliers) have to record a large amount of data from:

* customers' cheques (in the case of banks)
* meter readings (in the case of gas and electricity suppliers).

These companies employed what are called data-entry clerks to carry out this task. Technology has since developed easier ways to capture data than through the keyboard. Personal cheques have been largely replaced by credit and debit cards which contain a magnetic strip that can be read by magnetic card reader. The data entry is therefore done via a credit card terminal in the shop. Gas and electricity meter readers no longer write the meter readings down on a form; instead they use a hand-held computer and enter the data on site. The data from the hand-held computer is then downloaded into the utility company's computer when the meter reader returns to his or her office at the end of the day.

Bar codes are another example of how technology has made data capture possible. Prior to its use, shops and supermarkets had no easy way to capture sales information. But now, since almost every item in a shop has a bar code which can be simply and quickly read by a bar code scanner, item prices can be stored (and easily modified) on the shop's computer. As items are sold the shop's stock records can also be updated, making stock control and the reordering of goods an automated process.

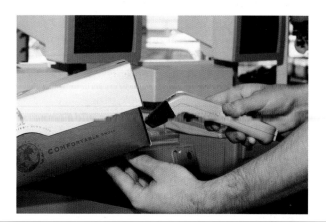

Bar codes have made the electronic capture of data possible

Presenting and exchanging information

Originally conceived as calculating machines, it wasn't long before the usefulness of computers was greatly enhanced by their being able to communicate the information they stored and processed. The World Wide Web itself was originally created to enable scientists to communicate and share the results of their research. Email has become the method of business communication, largely replacing the paper-based letter and memo. As well as sending text, email attachments can consist of pictures, music, documents and any machine-readable file. Other methods of computer communication include videoconferencing and online 'chat', where users can interact with each other in real time. All these methods of communication are used both for business and pleasure.

Conducting transactions

As we have already discussed, businesses are often involved in a complex series of customer and supplier relationships. Many large commercial and industrial organisations purchase large quantities of goods from a wide range of different suppliers. Supermarkets, for example, stock tens of thousands of items on their shelves, purchased from thousands of different suppliers. Motor car manufacturers also purchase many thousands of different components, ranging from nuts and bolts to tyres and radios.

Managing the purchase of these different items is a major task, and these transactions between buyer and supplier have also been revolutionised by ICT. Businesses that used to exchange order forms, invoices and other paper documents now complete their transactions electronically using EDI (electronic data interchange). The general public now rarely use a written cheque to pay for goods as credit and debit cards allow the transaction to be electronically authorised and recorded in real time. Although cash still remains popular for many transactions, that, too, may one day be replaced by a form of electronic money.

Marketing goods and services

ICT has not traditionally been used to market a company's goods and services. Radio, TV, billboard and newspaper advertising have been the media that have been most commonly used. However, the popularity of the Internet has meant that many companies, both large and small, have websites that provide information about their goods and services. While websites are still not the primary means of advertising for most companies, many companies direct interest to their websites from more direct forms of advertising. Website information is much easier and cheaper to update and add to than information contained in traditional sales leaflets and brochures. Websites can also include such media as sound, animation and video which cannot be included in leaflets and brochures. It is now unusual, therefore, to see an advert that does not suggest people should look up the company's website for more information.

Distributing goods

Commercial organisations (such as supermarkets) have a large number of stores, all of which need to be kept stocked with a huge variety of goods. It is a major task to plan and control the distribution of these goods to the stores in a timely and efficient manner. They also have to bear in mind that many of the goods may be perishable, so they need to be delivered to stores promptly. Computerised distribution systems control the movement of goods inside large regional distribution centres, ensuring the correct goods are loaded on to the correct lorry in the correct order. These systems not only ensure the correct goods are loaded for each store but also plan the route the delivery lorry will take to ensure the most efficient use of time and fuel.

Managing customer relations

The rise of the 'call centre' is another recent phenomenon which relies heavily on ICT. Many large organisations now provide customers with a central enquires telephone number which will connect customers to a computer-controlled telephone-response system. Some enquiries may be dealt with without human operator involvement. For example, in many cases bank customers can listen to their current account balance or make payments using an automated menu system with input from the customer via his or her telephone keypad.

For enquiries that cannot be dealt with by automated systems, customers may be routed to human operators. These operators, in order to reduce labour costs, may be situated across the globe, with many Asian countries being popular locations for call centre staff. Call centre staff use computers to access customer details and their purchasing or other transaction histories so that they can answer customer queries and resolve problems. Specialised customer relationship management software (often referred to by its initials, CRM) is often used to record details of customers' queries so that call centre staff can see the history of a query even though they may not have previously spoken to the customer.

Managing customer relationships is an important activity that, in the past, relied on personal contact. However, ICT has provided a number of cost-effective alternatives. Many organisations direct their customers to their websites for help and support, providing facilities such as FAQs (frequently asked questions) to deal with common problems, and email contact or support forms for more individual problems.

> **Think it over...**
>
> What are the benefits and drawbacks (both to the customer and the organisation) of locating call centres in remote locations?

Optimising just-in-time purchasing of stock and components

Manufacturing organisations that purchase large amounts of stock to be used in the manufacturing process often implement so-called 'just-in-time' (or JIT) manufacturing systems. Just-in-time systems aim to deliver components only as they are needed in the manufacturing process, thereby reducing the stock that has to be held in the warehouse. JIT techniques benefit from the use of ICT because they allow organisations to:

* keep accurate records of components kept in stock

* keep a close control on the manufacturing process so that the timing and quantities of required components can be monitored

* communicate electronically with suppliers so that orders can be placed promptly.

It's difficult to think of an area of business that has not been affected, if not revolutionised, by the computer. Even prior to the World Wide Web, computers had a profound effect on the way businesses operate, but since its explosive growth that revolution has spread out of the office and factory and has begun to change the way people sell goods and services.

Knowledge check

Select an organisation from each of the categories listed earlier (public, commercial, industrial) and list the different ways they use ICT to collect and process information.

2.2 From 'brick' to 'click'

Traditionally, those organisations that sell products or services have done so by one of two methods:

* a high-street shop, with customers visiting the shop and buying the goods in person

* mail order, with customers selecting goods via a printed catalogue and having them delivered.

With the advent of the Internet, online shopping has become possible. Online selling does not require a physical presence: traditional methods of selling took the form of the 'bricks and mortar' of the high-street shop or, in the case of mail-order selling, the paper catalogue and the telesales person at the end of a phone line. The term 'virtual' is often used to describe online selling since it has, or appears to have, no physical presence.

Key term

Virtual has become a commonly used term in the realm of computing and the Internet. The term literally means 'having the effect but not the physical presence'. So a virtual-reality computer game has the effect of being on a battlefield without you actually physically being there. The Internet, therefore, provides you with a 'virtual shopping mall' with all the features of a shopping mall but without you actually being in one.

The explosion in the growth of the Internet in the 1990s created sufficient online users for technically minded entrepreneurs to consider setting up online stores. Most of these were initially in the United States, but they soon spread to Europe and other countries where Internet usage is high. Online retailers, such as the bookseller, Amazon, were amongst the first to set up sites in the United States and Europe.

Setting up an online store

What is required to set up an Internet store? Many of the ingredients are similar to those needed for a traditional store, but there are some important differences:

* You must have a product or service to offer.

* You need a way to encourage buyers to visit your store, which is known as marketing. This is more difficult than with traditional stores since an Internet store has no physical presence and, therefore, without any marketing, no one will know the site is there. An important part of any online store's marketing is its domain name

CASE STUDY

The dot com 'bubble'

In the late 1990s, entrepreneurs and financiers became aware of the Internet and the potential that online selling held. Many people thought the Internet would become the 'next big thing' and that those who got in early and set up e-commerce sites would make large amounts of money. This was something like the 'goldrush' that occurred in America in the nineteenth century. Financiers lent these people millions of pounds to set up websites, and companies like lastminute.com were valued very highly, with their founders apparently being worth millions.

One of the websites set up at this time was boo.com. This online fashion clothing store was set up by three Swedish entrepreneurs and quickly attracted over £80 million in funding. They had an ambitious plan for a stylish and sophisticated website, which sold to 18 different European countries. However, technical problems meant that the site took a long time to develop and, when it was launched in November 1999, the problems did not stop. The extensive use of graphics, 3D images and pop-up windows made the site very slow to download and frustrating to use.

At that time only around 1 per cent of Internet users in Europe had a broadband link. The site also required the Macromedia Flash browser plug-in to work properly but, at that time, few people had this plug-in. People who tried the site found their bad experiences off-putting, and even though boo.com modified its site, many users did not return. The company was forced to close down only six months after it was launched, due to lack of funds (the company had spent the £80 million it raised!) and its inability to raise any more money.

The collapse of boo.com and a number of other dot.com companies scared investors and the 'Internet goldrush' came to an end. The high values placed on some companies nose-dived (for example, shares in lastminute.com went from £5 per share to 20p). Lastminute, unlike boo.com, survived the dot.com boom, but only became profitable in 2003.

How are 'dot com' companies doing today? You can find lots of up-to-date articles on the fortunes of companies like Lastminute, Amazon, eBay and others on the BBC News website, which has a section dedicated to e-commerce on its business pages.

---

or web address. An easy-to-remember address is important to make it easy for customers to find the site. Web addresses are unique: their use is controlled by a central authority, and new businesses in online shopping will have difficulty finding a memorable web address that has not already been registered.

* You need a way to accept orders. A transactional website must be designed and built.

* You need a way to accept money. Accepting cash or cheques for goods purchased over the Internet is not practical, so you need to accept credit or debit cards.

* You will need a way of delivering the goods or services you sell, which is known as 'fulfilment'. With traditional stores, fulfilment is easy: the customer picks up the goods when

he or she buys them. With an Internet store, unless the goods or services can be delivered electronically, they must be physically delivered, by post or courier.

* Since customers may not like what they buy, or the goods may be faulty, you will need a way to return goods. As customers cannot physically see the goods on an online site, this aspect is more important than with a traditional store. Customers will expect a guarantee that they can return the goods if they don't like them before they will buy from an Internet store.

* You will need a customer service department to help customers with problems, both technical (i.e. with the product they have bought) and with the purchasing process (i.e. with the website).

A *transactional website* is a site were visitors can complete some kind of transaction. The most common type is sites were visitors can order and pay for goods (such as books or computers) or services (such as airline flights). Other types of transactional website include sites provided by banks, where customers can check their account balance, transfer money and pay bills.

A *debit card* is issued by your bank and allows to you to make payments from your bank account to anyone who can accept your card. The payments are taken more or less immediately from your bank account.

Credit cards are slightly different. With a credit card you have an account separate from your normal bank account. Purchases you make with the card are added to your account and, at the end of the month, you are sent a statement, listing all your transactions. You can pay some or all of the outstanding balance. The use of stolen credit and debit cards to obtain goods fraudulently has become a major problem.

Chip and pin cards have been introduced to combat this. With these cards, rather than using a customer signature (which can easily be forged) to validate the card, the customer enters a PIN code into the credit card terminal in the shop though not online.

Why has online shopping proved so popular?

To understand this we need to consider the advantages both to the seller and the buyer. From the seller's perspective, there are a number of important benefits to selling online.

Access to a worldwide customer base

Traditionally, to achieve a wide geographic coverage, an organisation would need a large number of outlets spread across the country. With online selling such a coverage can be achieved without a large investment in buildings and the

people to staff them. Because, in most cases, goods have to be delivered to the customers and trading laws are different in different countries, most websites only sell within the country they are located in. Companies that have a international online presence, such as Amazon and eBay, have separate sites for each country they operate in.

Low set-up and running costs

Online selling has much lower costs that traditional selling methods. The operation can be run from a single, low-cost location rather than having to pay for a large number of shops in high-cost, high-street locations. As well as the reduction in cost associated with premises, there is a very significant reduction in the labour costs. Traditional selling through shops or mail order requires shopfloor or telesales personnel, but selling via a website does not require sales personnel. The customers themselves (via the website) select and pay for the goods.

Extension of product range

Once the infrastructure of an Internet shopping site has been set up, it is relatively easy to extend the range of goods that are sold. Certain goods are ideal for selling over the Internet (for example, goods that are relatively small and light in weight will not be expensive to deliver). The Amazon website provides a good example of an organisation that, over time, has extended its product range. Originally, Amazon just sold books, but it now also sells electronic goods (digital cameras, computer accessories, etc.), music CDs, videos and DVDs, games and computer software. Amazon also sells some Internet-specific goods, such as e-books.

E-books are not paper books but digital versions of books which can be instantly downloaded from a website (see Unit 1).

Amazon has also added what it calls 'Marketplace', a concept that is unique to

Internet selling. Amazon Marketplace allows customers to sell second-hand books and other goods on the site, alongside the new goods. Customers therefore have a choice of purchasing either new or second-hand items. Amazon makes money from their Marketplace concept by charging the seller a commission on every sale they make.

Many sites, especially those selling travel products, have partnerships with sites that sell related services, so most airline websites have partnerships with sites selling car hire, hotel bookings and other related services. This is convenient both for the customer, since he or she can book his or her flight and car hire at the same time, and for the primary seller, as they receive commission from these 'follow-on' sales.

Twenty-four hour opening

Modern lifestyles often do not fit with traditional shop-opening hours: people want to be able to shop at all hours but it is often not economic to open traditional shops late at night since the numbers of customers may be quite low. Also, in the UK, Sunday opening hours are currently restricted. No such problems face online selling, which can be open 24 hours, 365 days a year at no additional cost, thus maximising the opportunity to sell goods.

Faster response times

Online shops do not have queues and there is no waiting to be served. This, on top of all the other time savings involved, such as travelling time, makes online shopping a seemingly more 'instant' experience.

Real-time sales information

There is nothing more frustrating than setting off to the local shops or to the out-of-town shopping centre in search of a particular item only to find that none of the shops has it in stock. This is not a problem with online buying. Most Internet shops provide real-time stock level information so that you can see if the item you require is available

and, if it is not, many sites will give an estimated delivery date. If the site you normally use does not have the item, it is also easy to search for other sites that sell the item.

Customer expectation

Many customers expect large organisations to have an online presence and, in some cases, an online presence can complement physical stores. Buyers can do their research online in prices, specifications and such like but may decide they want to see the actual goods in store before purchasing. Or they may decide they don't want to wait for delivery, so the journey to the shop is worth the effort. Many organisations go to considerable efforts to project a good image of themselves to their customers.

A survey carried out by BT in 2004 of businesses in Britain and Germany showed that many businesses had created an e-commerce site mainly to make the company look modern and forward-looking in the eyes of their customers.

There are also many advantages to the customer:

* The ability to access a wide range of goods and services from the comfort of your home at any time of night or day is clearly a major benefit.

* Price comparisons are much easier to make online – you do not have to travel to different shops. Websites exist that will carry out price comparisons for the customer (such as those at **kelkoo.co.uk**; a link is available at www.heinemann.co.uk/hotlinks (express code 2016P)). While this is clearly an advantage to the customer, it does mean that sellers must be very price competitive, which can cut profit margins.

Disadvantages of Internet shopping

Internet shopping has many advantages for both the seller and the buyer. However, there are some important drawbacks.

Security

Probably the greatest concern for most people shopping online is security. Passing personal and financial information over the Internet poses a risk but, in many cases, the risks are exaggerated. According to Forrester research, for every £1,000 spent online, £1 is lost in fraud (this compares to £25 lost in off-line sales). None the less, there have been some high-profile errors involving online selling sites – the disclosure of credit card details, for example. In November 2004 a security loophole was identified in the Cahoot Internet Bank website. A customer discovered a way to view other people's account details, and provided details of the flaw to the BBC. The site was closed for 10 hours while the problem was resolved.

For the seller themselves, security is a headache as they must be constantly on their guard against attacks from hackers, who may try to steal customer details, and from people who are trying to obtain goods fraudulently.

Competition

The Internet shopping market can be very price competitive. People who shop via the Internet often know the product they want and are trying to find it at the lowest price. In many market areas there are a number of sites selling those products (for example, electrical and electronic goods, computers and accessories, travel) so competition is fierce, and a number of online shopping sites have failed. Internet-only sellers also face strong competition from traditional companies that have also set up websites (Argos, Comet, Tesco, etc.). These traditional companies have a well-known name, a reputation and greater marketing muscle than most Internet-only organisations.

Cannot physically see or try the goods

For certain types of goods, not being able to see or try the goods is not a problem, especially if the buyer knows exactly what he or she wants. With other goods (for example, clothes), people may prefer to see and try on the actual goods before purchasing.

Goods must be delivered

Physical goods purchased over the Internet must, of course, be delivered. This adds to the cost (especially for large or heavy goods) and means that the customer cannot have the goods immediately. Delivery can cause problems because many companies require goods to be signed for when they are delivered as a protection against fraud, especially if they are high-value items. This means customers may have to stay at home or arrange for someone to be at home to receive the goods.

The year 2004, and in particular the Christmas period, was the turning point for online retailers: a survey of shoppers that year showed that 44 per cent planned to make online purchases, compared with 21 per cent in 2003, and they were predicted to spend around £4 billion during the Christmas period, an increase of over 60 per cent on the previous year.

Theory into practice

Magazines, newspapers and websites such as the BBC News site have plenty of articles about the latest e-commerce issues. Reading these articles can help to develop your knowledge and understanding of the issues affecting this area.

2.3 Transactional websites

Websites that can be used to buy or sell goods or services are sometimes called transactional websites (see earlier in this unit) since they allow some kind of transaction to take place. These types of website should not be confused with the many websites which simply provide information. Transactional websites can be broadly divided into three categories. Sites which sell:

* physical goods, such as books or TV sets

* services, such as airline flights or insurance

* products that can be downloaded directly from the site, such as music and computer software.

CASE STUDY

The music industry

No other industry has been as dramatically affected by the rise of the Internet as the music industry. Since the invention of a cheap and simple audio recording system in the form of the audio cassette, the industry has faced the problem of the illegal copying of music. With the Internet the problem became a very serious one. Two other developments went along with the Internet in making large-scale music piracy practical. One was the MP3 digital music file format. This allowed digital music to be compressed into files which could be downloaded in minutes rather than hours while retaining good-quality playback. The other was peer-to-peer file sharing over the Internet. This allows users to share each other's collections of digital music directly from their own computers, rather than storing the files on a central server. These three ideas were brought together in 1999 by an 18-year-old called Shawn Fanning. He created a program which allowed searching and peer-to-peer file sharing of music files and he called it Napster.

Napster quickly became very popular since it provided a way for people to obtain music without paying for it. However, it was not popular with the music industry because it enabled people to obtain thousands of copyrighted songs without paying any royalty fee. The music industry fought for years to close down Napster, and eventually succeeded in May 2002 after a long legal battle. The illegal copying of music is still possible: a number of other peer-to-peer file-sharing programs exist, which, unlike Napster, do not maintain a central index server which lists all the users (it does not store the songs themselves), and which are therefore much harder for the music industry to find and close down.

Until quite recently no organisation had successfully set up a legal MP3 download site, where songs are available with the agreement of the music company that owns them and that can be downloaded for a fee. This was the result of the difficulty of obtaining the permission of a cautious music industry who were nervous about this new technology, and the ease with which music could be illegally obtained without charge. However, the music industry knew something had to be done because, during 2003–4, sales of legal CDs fell in some markets by as much as 30 per cent. In 2003 the music industry launched a worldwide crackdown on Internet music swapping and began to sue individuals who made large catalogues of music available over the Internet.

In May 2003, Apple computer launched the first successful legal music download site, called iTunes. Apple managed to persuade the music industry to give them permission to sell their songs, and the site linked with the enormously successful Apple MP3 player, the iPod. The iPod is stylish and sophisticated, and its success has transformed the fortunes of the Apple company, with more than 3 million iPods sold in 2004, giving Apple 50 per cent of the MP3 player market and boosting the company's profits by 50 per cent.

The iPod is stylish and sophisticated

Continued…

The iTunes site sells single songs for around 90p each, and it has sold more than 100 million songs, with 70 per cent of the market share in legal downloads. The iTunes site is a little different from many other successful e-commerce sites. Apple is a computer company, not a music company, and, unlike many sites, the product is delivered instantly and electronically over the Internet.

Napster has recently been re-launched, this time as a legal music download site, where music must be paid for.

The success of the iTunes site was partly linked to the success for the iPod player, but what other factors help the site to succeed?

You need to study such sites and, as you do so, you need to consider the following:

* the purpose of the site and how successfully it meets this objective
* how it is structured
* the goods and/or services it offers
* the product information provided
* the types of transactions that can be made and how easy it is to do so
* the methods used to capture customer information (both overt and covert) and to authenticate the identity of customers
* the techniques used to engage, retain and entice customers
* its usability and accessibility
* the 'customer experience' it offers.

In this section we will look at a number of sites to see how they address the above issues.

The purpose of the site and how it is structured

Most transactional websites which sell physical goods take the purchaser through a number of stages.

Product search, selection and information

This stage allows the customer to search for the item he or she requires, perhaps by type or name. Customers can view details of the product, and some sites show additional information about the product, such as customer reviews, etc. Figure 2.1 shows the front page of the Heinemann FE and vocational website. The name of a book (or qualification) can be entered in the Search box on the top right and this will produce a list of books that match the criteria entered.

More powerful search facilities need to be provided on sites that sell items such as holidays or airline flights as there are more criteria which need to be set. Figure 2.2 shows the home page of the British Midland Airways company, which is called flybmi.com.

The results of the search are then displayed, allowing the user to select the most suitable one. Figure 2.3 shows the search results page of the flybmi.com website, with a number of different flights to the chosen destination on the days selected. The page lists them with an **Option** button next to each.

Having searched for and found the required product, the site may provide more information about the item. The Heinemann site, for example, gives a brief description of the book, allows you to read some reviews and gives you a preview of some sample material from the book (see Figure 2.4). This page also has a link to additional items which may be relevant, such as teacher resources.

Virtual shopping basket

This allows customers to select the goods they wish to purchase and to make a list of these items. The customer can then either continue shopping and add additional items to the basket or move to the checkout. The Heinemann website has a button on the right site of the product details page

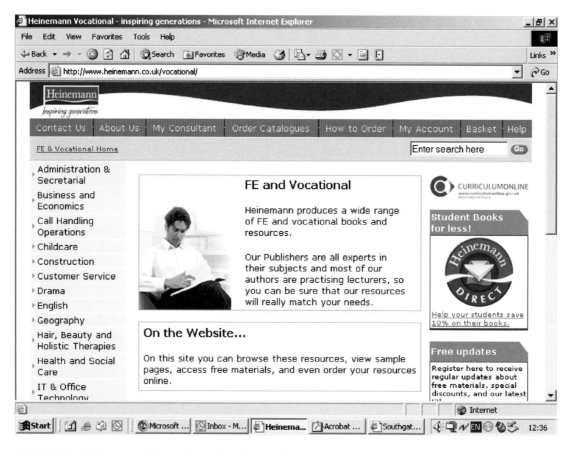

FIGURE 2.1 *Heinemann FE and vocational website*

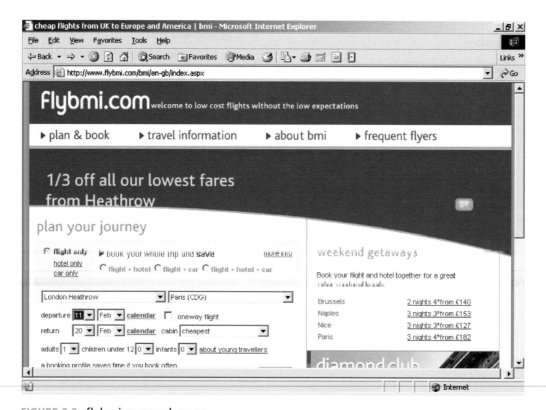

FIGURE 2.2 *flybmi.com web page*

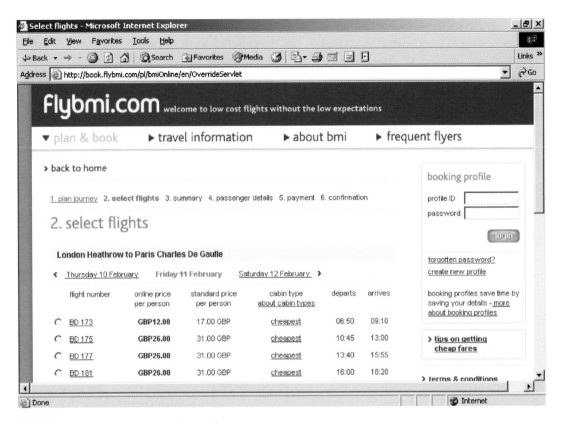

FIGURE 2.3 *flybmi.com search results*

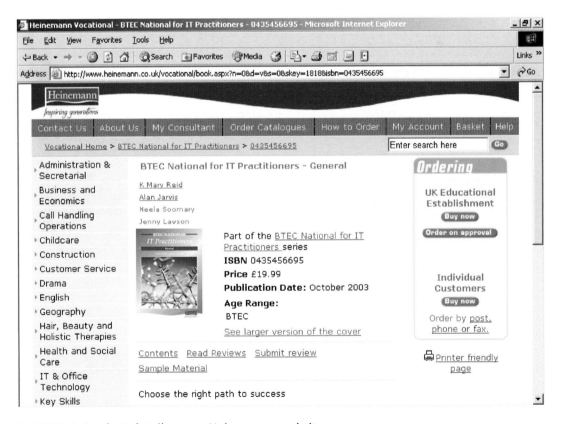

FIGURE 2.4 *Product details page, Heinemann website*

(labelled **Buy now**), which will add the currently displayed item to the basket. Clicking this button adds the product and displays the basket's contents, as shown in Figure 2.5.

The shopping basket page usually has facilities to remove or modify the quantities of items previously added (the **Delete** link on the Heinemann page allows items to be removed).

Travel websites often do not have a shopping basket concept since most people only buy one flight or holiday at a time. The flybmi.com website is an example of this: once the flights (outward and, if required, return) have been chosen, a summary page is shown, with no facility to add more flights, as shown in Figure 2.6.

Types of transaction and customer registration

Checkout

Once the customer has finished shopping, he or she needs to pay for his or her goods. The transaction stage requires that the customer is registered with the site. Customers who are already registered can enter their authentication details and confirm the delivery address and payment details. Customers who are not registered must go through the registration stage.

Registration

This stage involves the customer providing his or her personal details, including delivery address, email address and payment details in the form of the credit or debit card number, security code and expiry date. Figure 2.7 shows the customer registration page from the Heinemann site.

Confirmation

Having registered, the customer's credit card details will be validated and authorisation for the sale obtained from his or her credit card company. The final stage in the process is the display of the confirmation page, which gives details of the purchase that has been made.

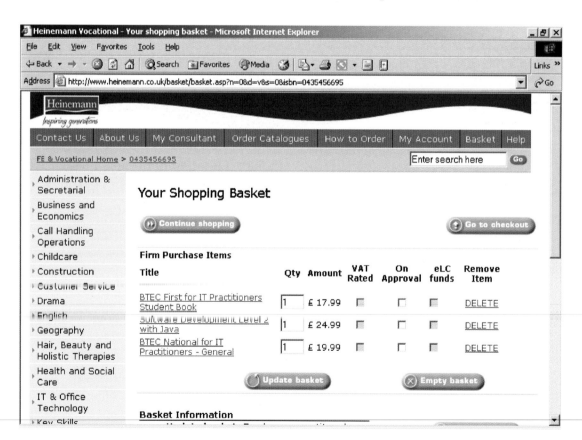

FIGURE 2.5 *Heinemann website shopping basket*

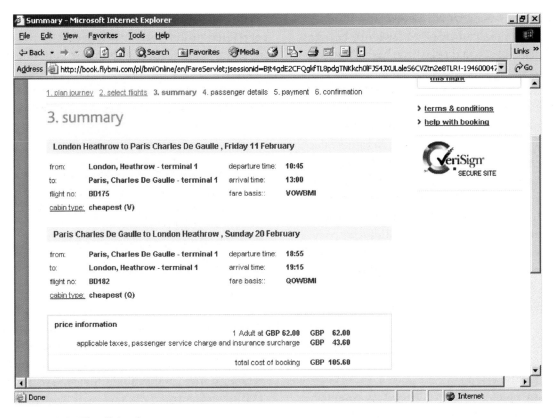

FIGURE 2.6 *The flybmi.com summary page*

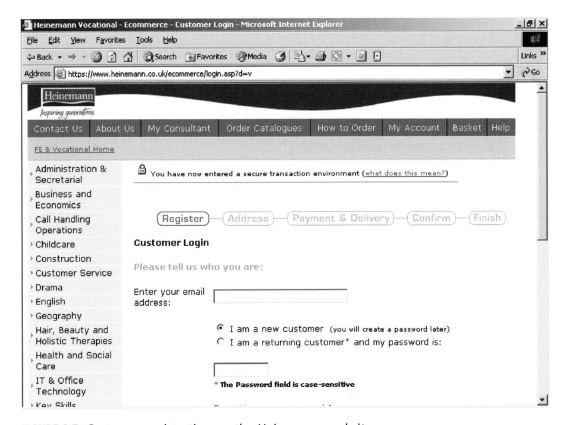

FIGURE 2.7 *Customer registration on the Heinemann website*

Confirmation is normally also sent to the customer's email address. An order or booking reference code is also usually issued. This can be used if there is any query about the order or, in the case of the flight, it is used at the airport check-in to identify the customer's flight booking.

Airline tickets and books are, of course, not the only things you can buy online, but most sites follow the same structure. For example, another popular type of transaction website is online banking. Most traditional banks allow customers to access their account details online and provide facilities for them to view their statements, to transfer money and to pay bills. An number of Internet-only banks have also sprung up. The key benefit of online banking is convenience, but security is a major headache (see the section on security page 47).

The two transactional websites described here (flybmi and Heinemann) are fairly typical, but there are many more examples. Most follow a similar layout but there are differences between them. Many sites provide more sophisticated facilities to assist the purchaser in making his or her choices. Some sites also encourage the customer to purchase related items. Amazon, for example, features lists of additional items that people who bought a particular product also purchased. Sites which sell computer hardware and electronic goods also often feature lists of related items or accessories that can be used with the items chosen.

Attracting customers

Transactional websites use a variety of techniques to encourage customers to spend time on their sites, visit them regularly and purchase items. Large sums of money are spent on designing and developing a visually interesting site with images and animations that encourage users to visit and explore it. Sites also need to be updated regularly to maintain the interest of returning customers.

Sites attempt to retain existing customers in a number of ways. Personalised offers and suggested purchases is one way this can be done and most sites will send registered customers regular e-mails reminding them of special offers and the latest products.

The site's usability and accessibility

No one likes using a site that is slow, keeps crashing or is difficult to use. This was one of the

---

CASE STUDY

eBay

eBay is something of an Internet phenomenon. The site has been enormously successful with versions in 29 different countries and profits of over $182 million in the three months to the end of September 2004. eBay has been likened to an online car-boot sale: unlike the sites we have discussed so far, eBay does not sell its own products; instead, anyone can auction his or her goods on the site. With something like 25 million items for sale at one time, eBay has 114 million registered users worldwide, with 8.7 million in the UK alone. Items up for auction include anything from a Gulf Stream jet aircraft (sold for £2.57 million – the most expensive so far) to cars, jewellery, computer goods and antiques.

eBay was founded in 1997 by an American called Pierre Omidyar who wanted a way for his wife to trade her collection of Pez dispensers (Pez is an American sweet that comes in different styles of plastic dispensers).

eBay makes its money from the commission charged to people who sell their goods on the site; it does not handle, stock or ship the goods it's down to the sellers to do that.

1 What is it that makes eBay so successful?
2 What benefits for the company that runs the site does eBay have over more traditional e-commerce sites?

major problems with the boo.com site mentioned earlier. Site designers need to strike a delicate balance between making the site interesting and making it too complex. The site design needs to be intuitive so that it is obvious to users how to use it and they don't get lost within the site or confused about how to use its various features. The topic of user interface design is a subject in itself, known as Human Computer Interface (HCI) and there are many guidelines and rules on producing easy to use websites. The 'web pages that suck' site includes many examples of bad web page design, as well as articles on good page design: http://www.webpagesthatsuck.com/

A transactional website also needs to run on systems capable of providing a reasonable response time during periods of high demand, since people quickly get bored with a site whose pages load very slowly.

Shopping from home via the Internet is clearly beneficial to some disabled people for whom a trip to high-street shops may be difficult. Most sites however would be difficult for the visually impaired to use. In April 2005 Queen's University in Belfast started a three-year project to help open the Internet to blind people. You can read more about this project at http://news.bbc.co.uk/1/hi/northern_ireland/4457793.stm.

The customer experience

Unless a customer knows exactly what they want, they typically want to browse through items, view detailed specifications (especially with computer and electronic equipment) and compare prices. With a well-designed interface, a website can provide all these facilities to the customer, which is often difficult to achieve in a traditional store. All sites allow customers to search for items. Some sites only provide a simple key word search, more sophisticated sites include multiple criteria searches and searches within restricted categories. Some sites also allow search results to be ordered (most or least expensive first, for example) in a particular way. Many sites provide extensive information on the specification of the products they offer, some offering manufacturers data sheets

or links to the manufacturers website for further details. Some sites also allow customers to rate products and make these comments available to prospective purchasers (online book seller Amazon is an example of this). This can help buyers make up their mind and is another example of a feature that is not available with traditional shopping.

As long as their facilities are reasonably easy to use, they can enhance the customer experience and provide another reason to shop online and return to the sites that provide the best experience.

Theory into practice

Investigate the design of another commercial website. In terms of design, ease of use and navigation, what are its strengths and weaknesses?

You could also ask other people, such as members of your family, to rate the different sites based on the facilities they provide.

Assessment activity

Research the various types of e-commerce website and evaluate them in terms of ease of use and the facilities they provide. The questions you should ask include:

✳ How easy is it to find the products you want?

✳ Is a range of search options provided?

✳ Can lists of matching items be displayed in different orders (cheapest first, most popular first, etc.)?

✳ Was sufficient information provided to enable you to choose between similar products?

Assessment hint

✓   Briefly describe the main features of the site's design.

✓✓✓ Find and investigate suitable sites independently and provide a comprehensive description of the site

Signpost for e-portfolio evidence

Save this work in your portfolio. It could contribute towards covering assessment evidence (a).

2.4 Back-office processes

While the web pages you interact with are the most obvious part of a transactional website, it is the software that runs on the server computers that make the whole shopping process work. The choices you make on the web pages and the information you enter are all transferred back to the website's server computers for processing. This processing includes the following:

* real-time tracking of customers' actions
* the maintenance of the virtual shopping basket
* identification and authentication routines
* payment processing
* stock control
* despatch and delivery.

These software systems are connected to other systems within the company, some of which may predate the web-based system, and also to other systems outside the company, such as the credit card authorisation system. In this section we shall look at each stage of a typical online purchase again, this time concentrating on what happens in the 'back office' where the seller's web server computers are located.

> ### Key term
>
> A *web server* is a computer which runs software that responds to requests to display web pages. A website is accessed using its Internet address (i.e. www.domainname.suffix), which is used to find the appropriate web server computer that holds the page.

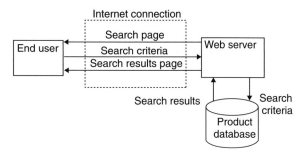

FIGURE 2.8 *The search phase*

During the search and select phase, the user makes choices and enters information into the web page he or she is viewing. This data is transferred back to the server and used to query the product database. The resulting data is used to produce a web page that shows the products that match the search criteria. This page is then transmitted back to the user. As well as including product and price information, stock or estimated delivery date information may also be extracted from the product database for inclusion in the data that is sent back to the user. This process is show in diagrammatic form in Figure 2.8.

Real-time tracking of customer's actions

Each time a user visits the transactional website, a record is created in the server's database of the visit, which is commonly known as the session. Each session is identified by an ID number. The session record is used to track and hold information about the user's visit while he or she is using the site.

Maintenance of the virtual shopping basket

Having found the product he or she requires, the user may then place it in the virtual shopping basket. The details of the product

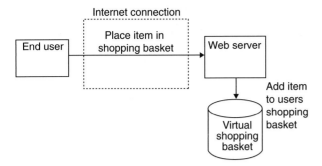

FIGURE 2.9 *The shopping basket*

Key term

A *secure connection* is used to protect information (such as credit card numbers and personal information) as it is transmitted from the customer to the website he or she is using. The data sent is encrypted so no one else can read it. When you enter a secure connection, a dialogue box appears telling you that you are about use a secure connection, as shown in Figure 2.11. A similar dialogue box also appears when you exit the secure connection, warning you that you are about to do so. While you are using a secure connection a padlock icon appears in the Status bar at the bottom of the browser window.

that has been chosen and the quantity required are recorded as part of the session data. The user may search for and add many different items in the shopping basket, and the session record maintains a list of the items in the basket. In some cases a user may browse the website and add items to the basket but leave the site without purchasing anything. Some sites do allow users to maintain a saved shopping basket or wish list, which they can access next time they visit the site. The diagram in Figure 2.9 shows the main data flows associated with placing an item in the shopping basket.

Identification and authentication routines

When the user has finished shopping and goes to the checkout page on the site, he or she must first log on. If he or she is a new user, he or she enters his or her personal details and this information is transmitted to the server and recorded in the registered user database. If the customer is an existing user, his or her authentication information (username and password) is transmitted to the server and checked against the database to ensure it matches the recorded credentials (see Figure 2.10).

From this stage on, the transactions between user and website are usually done using a secure connection.

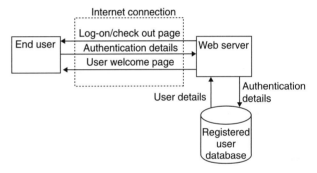

FIGURE 2.10 *Log on*

Payment processing

Once the user has logged on or registered, the server will calculate the total sales price using the session data about the items in his or her shopping basket and will apply the site rules about postage and packing, etc. The user will then be asked to confirm that he or she wishes to proceed with the purchase. If the user does, the server must then either ask the user for his or her credit card details and obtain authorisation for the sale from the user's credit card company. This involves transmitting the user's credit card details and the amount of the sale to the credit card company's authorisation computer. (Some servers may already have the user's credit card details on their registered

FIGURE 2.11 *Opening a secure connection*

user database with the user's authorisation. In this case, they simply extract the relevant details from the database to transmit to the credit card company.) Once authorisation has been obtained, the server will create a record on the transaction database, recording all the details of the sale. It will also update the stock levels on the product database since the items in the sale are no longer 'in stock': they are awaiting despatch to the customer.

Stock control, despatch and delivery

The server will also send a message to the warehouse computer notifying it that a sale has been made and that the goods need to be despatched. Using the data recorded on the transaction database, the warehouse computer will print off a picking list and an address label so that the warehouse personnel can pick and pack the items purchased and stick the address label on the package ready for it to be collected by the delivery company. The main data flows for this step are shown in Figure 2.12.

Theory into practice

What software do people use to create transactional websites? There are a number of software systems that are currently in use, including Dreamweaver and Cold Fusion from Macromedia and ASP® from Microsoft. Find out what features these and other systems provide and how they can be used to create transactional websites.

Assessment activity

Using an e-commerce website you are familiar with, create detailed diagrams showing the events involved in an online purchase. The diagrams should show the flow of information between the user, the website and other back office processes. The diagrams should show how the virtual shopping is maintained, how customers are identified and authorised, and how payment is processed. They should also show how the system links with stock control, despatch and delivery.

Assessment hint

✓   Produce a diagram which gives an outline of the purchase process.

✓✓✓ Produce diagrams which give a complete and accurate picture of the process and are effectively presented.

 Signpost for e-portfolio evidence

This activity covers assessment evidence (b).

2.5 E-customers

As you discovered when investigating transactional websites, an essential part of completing an online transaction is registering the customer and collecting his or her details. This provides an vital information bank that is an important resource for the selling organisation, and one that it is not always possible for traditional (non-Internet) sellers to collect. One of the most important pieces of information is the customer's email address. Once this has been collected, the seller has a way to update the customer regularly on the latest offers and new products. Anyone who has purchased from an Internet site will know that he or she is guaranteed regular emails from the organisation advertising their goods or services.

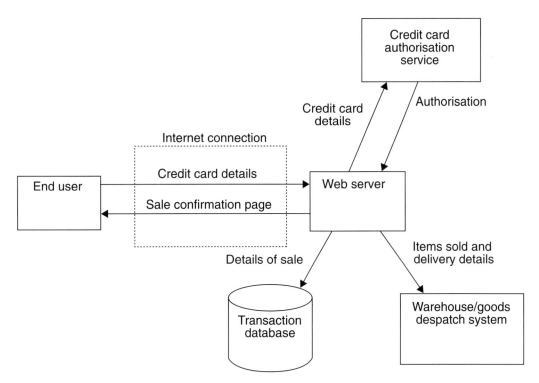

FIGURE 2.12 *Completing the sale*

Analysis of purchase histories and sales information

In addition to the personal information collected when a customer registers with a site, data is also collected about every sale that is made. This information needs to be collected in order to complete the sale. However, it is also analysed for marketing purposes. Such information can help to identify a number of important things:

* which products are selling the best, and which are increasing and decreasing in their sales

* what category of products sells the best

* how sales vary at different times of the year

* which region of the country sales come from.

This data can be used to:

* plan capacity at the warehouse

* measure the effectiveness of advertising

* plan new products or product ranges

* forward-order stock to meet anticipated demand.

The careful analysis of this kind of data can ensure that the company is run in a efficient way: it can help make sure that there is the right kind and quantity of goods in the warehouse and that the warehouse in not overstocked (no one wants to have a warehouse full of Christmas decorations on the 26 December!) as this costs money.

Think it over...

What website and traditional sellers have you come across that run loyalty schemes? What sort of companies tend to run these schemes? Why do they run them? What benefits are there for the companies that run the schemes?

Loyalty schemes

Many online stores, in common with many traditional sellers, operate loyalty schemes. These provide purchasers with points or e-vouchers that can be collected and exchanged for discounts on goods. These schemes are designed to encourage purchasers to visit the store repeatedly.

Surveys

Surveys or questionnaires are used by some sites to collect information about customers. Sites often ask new users where they heard about the site. This information is used to judge the effectiveness of various types of marketing. However, it is difficult to collect very much information this way as users are often unwilling to spend a lot of time filling them in.

Competitions

Competitions and special offers are used by some sites to encourage users to buy items and to return to the site. Some companies also run traditional competitions on chocolate or drinks wrappers that require the entrant to go to the company's website, thereby encouraging visitors to their site.

Cookies

A cookie is a text file that a web server can store on a user's hard disk when he or she views a page from that server. Cookies store some information about your visit to the web page, and they are generally used so that the web server can identify you. For example, many e-commerce websites use cookies to identify users who have visited the website previously. They are also used by the server to keep track of users and their shopping trolley contents. When you open a shopping web page, a cookie is normally created on your machine with a unique session ID number in it, allocated by the server. Each time you put an item in your shopping trolley, the web server checks and records the ID number from the cookie and so keeps track of which shopping trolley items belong to which user.

Cookies do sometimes get users worried as they don't like the idea of other people saving files on their computer, but it is important to realise that the cookies by themselves are just files (not programs) and therefore they do not represent much of a security risk. There are also some concerns over privacy and cookies. Cookies can be used to record information about which pages within a site you have visited and therefore they build up a profile of the products you might be interested in but have not yet bought. This information could be used to target marketing specifically at you, and your interests.

Theory into practice

Investigate the cookies on your PC at home or in the classroom. What picture do they build up of you? Look at the way cookies track which websites you have visited.

Spyware

Spyware is the name often given to advertising-supported software. This is normally used by shareware authors to make money from a product, other than by users paying for the licence. An example is the 'Gator' program which is included in some freeware and shareware programs. This program helps you fill out online forms (by remembering your details), but it also sends information about your web-surfing habits back to the company that produces the program and pops up adverts on your PC.

Key term

Shareware is software that can be obtained and downloaded free of charge. The software, however, is copyright and can only be used for an evaluation period before a payment needs to be made.

Advertising and media companies offer software that displays banner adverts to shareware authors to add to the products they have created. In return, the authors receive a portion of the revenue from the advert sales. This might seem fairly harmless, even if the adverts are annoying, but the problem with these spyware programs is that, as well as displaying the adverts, they also gather statistics of various types (the Internet sites you visit and the products you might be interested in, for example) and transmit these statistics back to the organisation that originally provided the spyware program. Most of the statistics gathered are quite harmless, and spy ware is not illegal. Nonetheless, many people are uncomfortable with the idea of data about them being gathered and transmitted.

All these techniques are used to enable the online seller to gather as much information as possible about their customers. Unlike traditional shops, there is no personal contact between the buyer and seller and the opportunity to build loyalty based on a personal relationship does not exist. This, coupled with the ease with which searches and price comparisons can be made, makes customer loyalty difficult for the online seller to build. Collecting information about a customer's interests and the sort of products they like enables a site to provide customised marketing targeted at individuals and groups of customers. Sites can also attempt to obtain a competitive advantage over their competitors by the following methods:

* *Offering a personalised service*: this can be done, for example, by sending what appear to be personalised emails that offer goods and services that the customer's profile suggests he or she may be interested in.

* *Persuading customers to spend more*: a number of sites provide encouragement to purchase additional items with 'other customers who bought this item also bought the following' sections (Amazon is an example of this), or lists of accessories or additional items which relate to items already selected.

* *Predicting market trends*: by analysing sales trends, sites can see, for example, which items are becoming less popular, and so can offer them at a discount to get rid of stock. They may also be able to spot which products are becoming more popular and so order more to meet the anticipated demand.

* *Reduce wastage*: this is also linked to spotting trends in sales and is particularly important for sites that sell perishable goods, such as supermarkets or sites that sell flowers. If they buy in too little stock they will be unable to meet the demand; if they buy too much, goods will be wasted.

Knowledge check

1 Why do companies collect information about the individuals who visit their website?

2 What methods are used to attract and retain customers?

2.6 E-consumer awareness

While collecting information about customers and their purchases is useful for the seller, e-customers need to be aware of what information is held, how accurate it is, who has access to that information and how it is used. They need to be sure that the information collected is being protected against theft and misuse. They need to know how accurate the information being held about them is. They also need to be aware of some of the more intrusive methods that can be used to collect information and how to protect themselves against methods that may be used by some unscrupulous sites.

People are naturally worried about handing over personal and financial information, especially with the recent increase in identity fraud, where criminals steal individual's identity (personal details, account numbers, etc.) and then use this data to obtain money from their bank accounts or on their behalf (by taking out loans, etc. using the stolen identity). Transactional websites need to make sure customers are confident to hand over such information, and assure them that it will be used properly and stored securely.

Data Protection Act

Customers purchasing from UK-based sites are, of course, protected by the Data Protection Act (DPA). This requires companies that hold personal information about living individuals to keep that information:

* secure from unauthorised access
* accurate and up to date

* for no longer than is necessary
* only for the purpose it was gathered.

Companies that keep personal information must register with the Data Protection Registrar and, if they break the rules, they face legal action.

Customers are also protected by the Distance Selling Regulations which apply to goods purchased by phone (mail order), over the Internet or via TV. The protection provided includes:

* the customer has the right to receive clear, accurate information about the goods
* goods must be delivered within 30 days unless agreed otherwise
* the customer has a 'cooling-off period' that allows him or her to withdraw from the sale for up to seven days after the sale is made (this does not apply to some goods, such as perishable items and unsealed CDs and DVDs)
* the company must refund the customer if his or her credit card is used fraudulently.

The online buyer is also protected by the same regulations that cover goods sold by traditional methods, such as:

* the Sale of Goods Act, which requires that goods are of satisfactory quality and gives the customer the right to obtain a replacement if a fault is discovered

CASE STUDY

'Phishing'

Online banking has naturally been a target for criminal activity. So called 'phishing' (a misspelling of the word 'fishing') involves an attempt to get an unsuspecting customer of the online bank to reveal his or her personal details, such as username, password and security codes. This is done by sending an email to the customer which purports to be from the person's bank, and which asks the person to follow a hyperlink that takes him or her to a page which is made to look like one of the genuine bank's pages. Once at this bogus page, the customer fills in his or her account details

and these are collected by the criminals, who can use this information to transfer the money into the criminals' account. Up to November 2004, around 2,000 people had been victims of these scams, with £4.5 million lost (although the banks have refunded the money to the customers).

How can banks protect their customers from these types of attacks? You may find it helpful to visit the anti-fraud website set up by the banks at www.banksafeonline.org.uk (a link to their site is available at www.heinemann.co.uk/hotlinks (express code 2016P)).

* the regulations of the Advertising Standards Authority, which require that adverts are legal, decent, honest and truthful.

Theory into practice

Find more about the distance-selling regulations at the DTI (Department of Trade and Industry) website (*www.dti.gov.uk/ccp/topics1/ecomm.htm;* a link to their site is available at *www.heinemann.co.uk/hotlinks* (express code 2008P)).

2.7 Security

As we have already mentioned, security is a big issue with online buying. People are naturally cautious where money is involved, and the thought of personal details, particularly credit or debit card information, being hijacked by cyber criminals puts some people off shopping on the Internet. Organisations that want to operate successfully online must take the threats to data security seriously in order to win their customers' confidence and trust.

Organisations can try to protect themselves against these kinds of attacks by using:

* risk assessments
* physical security
* user IDs and access right
* encryption
* secure electronic transactions
* firewalls
* virus protection.

Each of these techniques is described below.

Risk assessment

Before any organisation can arrange with its bank to accept payments electronically over the Internet, it must carry out a risk assessment which estimates how exposed the organisation is to the risk that the customer will not pay for the goods. There are two main reasons why a customer may not pay for the goods:

* the customer may request a refund from the credit card company (for example, if the goods are faulty or are never delivered – known as a charge-back)
* the customer's card has been stolen.

Key term

Exposure to risk is an estimate of how likely an event will take place. The estimation is based on a number of factors. Insurance companies, for example, estimate how exposed to risk a person or organisation is when they calculate premiums.

Risk assessment for an online business is based on a number of factors:

* *The amount of goods the company estimates it will sell*: the more goods that are sold, the greater the likelihood of problems
* *The average transaction size*: higher-value items are more likely to cause problems
* *Time taken from payment to order delivery*: the longer it takes the company to deliver the goods, the greater the risk that the customer will cancel his or her payment
* *Length of time in business*: a start-up company represents a greater risk than an established one
* *Business classification*: different business sectors have different risks. For example, if you purchase an airline ticket online, you have to turn up at the airport to take the flight. However, if you purchase a CD online you can always claim it was never delivered, or copy and return it and claim a refund
* *The security the organisation puts in place*: the more secure the bank thinks an organisation's website and overall system is, the less the risk.

Having estimated the risk, the bank will require the organisation to pay a bond (like an insurance premium) to cover the risk. You can find more information about electronic payments and risk assessment at the Electronic Payment website (www.electronic-payments.co.uk; a link to their site is available at www.heinemann.co.uk/hotlinks (express code 2016P)).

Physical security

The data held on the selling organisation's web servers and other computers must be physically secure as well as secure from attack via electronic means. This means the computers must be locked in a room to which only authorised staff have the key. Copies of backup disks or tapes must also be kept secure. It is unwise to store backups in the same room as the server (since a fire or other catastrophe could destroy both), so they should be stored securely at another site.

User IDs and access rights

Networked multi-user computer systems have usernames to identify individual users. Local users of the web servers of an Internet shopping site would include technicians, managers, customer service staff and warehouse personnel. Each of these users must have his or her own username and password. Different users will need to gain access to different parts of the system and the data held on it. Personal data about the site's customers, for example, must be protected against unauthorised access because:

* it is a requirement of the Data Protection Act that personal information cannot be viewed by people who do not need to see the information

* this information is commercially sensitive. The organisation would not want a competitor to able to get hold of a list of customers' email addresses, for example

* details of people's credit cards must be protected from unauthorised access.

In order to protect data held on the system, the administrator must set the access rights to sensitive data files so that only those users who are authorised to see them can do so.

Encryption

This is a technique for encoding sensitive information (such as credit card details) when it is sent over the Internet so that only the site that the data is intended for can decode it. Most e-commerce websites use a type of encryption known as secure sockets layer (SSL) encryption when this type of data is being sent.

Secure electronic transactions (SET)

SET is a networking protocol developed by the credit card organisations Visa and MasterCard. It is designed to ensure the security of electronic credit

CASE STUDY

The Sasser Internet worm

In May 2004 the Sasser Internet worm virus caused chaos. It hit hundreds of thousands of computers across the world, causing them continuously to shut down and then reboot. The virus was created by an 18-year-old German student. Unlike other viruses, Sasser did not require the computer users to download a file or open an email – it invaded the machines directly via the Internet exploiting a loop-hole in recent versions of Microsoft operating systems including Windows 2000 and XP. Only those computers which had the very latest Microsoft updates could prevent the virus infecting them. The required update was only released a couple of weeks before the virus started infecting machines.

card transactions made over the Internet. SET encrypts messages sent between the buyer and the seller so they cannot easily be read by anyone else.

Firewalls

To protect their web servers and other computers from outside electronic attack, Internet shops commonly use a firewall. This is device that provides a gateway between the company's internal network and the external Internet. The software in a firewall inspects incoming data and only allows data through into the internal network if it is legitimate. This helps to prevent hackers from trying to gain information about the systems and data within the organisation.

Virus protection

Viruses are a major problem on the Internet. Viruses can damage data held on computers and can also use infected computers for unauthorised purposes, such as sending emails and replicating themselves. It is vital, therefore, that organisations running e-commerce website protect their machines from virus attack by installing virus-detecting software and updating it regularly so that it can catch the latest viruses.

Assessment activity

Investigate three ways in which the customer data that is collected by organisations via their website could be misused. You will need to describe these threats and evaluate their likely impact. You will also need to describe and evaluate the protective measures that organisations can take to defend themselves against each of these threats. In addition, describe and evaluate two examples of legislation which is relevant to this area.

Assessment hint

✓ Describe some of the potential threats and the measures taken to protect customer data.

✓✓ Include some assessment of the effectiveness of the protective measures taken

Signpost for e-portfolio evidence

This activity covers assessment evidence (c).

2.8 The database

As you discovered when we looked at the back office processes that take place on the web server of a transactional website, databases have a very important role to play. They store key information which makes the site work:

* details of the products on offer (prices and specifications, etc.)

* stock levels of the products

* registered customers' details

* details of orders placed.

Each of these sets of information is stored in a table so that the complete database contains many different tables.

Through out this section we shall be using an example database to demonstrate how the database can be set up and analysed. The database is designed to support an imaginary online DVD store called AJ's DVDs.

Selecting appropriate field types and formats

Before you use a database you must decide how the data to be stored in the database will be structured (i.e. how the data is divided up into tables and fields). A table is a collection of data about a particular subject, such as customers or products; fields are individual items of data within the table. The decisions you make about the database structure will depend upon the nature of the data (i.e. where it comes from and what it describes) and what information you will want to extract from the database.

A single table consists of many records, and each record is split into different fields which store a particular piece of data. So, for example, the DVD list table would have fields for the DVD number, Title, Category, Rating, Price and so on (see Figure 2.13).

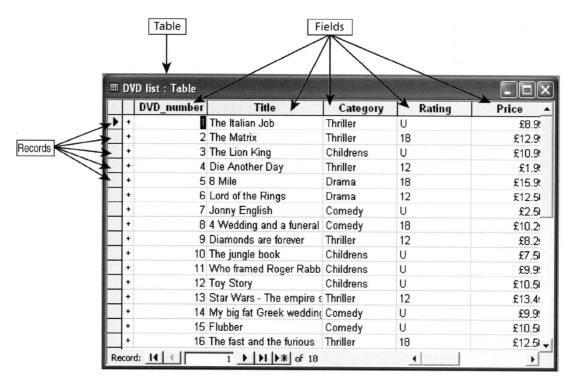

FIGURE 2.13 *Tables, records and fields*

When creating a database table, you will need to decide what fields are needed in the table and what format the data in the fields will be in. There are two basic data types, numbers and text, but there are many variations of the basic types. For example, numbers can be whole numbers, numbers with a certain number of digits after the decimal point or numbers formatted in a particular way, such as currency. A date is another type of numeric data type, and with this type different formats can be set (for example, a short date format such as 26/10/04 or a longer format such as 26th October 2004).

Theory into practice

The database for AJ's DVD store contains information about the customers who are registered with the site in the Customer table, and details of the DVDs which are offered for sales in a table called DVD list. The fields within the Customer table and the data types for those fields are shown in Figure 2.14.

Customer : Table

Field Name	Data Type	
Customer Number	AutoNumber	
Title	Text	
First name	Text	
Family name	Text	
Age	Number	
e-mail address	Text	
Address	Text	
Town	Text	
Postcode	Text	

FIGURE 2.14 *Fields in the Customer table*

Most database tables have a special field which is used as a unique identifier for each record. This is called the primary key, and it is usual to choose a made-up value, such as an ID or account number, rather than some real data such as a person's name, to ensure the value is unique.

Creating simple validation rules

It is important that the data contained in a database is accurate and valid. Creating validation rules can help ensure the data entered into the database is valid. Some validation is done automatically by the database software. For example, if you create a field with a date data type, the software will not allow you to enter an invalid date, such as 26/13/04. However, you can add further validation to ensure data is reasonable. For example, if you have a field in the Customer table for the customer's date for birth,

Theory into practice

The Customer table in AJ's DVD store database contains a field called Age, which is used to store the customers' ages. The store does not accept orders from anyone under 18 and a value higher than 120 would of course be invalid! Therefore a validation rule can be applied which says that Age must be equal to or greater than 18 and less than 120. Figure 2.15 shows how this validation rule can be applied using Microsoft Access. The validation text is the message that appears on the screen if an age outside these boundaries is entered.

What other validation could you add for the fields in the Customer and DVD list tables?

today's date, although a valid date, could not be a correct entry. In fact, since all online shops require payment to be made by credit or debit cards and these are only available to people aged

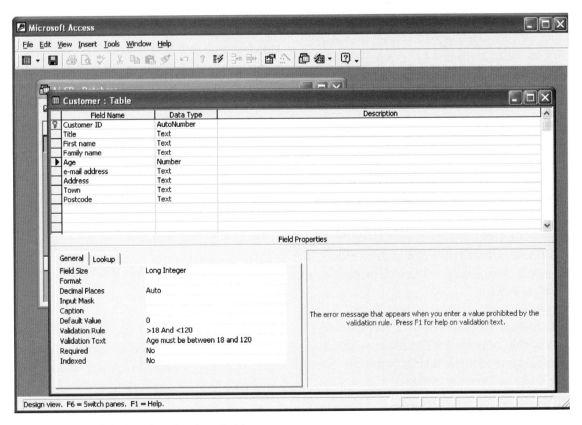

FIGURE 2.15 *Validation for the Age field*

18 or over, you could create a validation rule for the date of birth field that says the person must be 18 or over.

Creating a one-to-many relationship between tables

Database systems allow relationships to be set up between different tables so that, for example, records on the Order table can be related to the customers who placed the order, and whose details are stored on the Customer table. This type of relationship is sometimes called a one-to-many relationship, because one customer on the Customer table may have many related orders on the Order table.

> **Key term**
>
> A *one-to-many relationship* can exist between records on two different tables. The table which is at the 'one' end of the relationship has individual records which can be related to many records on the other table. So, for example, in a doctors' surgery database each doctor on the Doctor table can be related to many patients on a Patient table.

Relationships like these are created by using a field from the 'one' side of the relationship, usually the primary key field, and placing the value in that key field into a field on the 'many' side of the relationship. Therefore when you look at records on the Order table, you know which customer placed the order because Customer number is one of the fields in the order record. (See Figure 2.16 for a diagrammatic representation of this relationship.)

In a similar way, all the details of the DVD that has been ordered do not need to be recorded on the Order table, only the DVD number is required. This is also a one-to-many relationship since one DVD will appear on many orders.

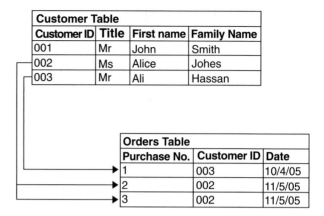

FIGURE 2.16 *The relationship between customers and orders*

Using a single table to record an order has a serious restriction. What if a customer wanted to order more than one DVD? To deal with this possibility, you need to split the Order table into two tables. One, which we shall call the Order header, will store the information about the order that does not change no matter how many DVDs are on the order, such as the order number, the customer number and the date of the order. The other table we shall call the Order items: this has one record for each DVD ordered. It is related to the Order header table using the order number and it also has fields for the DVD number and the quantity. The DVD number is used to link records on this table to the DVD list table, where the full details of the DVD, such as the title, price and rating, are held. The relationships that exist between these four tables are shown in Figure 2.17.

Importing a given data set

In order to investigate how databases can be used to analyse data and to identify trends such as buying habits, you need to deal with databases that have a large number of records.

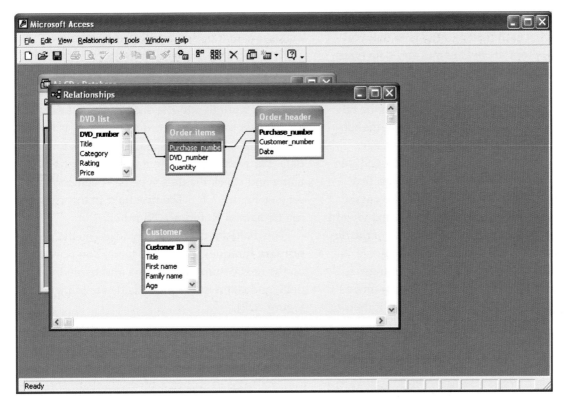

FIGURE 2.17 *Relationships between tables*

Rather than having to key in hundreds of records it is much simpler to import a ready-prepared set of data. Data sets are normally prepared in a text file, so they can be imported into a variety of different database programs.

Key term

A *comma separated values (CSV)* file is a text file which can be used to store database records. Each field on the file is separated by a comma, and each record is separated by a carriage return. CSV files are sometimes used to transfer data between systems since they can be easily exported and imported.

```
DVD list.txt - Notepad
File  Edit  Format  View  Help
1,"The Italian Job","Thriller","U",£8.9
2,"The Matrix","Thriller","18",£12.99,
3,"The Lion King","Childrens","U",£10.9
4,"Die Another Day","Thriller","12",£1.
5,"8 Mile","Drama","18",£15.99,
6,"Lord of the Rings","Drama","12",£12.
7,"Jonny English","Comedy","U",£2.50,
8,"4 wedding and a funeral","Comedy","1
9,"Diamonds are forever","Thriller","12
10,"The jungle book","Childrens","U",£7
11,"Who framed Roger Rabbit","Childrens
12,"Toy Story","Childrens","U",£10.50,
13,"Star Wars - The empire strikes back
14,"My big fat Greek wedding","Comedy",
15,"Flubber","Comedy","U",£10.50,
16,"The fast and the furious","Thriller
```

FIGURE 2.18 *A CSV file*

The most common way of formatting data in a text file is to use a comma to separate each field and a carriage return to separate each record. These type of files are sometimes called CSV files, which stands for comma separated values.

As these are text files you can view them in a text editor such as Microsoft Notepad (Figure 2.18 shows a CSV file displayed in Notepad). The data in it could be used to populate the DVD list table on AJ's DVDs database.

In some CSV files, the first line contains the field names, but in this example it does not. This is not a problem as you can assign field names when the data is imported. However you will need to decide or find out what each field represents so that you can choose appropriate field names and data types.

To import a CSV file into Microsoft Access, you need to have an existing database open, even if it does not yet contain any tables. Then from the **File** menu, select: **Get external data**, and, from the sub-menu: **Import**. You will then see the Open File dialogue box where you need to select the CSV file you want to import. Make sure you choose **Text Files** from the **Files of type** drop-down box at the bottom of the dialogue box. The Import Text Wizard will then start, showing the first few lines of the file you have selected, as shown in Figure 2.19.

You should not need to make any changes to the standard setting, so just click: **Next** to move to the next step. This will show the data split up into fields. If your data has field names as its first row, make sure that option is selected (see Figure 2.20).

The next step allows you to choose whether the data should be appended to an existing table in the database or placed in a new table. You will probably want to add the data to a new table. Click: **Next** to go to the next step, which is where you will add field names and data types to the data. For each field you will need to enter a field name and check the data type has been correctly set (see Figure 2.21). The first field in this example can be named **Reference Number.**

This field should also be indexed as the primary (unique) key for the table. You now click on the next column of the data and name this field, and so on until all the fields are named (see Figure 2.22).

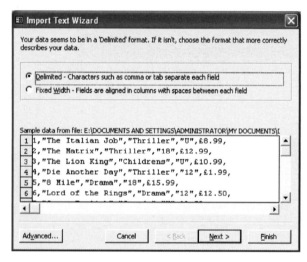

FIGURE 2.19 *Import Text Wizard, step 1*

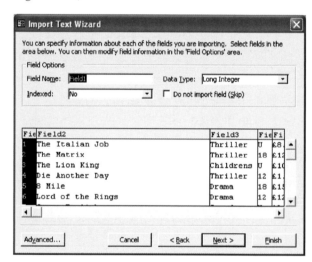

FIGURE 2.21 *Naming the first field*

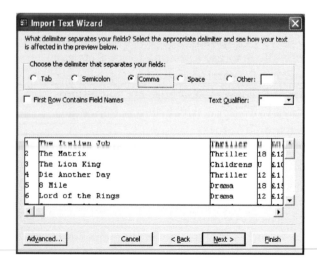

FIGURE 2.20 *Import Text Wizard, step 2*

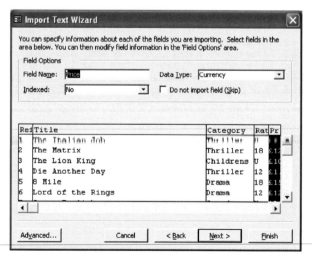

FIGURE 2.22 *Naming the fields*

The next step of the wizard will ask you for a primary key, so you can choose the name of the first field (Reference number) we named from the drop-down box.

The final step of the wizard will ask you to name the table itself. You will need to check that all the data has been imported correctly by comparing the contents of the original text CSV file with the table that has been created.

Using queries to sort and extract valid and meaningful information

Queries answer questions about your data. They are able to combine data from different related tables and to select records which match certain criteria. Queries can also select the fields you wish to view and sort the data in whatever order you choose. Because of their powerful ability to manipulate data in these ways, queries are the key tools for analysing data. We shall investigate how queries can be used with a number of examples.

Selecting fields and sorting data

The ability to sort data by any field and by multiple fields is a useful tool. You could, for example, sort the records on the DVD list table in order of the number of sales made. This would tell you which DVDs were most popular. You could also sort the records first by the category the DVD is in, then by sales made. This would show what the most popular DVD in each category was.

Theory into practice

In order to create a query in Microsoft Access you first have to choose the *Queries* option from the database control centre, then select: *Create query in Design view* from the panel on the right, as shown in Figure 2.23.

This will display the Query grid, with the Select Table dialogue in front of it. Choose the DVD list table from the Select Table dialogue box, click: *Add* to add the table to the Query grid, then click: *Close* to close the Select Table dialogue box. Your screen should now look like Figure 2.24.

In this example we shall only display the fields Title, Category and Sales_made. Select each of those fields in turn and drag them from the table into the top row of the Query grid, each in their own column (see Figure 2.25).

Finally, we want to sort the records by the Sales_made field, so click in the row labelled *Sort,* in the Sales_made column, and select: *Descending* from the drop-down list (see Figure 2.26).

The query can now be run by going to the *Query* menu and choosing the *Run* option. This will show the list of DVDs with the DVD with the highest number of sales first (Figure 2.27).

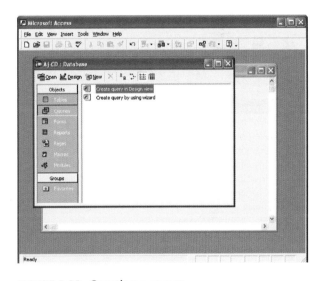

FIGURE 2.23 *Creating a query*

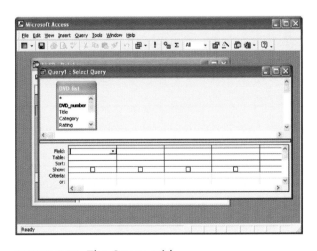

FIGURE 2.24 *The Query grid*

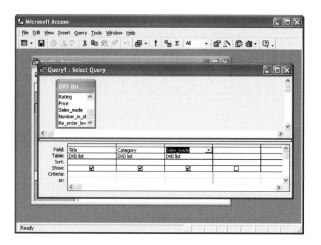

FIGURE 2.25 *Selecting the required fields*

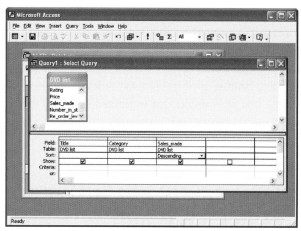

FIGURE 2.26 *Sorting the records*

FIGURE 2.27 *The DVD with the highest number of sales*

You can also sort records by multiple fields. If you click in the **Sort** box below the Category field and choose **Ascending** and run the query again, you will see the DVDs listed alphabetically (since Category is a text field it is sorted alphabetically), and then within each category the films are listed with the highest-selling one first. Because the Category field is shown before (to the left of) the Sales_made field in the Query grid, the data is sorted by that field first. If you have these fields the other way around you will not get meaningful results. You can, of course, save a query so that you can run it anytime you wish by going to the **File** menu, choosing: **Save** and giving the query a suitable name.

Combining data from different tables

With a query you can display fields from different, related tables.

Theory into practice

For example, suppose you wanted to see how many orders each customer had placed. To create a query to show this information, you would return to the Query section of the database control centre and double-click the *Create a new query in Design view* option as before, click on: *Customer* in the Select Table dialogue box, then click: *Add*, then on the *Order header* table and also *Add*, then *Close*. The two tables will now be shown with the relationship between them also visible, as shown in Figure 2.28.

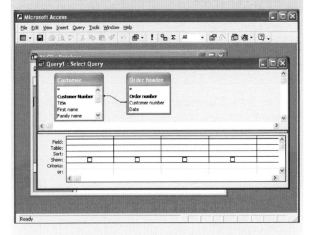

FIGURE 2.28 *Related tables in the Query grid*

Now drag the First name and Family name fields from the Customer table and the Date field from the Order header field into the Query grid. Set the *Sort* box for the Family name field to

Ascending so that the customers will be displayed in alphabetical order, then run the query. Don't forget to save this query, calling it *Customers and Orders* as we will use it later to create a report.

Filtering records using selection criteria

One of the most powerful data analysis tools is the ability to select certain records from your data based on the criteria you set.

Theory into practice

Each of the DVDs on the database is categorised into children's, drama, comedy, etc. Suppose you wanted to list only those DVDs in a certain category – comedy, for example. To do this you would create a new query as before and add the DVD list table to the query. Then drag the Title and the Category fields into the Query grid and under the Category column. In the row labelled *Criteria* you would key in *Comedy*, as shown in Figure 2.29.

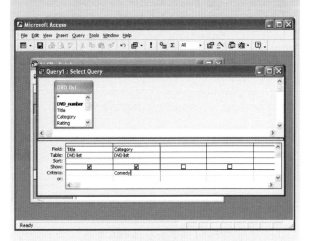

FIGURE 2.29 *Entering a simple query criterion*

Now run the query and only those DVDs in the comedy category will be displayed

Let's look at a slightly more complex example of how to use criteria within a query. How could you list all the orders placed in a certain month, say, for example, November 2004?

Follow the instructions given previously to bring both the Order header and the Customer tables into the query, and drag the Order number, Customer number and Date fields from the Order header table into the Query grid and the First name and Family name fields from the Customer table. In the Query grid under the Date column and in the row labelled *Criteria* key in *Between 1/11/2004 And 30/11/2004*, as shown in Figure 2.30.

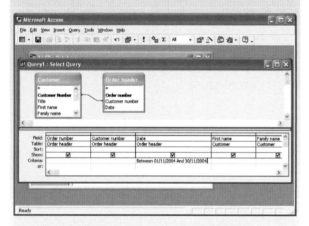

FIGURE 2.30 *Entering a more complex query criterion*

Now run the query and only those order placed in November 2004 will be displayed.

To show how a report can be created we will use the Customers and Orders query created earlier. Before starting work on the report we will make the query a little more sophisticated so that it shows not only when each customer placed an order, but also what he or she actually ordered.

Open the query in Design view and then go to the *View* menu. Choose: *Show table* and then add the Order items and DVD list tables. Drag the DVD title from the DVD list table and the Quantity from the Order items table into the Query grid. Also drag the Order number field from the Order header table to the first column of the Query grid and set this field to be sorted *Ascending* (that way all the orders will be shown together in order). Your query should now look like that show in Figure 2.31.

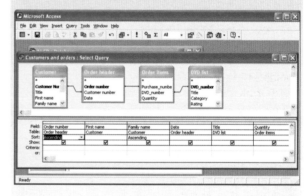

FIGURE 2.31 *The modified Customers and Orders query*

Producing reports to present information clearly

Database reports enable you to format the information that has been extracted from the database using a query and to present it clearly, professionally and neatly.

If you now run the query, you will see a list of all the orders along with details of which DVDs were ordered. However, the data is not displayed in an organised way since the customer's name is repeated for each DVD he or she ordered. With a report the data can be formatted so that the customer name and the date of the order are displayed first, then the DVDs ordered shown underneath.

Save this modified version of the query then return to the database control centre and choose the *Reports* option and double-click the *Create report by using wizard* option (see Figure 2.32.

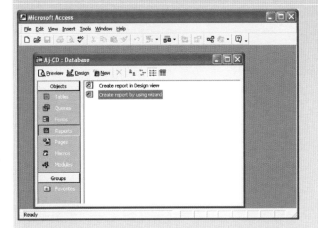

FIGURE 2.32 *Creating a report using the wizard*

You will then see the first step in the wizard process. Choose the *Customers and Orders* query from the drop-down box, then use the double arrow button to add all the available fields to the list of selected fields (you can, if you wish, only display some of the fields from the query in your report, but in this example we need them all) (see Figure 2.33).

Then click: *Next* to go to the next step in creating the report. This step allows you to choose by which field you would like the data grouped. We want the data grouped by Order header so that all the details of the order (date, customer, etc.) are displayed first and then the items on the order are listed underneath each order (see Figure 2.34).

Click: *Next* and the wizard will ask if you want any groups within the Order header group, but you don't need any in this example, so just click: *Next*. This step asks what sorting and summary options you require for the report. The query is already sorted by Order number, so there is no need to choose any sorting here. The *Summary* button allows any numeric fields to be totalled up (sum) or the

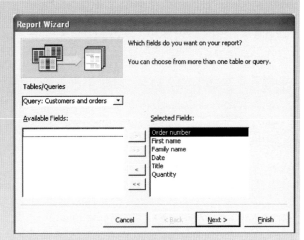

FIGURE 2.33 *Selecting the fields*

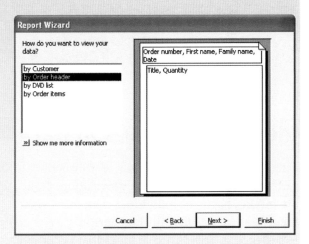

FIGURE 2.34 *Choosing how to group the data in the report*

average, minimum or maximum values displayed. It is quite useful to know how many DVDs were ordered on each order and in total, so select: *Sum* for the Quantity field (see Figure 2.35).

Click: *Next* to go to the next step, where you can choose the layout options for the report. You can leave this set on the default *stepped* layout, and the same is true for the next step where you can choose the style of the report.

(Continued)

Finally, you will be asked what title you want for the report. Something like *Orders Report* would be suitable. The wizard has now been completed and, when you click: *Finish*, the report it has created is displayed in Print Preview, as shown in Figure 2.36.

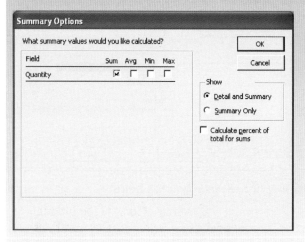

FIGURE 2.35 *Summing the Quantity field*

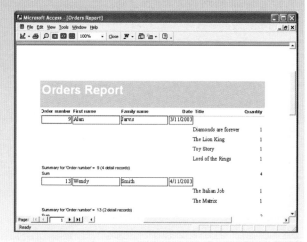

FIGURE 2.36 *Completed report*

Identifying trends in data

Data collected in the databases of transactional websites contains important information about the buying habits of individual customers and the overall trends that the business is experiencing. Trends are changes that occur over time. For example, in an organisation that sells several types of products, the number of sales made of one type of product may be rising while sales of the other type of product may be falling. It is important that the management of the company is aware of these trends and carries out marketing activities or makes other changes in the business to take advantage of positive trends and to avoid the consequences of negatives ones. To identify and analyse trends within data, you will need to produce summary reports which show how values, such as the number or value of sales made, have changed over time.

Suppose we wanted to look at the total value of the sales made each month by AJ's DVDs. The first step it to create a query which brings together the required data. To do this you create a new query in Design view as before, bringing in the Order header, Order items and DVD list tables. From the Order header table you include the Date field in the query, from the Order items you include the DVD number and Quantity and from the DVD list table the Price is included. This query also needs some data added that is derived from these fields. You want to look at the sales made each month over a whole year so you need to include a field which shows the month the sale was made. This can be derived from the Date field. To do this, go to the next blank column in the Query grid and key in the field row:

(Continued)

Month: DatePart("m",[Date])

This creates a new field in the query called *Month*. It uses the DatePart function to extract the month (as indicated by the "m") from the field called Date (as indicated by [Date]).

In order to restrict the data to a particular year, a criterion needs to be added to the Date field column. So to see orders in 2003 you would enter *Between 01/01/2003 And 31/12/2003.* This field should also be sorted to ensure the orders are shown in date order. The Query grid should now look like Figure 2.37.

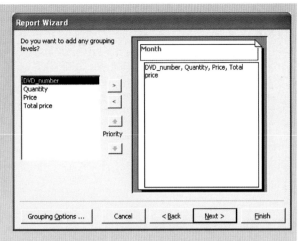

FIGURE 2.38 **Grouping the report by Month**

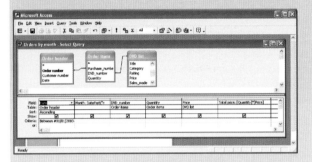

FIGURE 2.37 **Adding a Month field to the query**

Summary Options is used to sum up the total prices for each order item for each month, as shown in Figure 2.39.

The other options in the Report Wizard can be left at their default values, and the resulting report will list the sales made each month, with the number and value of sales made shown at the end of each month's list, as shown in Figure 2.40.

The other field you need to add is the total price of each order item. The price of the individual DVD is already in the query, but this needs to be multiplied by the quantity in order to give the total price. To do this the following statement is added to the next column in the Query grid, in the Field row:

Total price: [Quantity]*[Price]

This adds another field to the query, called Total price. If the query is now run, this new field will be displayed.

The query in now complete, but is in not very easy to identify any trends from its output because it does not total up the orders each month. To do this you need to create a report. The Report Wizard can be used as before, but the data must be grouped by Month, as shown in Figure 2.38.

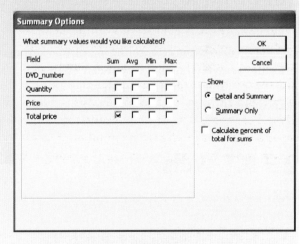

FIGURE 2.39 **Summary Options**

Looking at the completed report will enable you to identify whether sales have risen or fallen over the year, and which months are the most successful. By modifying the query you could run other reports showing the data from different

(Continued)

years and comparing the monthly sales totals between years.

1 What recommendation might you make to AJ's DVDs based on the analysis of the data that has been done?

2 What other fields could you analyse to attempt to identify relevant sales trends in this data?

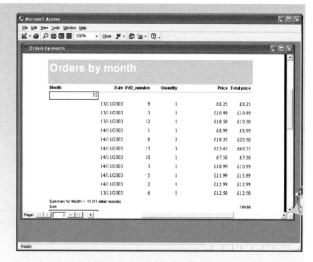

FIGURE 2.40 *The completed report*

Databases are at the heart of transactional websites. The day-to-day running of sites relies on them as they the provide product, stock and user information which drives the website. They are also used to record and process each sale. Databases also provide a goldmine of marketing information which management can analyse and use to target and direct their sales and marketing strategy.

2.9 ICT skills

There are a number of ICT skills you will need to complete this unit:

* production of information flow diagrams
* production of reports
* internet research skills
* use of database software to store and manipulate data.

Internet research skills are covered in Unit 1 and use of database software in section 2.8 of Unit 2; this section discusses production of information flow diagrams and reports.

Producing information flow diagrams

There are many different software applications which provide graphics and diagram drawing facilities, however to add simple diagrams to word processed reports the drawing tools provided in Microsoft Word are perfectly adequate.

Before you can use the drawing tools you must ensure the drawing tool bar is displayed (normally shown at the bottom of the editing window) by clicking the Drawing button in the standard tool bar (see Figure 2.41).

To draw a simple text box, just click on the text box button, then drag out a box where you want it to appear on the page. You can type in the box and apply all the text formatting options you can use with normal text. You can move the box around the page by dragging on the shaded outline, or resize the box by dragging on the handles. If you double click on the shaded outline the **Format text box** dialog will appear where you can modify settings like the colour and thickness of the line around the box and the fill colour of the box.

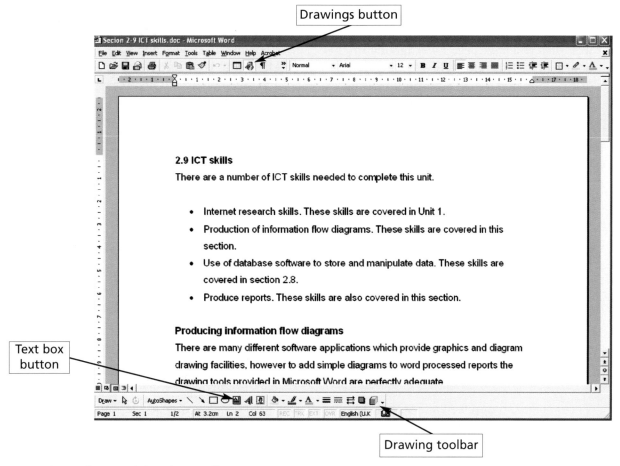

Drawings button

Text box button

Drawing toolbar

2.9 ICT skills

There are a number of ICT skills needed to complete this unit.

- Internet research skills. These skills are covered in Unit 1.
- Production of information flow diagrams. These skills are covered in this section.
- Use of database software to store and manipulate data. These skills are covered in section 2.8.
- Produce reports. These skills are also covered in this section.

Producing information flow diagrams

There are many different software applications which provide graphics and diagram drawing facilities, however to add simple diagrams to word processed reports the drawing tools provided in Microsoft Word are perfectly adequate.

FIGURE 2.41 *The Word drawing toolbar*

When drawing flow diagrams you may want to include other shaped boxes, for example a decision box is always a diamond shape. All the standard flow chart box shapes can be found in the **AutoShapes** menu, under the flowcharts sub-menu. You can draw these shapes in the same way as the text box. To add text inside them, right click on the shape and choose the **Add text** option. You can format these shapes in the same way as text boxes.

To draw arrows joining up your boxes click on the **Arrow** button in the drawing toolbar and drag out the arrow to where it is required. By default the arrow head goes at the end of the line you draw. You can change this, and the thickness, colour and other format setting by double clicking on the arrow to display the Format shape dialog.

Producing reports

You probably already have the skills to use word processing software, but you need to make sure you use them to produce reports that are professional in appearance. Make sure you:

✳ *Structure the report properly*: your report needs to be divided into sections, including an introduction at the beginning and a summary or conclusions at the end. Sections should have headings and subheadings which are formatted in a consistent and appropriate way.

✳ *Check your report for accuracy*: this involves more than just spell-checking your document. You need to proof read it for errors that the spell-checker will not spot and check that the text makes sense and explains the topics required in your course work.

* *Include information from other types of software*: you will need to include screen shots of the web sites you have been investigating in your report. This can be done simply by displaying the required page and pressing the 'print screen' key on the keyboard. The screen image can then be pasted into your report. You can scale and crop the screen print using the image editing tools which can be found on the **Picture** toolbar (if it is not shown when you select the image, go to **View** menu, choose **Toolbars**, then **Picture**). Make sure your screen prints are given a title and are annotated if necessary. You can also include information from a database such as Microsoft Access using screen prints, or you can copy and paste sets of database records into your report.

UNIT ASSESSMENT

For this assessment task, you will need to download one of the example datasets from the Edexcel website. You will need to import this file, which is in CSV format, into a database program such as Microsoft Access as described in the text. Having imported it you will need to check that the record structure is correct (using appropriate data types and validation, for example) then carry out the following tasks:

1 Design three queries which, by sorting and/or selecting certain data, will help you to analyse trends within the data.

2 Create reports to format the data from your queries in a clear and professional way.

Once you have completed these tasks, write a report identifying significant trends within the data (for example, changes in sales patterns) and making recommendations for future action.

Assessment hint

✓   Create a simple database structure, carry out some limited testing on the database and extract some valid and meaningful data.

✓✓   Create a customised database structure. Test the database to ensure all the functions work correctly, extract valid and meaningful data, and identify some significant trends

✓✓✓ Include data validation in the database. Identify significant trends in the data, interpret the output and make recommendations.

 Signpost for e-portfolio evidence

Save this work in your e-portfolio. It could contribute towards covering evidence (d) and (e).

UNIT 3

The knowledge worker

Introduction

This unit examines the role of the knowledge worker and his or her ability to make informed decisions using modelling tools and techniques. This unit has a user focus and will explore a range of different spreadsheet models.

In this information age, ICT provides us with vast quantities of information and, as ICT users and knowledge workers, we have to make judgements about the sources and accuracy of any information we acquire and must be able to select and manipulate this information so that we can make the correct decisions.

This unit will give you a better understanding of how spreadsheets can be used as a modelling tool to facilitate the decision-making process. In addition, it also explains how problems can be addressed, informed decisions made and which factors impact on the choices we make.

What you need to learn

In completing this unit, you should achieve these learning outcomes:

* Know about the different stages involved in the decision-making process

* Understand the underlying logic and assumptions of decision-making models

* Evaluate decisions made by others in the light of available information

* Assess and evaluate the quality of information given by others

* Make decisions based on information provided by others.

Resource toolkit

To complete this unit, you need these essential resources:

* access to computer hardware including a printer

* access to computer software, in particular Microsoft Word, Excel and PowerPoint and graphics software

* sufficient storage space.

How you will be assessed

This unit is externally assessed through an examination. Further information on the conduct of the examination will be published on the Edexcel website in advance of the examination. In the examination:

* You will work with information provided in a number of e-resources, including a spreadsheet model

* You will use the information provided to add to your knowledge of the scenario and inform you decision-making

* You will be expected to use standard office software effectively (such as spreadsheet software) to help you make, present and justify your decision

* Marks will be awarded for evidence of adherence to relevant standard ways of working.

In preparation for assessment you will be encouraged to:

* work safely and adhere to relevant legislation and codes of practice when carrying out the externally-set practical computer-based activities required for this unit

* investigate the underlying logic/assumptions of models

* learn how to question quality of information they have available

* think critically when analysing problems

* practise using models to help make decisions.

How high can you aim

We have already identified a knowledge worker as 'anyone whose job involves the development or use of knowledge'. Throughout this unit you will be preparing yourself for the external assessment. To support you in this preparation, there are a number of activities and practical tasks such as **Theory into practice**, **Think it over** and **Knowledge checks** that will help you to focus on your external assessment requirements. You will be given more up-to-date examination tips and guidance by your teacher.

To start you in the right direction a **Theory into practice** task has been provided that should enable you to develop your understanding of knowledge workers, what they do and how they use information and ICT in their job roles.

This task will enable you to identify the role of a knowledge worker and help you to understand and appreciate your own role as a knowledge worker.

* Keep a journal or a scrapbook about knowledge workers. The types of evidence you could collect include:

    – information about knowledge workers (possibly job descriptions from adverts or vacancy sheets)

    – articles that you may find on the Internet or in newspapers.

* In one section of your journal/scrapbook, design a table and list the range of different knowledge workers, for example designers, programmers, analysts, and the types of ICT that they may use in their job role.

Ready to start?

Why not keep a log of the time you take to complete this unit. Devise a blank form that you could use to record the time that you spend on this course.

3.1 Problem-solving

We all encounter problems on a daily basis, and some of these are routine, such as the decisions we make in terms of what we wear, how we travel to college, what we eat, etc. Some, however, are more complex, and these more complex problems require more thought as to how they can be addressed. Some sort of decision-making process, therefore, needs to be applied.

If we liken a problem to a system, certain inputs will be needed to initiate the thought process, thus leading to a decision being made. The decision we make will be based on any information we have collected and any prior knowledge we have of the problem. This process can become more complicated, however, because we may suffer from 'information overload' – we have too much information and do not know what to do with it all. For the problem-solving process to work, therefore, we must be able to distinguish between information that is relevant to the problem and information that is not. Anything that is not relevant must be discarded. Finally, we must also be aware that ICT simply provides information – it does not supply knowledge. To acquire knowledge, we must read and assess information so that we understand it and can apply that understanding to other areas of our lives.

To help us understand information and thus acquire knowledge, we can use what is known as a 'systems model'. We add inputs to this system, process these inputs and, from the output we obtain, come to a conclusion, as shown in Figure 3.1.

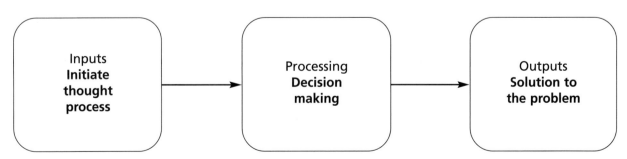

FIGURE 3.1 *A basic systems model for problem-solving*

The processing activities that occur within this systems model will differ depending upon the type of system being used (for example, you might sit down with a pen and a piece of paper to solve a problem – a pen-and-paper system – or you might feed data into a computer – a computerised system). The decision-making process can also be simple or complex (see Table 3.1).

TYPE OF PROBLEM	TYPE OF DECISION-MAKING PROCESS
Simple Doing an assignment	*Simple* Reading through tasks Carrying out research Produce a draft copy Submit final copy
Complex Finding information about a customer on a database	*Complex* Accessing a central resource such as a database Searching information Sorting and selecting specific details

TABLE 3.1 *Examples of simple and complex decisions*

TASK	RESOURCES	PROBLEMS ENCOUNTERED	DECISIONS
Booking a holiday			
Completing an assignment			

TABLE 3.2 *Problem-solving and decision-making*

3.2 The decision-making process

When you are making decisions, you need to ensure that you are in possession of all the facts to enable you to make the right decision. The decision-making process should, therefore, be based on all the information you already have or can acquire.

You make decisions every second of every day, at home, at work, at college or socially. At work or college, the decisions you make vary from being quite simple (for example, what time shall I have a coffee break?) to quite complex (for example, how should I market this new product?). For knowledge workers, the decisions that need to be taken may be based on the criteria shown in Figure 3.2.

These criteria are explained in detail in the rest of the unit, and this is a brief outline of each one:

* *Understanding the situation fully*: if you do not fully understand the environment or situation you are working in, you may make incorrect or inaccurate decisions. It might be that the situation is quite complex or unfamiliar, in which case additional research may be required to help you understand and appreciate the situation better.

* *Searching for information related to the problem*: when you are searching for information about the problem, you need to establish what sources you need. If, for example, the problem concerns inefficiencies in a payroll system, you may have to speak to staff in the finance department and human resources department and examine documentation and procedures relating to the payroll system.

* *Establishing sources of information and their reliability*: once sources have been identified, you need to check whether or not the information gathered is reliable. One way to ensure this is to compare (or 'triangulate') the information source with that of another/others. By checking against other sources of information, you should be able

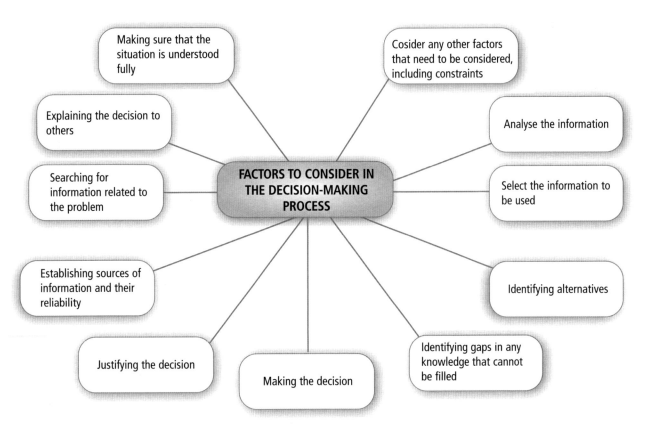

FIGURE 3.2 *Criteria involved in the decision-making process*

to guarantee the consistency and reliability of the information.

* *Identifying gaps in your knowledge*: if gaps exist in your knowledge, you might have to spend longer researching the problem and finding information to help you understand it. One way you could overcome this difficulty is to ask somebody else who does understand the problem to assist you. For example, if a company has requested a custom-made piece of software to be developed for their new system and you cannot provide this yourself, you could ask somebody to develop the software for you, but you would need to ensure that the level of expertise and quality of service are maintained.

* *Other factors and constraints*: as you work through a problem-solving exercise, you might find that other factors need to be considered, some of which could constrain the proposed solution. For example, a company may have asked for a new computerised system and specialist software for their finance department. However, no training has been discussed or agreed – so how will the users know how to operate the new system? This could be considered to be a constraint because additional costs, time and possibly resources may be required.

* *Selecting the information*: the information you select for a problem-solving activity must be appropriate, valid, current and authentic. There is no point in basing a decision on hearsay; you must have accurate information to support your decision.

* *Analysing the information*: sometimes information analysis is simply a process of elimination – because an option does not meet the specified criteria, it can be ignored. Information analysis, however, is usually more complex than this, and this complexity will depend on the size and nature of the problem. You will need to ensure that all options are fully addressed and fully justified before making a final decision.

* *Identifying alternatives*: identifying alternative solutions to the problem is considered to be good practice: it shows you have applied some thought to the problem and to the decisions

you made in arriving at your final choice. Alternative solutions may be based on varying costs, specifications, resources or time frames. The solution you choose should be the best option of the alternatives available.

* *Making and justifying the decision, and explaining it to others*: when you make and justify your decision, this should be the result of extensive research and of an analysis of all the facts available. Your decision should then be communicated to the end-user(s) in an appropriate format, such as a business report.

To ensure you make the right decision, ask yourself these questions:

* Has the problem been fully investigated?
* Has adequate time been allocated to the decision-making process?

* Are there adequate resources available to support any decisions I must make?

* Have I considered alternative solutions and on what grounds have I rejected them in favour of the actual working solution?

* Is there adequate documentation to satisfy the decisions I made during the solution specification process?

3.3 Understanding the situation

To arrive at the right decision, you often have to go through a methodical process of problem-solving. There are certain things you will need to think through in order to gain a better understanding of the situation, and this will allow you to make a more informed decision. The things you will need to address include the following:

* What exactly is it you have to decide?

* Are there different viewpoints?

* How does the decision compare with similar ones you may have made already?

* Are there variations from time to time or place to place?

* How long have you got to decide?

* What resources are at you disposal?

Trying to understand the problem is half the battle in overcoming it. If you know exactly what decisions need to be made, the process of trying to solve the problem will become more apparent.

What exactly do you have to decide?

The following activity is designed to get you thinking about actions that are taken as a result of making and carrying out a certain decision.

When you are trying to make a decision there might be alternatives or different viewpoints you need to consider. These viewpoints may arise from other people who suggest alternative options or they might arise from further research.

Think it over...

In small groups, consider the following decisions:

Shall I take the bus or walk to college?

Shall I do my assignment or go out with my mates?

Try to establish for each situation exactly what it is you need to decide. For each situation, weigh up the pros and cons of each course of action.

Are there different viewpoints?

When making a decision, there may be different ways of looking at the problem, and there may be different viewpoints that you have to take into consideration.

There are many ways to arrive at different viewpoints:

* by doing some research I have discovered there are four different laptops that offer the same level of functionality as the one I have found

* by speaking to my lecturer I have found an alternative way to design my website

* by watching my mentor at work I now know how to use shortcuts on my PC.

How does the decision compare with similar ones made already?

The decisions that you make may be based on similar decisions and choices you have made in the past. If, for example, you used a particular website to gather information about a certain topic area, you may be tempted to go back and use that website again to find out information for a current assignment.

Are there variations in time or place?

Decisions can be affected by time or place, and you will have to take these into account when you arrive at your solution. For example, if you are planning a trip and the train timetable has changed since you last made the journey a month ago, you might have to take a later train or use a different mode of transport.

How long have you got to decide?

Decisions can be made in milliseconds, minutes, hours, days, months and even years. Everyday we make time-framed decisions: when we cross the road we scan our environment to check for moving cars and safety conditions; we also make estimates about how long it will take to cross (do we need to run, do we need to weave between other people who are trying to cross the road?). Some decisions do need to be made in split seconds – for example, if a saucepan of water is about to boil over, we would instinctively turn down the heat or move it off the heat. If a programme we want to watch is just about to start, we would instinctively change the channel to watch it. Other decisions, however, require thought processes rather than instinct.

What resources are at your disposal?

Resources play a big role in some of the decisions we make, and the sooner resources are identified and put at your disposal, the sooner the decision-making process can begin. Resources will vary depending on the type of decision that has to be made. For example, the resources required to plan a birthday party might include a function room,

Theory into practice

You have been asked to take part in a study that will examine the recreational activities of teenagers. The study will involve you identifying what you do in the evenings, at weekends and during non-term time and comparing your findings with other people taking part in the study.

The study will be confined to your class. You need to think about four or five recreational activities that you do and try and address the following questions that may affect your choice of activity:

* On what basis is your decision to do one recreational activity rather than another based?

* Is your activity confined to a certain time or place, or are there variations?

* How long does it take you to decide whether or not to do the activity? Is there any planning involved?

* What resources do you need, for example your friends, money, etc.?

When you have addressed all of these points, the information can be collected from the rest of the class and put together as a recreational yearbook. Class members can read out certain extracts to the group to see if anybody can guess who does what, and when.

catering facilities, invitations and a party co-ordinator, etc. The resources required to complete an assignment might include books, the Internet and access to organisational information, etc.

3.4 Sources of information

You should only arrive at a decision when you are in possession of all the facts. Without this information, the accuracy and validity of any decisions you make may be distorted. To ensure you have access to these facts, therefore, you should ask yourself the following questions:

* what do I need to know

* what relevant knowledge do I already have

* what are the gaps in my knowledge and can they be filled

* what information do I already have access to

* where will any additional information come from

* how will I evaluate sources of information to ensure that content is reliable?

If you work your way through these questions, you should be able to establish if there are any gaps in your existing knowledge and, therefore, whether you need to undertake further investigations to acquire more information and where this information will come from.

What do I need to know?

To find the answer to this question, try asking some more questions. Produce a list of all the questions you need to answer. You will probably add extra questions as you go deeper into the problem, but the initial list will give you a framework.

Type your list of questions into a word-processing package. You can add notes under each question as you find out the information.

There are some techniques you can use to identify the key questions that have to be answered before a problem can be solved.

Brainstorming

This is done in a small group and everyone contributes any ideas that seem at all relevant. The important thing is for everyone to agree to stick to the one rule, which is that no-one makes any comments on any of the suggestions, however odd they may seem. This allows ideas to develop and flow. Sometimes one person will contribute a really wild idea, but that thought gets other people thinking and then they may come up with more useful ones.

One way to run a brainstorming session is to give everyone 'post-it' notes on which they write their ideas. When each person writes down and reads out an idea, the note is then stuck on a large sheet of paper or a wall panel. At the end of the session the notes can be moved around and clustered into themes. These themes can then be reworded as questions.

Spider diagrams (semantic maps)

Get a large sheet of paper and in the centre draw an image or circle that represents the problem. Draw branches off this to represent the different aspects of the problem that you need to explore. Write key words on the lines. At the end of each line draw extra lines to represent aspects of that part of the problem. If you can see things that relate to each other then link them with lines.

Using colours and images helps to bring the diagram alive. When you have finished, you should be able to write down the questions that you need to answer.

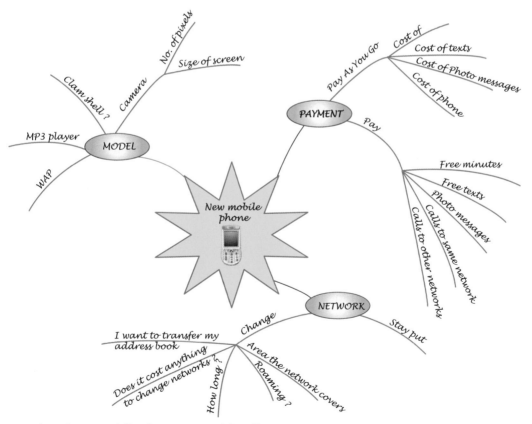

FIGURE 3.3 *Choosing a mobile phone – a spider diagram*

Suppose you are thinking of applying for a degree course in Information and Communication Technology. There are hundreds of courses spread across many different universities. You need to whittle them down to six for your UCAS application.

Draw a spider diagram to help you think about what you need to know each course or university to help you make that decision.

1 List the important questions that you need to ask.

2 Compare your list of questions to those of other students.

3 Have you left any questions out?

4 Would you expect everyone to ask the same questions?

What relevant knowledge do I already have?

You already have a large amount of knowledge, but sometimes you do not recognise the relevance of what you know to the problem in hand. Look at your list of questions again, and this time ask yourself 'Do I know anything at all about this?'

You may decide that you know someone who seems to know a lot about the subject, or you recall having read something about it in a magazine. Add these notes under the relevant question in your list. These may be pointers to the answers rather than the answers themselves, but they are very useful starting points for further investigation.

What are the gaps in my knowledge?

You should soon see where the gaps are in your list. They will probably fall into one of these categories:

* you have some information although you are not quite sure about it and need to check

* you do not have the information you need, but you know where to find it or who to ask

* you have no information at all, as yet.

What information do I already have access to?

You can get information from a wide variety of sources, including:

* books
* documents
* magazines and newsletters
* newspapers
* maps
* pictures
* photographs
* audio
* television and video
* emails and discussion groups
* databases, spreadsheets and other computer files
* websites
* other people.

Go through your list of questions and list the sources of information that you can easily find. For example, if you know that you already have a book with some relevant information in it then add its title to your list of sources.

Primary and secondary sources

You need to distinguish between two types of sources of information:

* primary sources of information are the original documents or first-hand reports

* secondary sources of information are summaries and accounts which have been put together from primary sources.

For example, if you see a live news report on the television, which shows an event as it actually happens, then you are viewing a primary source. But if you see a reporter describing what happened after the event then you are watching a secondary source. Similarly, a history text book is a secondary source, based on the primary sources which were the original documents and objects from the period of time when the events occurred.

The problem is that when you use a secondary source you have to judge how accurate the information is. All secondary sources interpret the primary sources to some extent, however careful they are to be as objective as possible.

You may decide that the information you have is all from a secondary source and you would like to look at the primary sources. On the other hand, the author of secondary source may be an acknowledged expert in the subject and you feel you can trust them to give you unbiased information.

Where will any additional information come from?

You now need to work out how to answer the questions that you have no information on, or how to get the detailed information for questions where your knowledge is rather sketchy. There are three main collections of knowledge that you can use, and you are advised to try all of them:

* libraries – librarians are highly skilled at tracking down information so do ask them for help

* experts – it is very useful if you can identify a few people who know a great deal about the subject. They may be knowledgeable through their work, or they may have a strong leisure interest, or they may just be clever. Most people are flattered if you ask their views and opinions so do not be afraid to ask for advice.

* the Internet – this offers both the huge resources of the Web itself, and also access to other people through email, discussion groups, online chat, newsgroups etc. See below for some ideas on how to use the Web effectively as a source of information.

Using the Web to find information

To use the Web effectively you need to learn how to use search engines. A search engine can search a particular site or search the whole of the Web. In both cases you enter a criterion of the search – this is usually one or more keywords. Most search engines also offer you an advanced search, where you can add extra criteria and so narrow down the search. Some search engines, such as Ask Jeeves, allow you to ask a question in normal English.

The best known search engines are Google (www.google.com), Ask Jeeves (www.ask.com) and Yahoo (www.yahoo.com). They all have UK versions (www.google.co.uk, www.ask.co.uk, www.uk.yahoo.com) which allow you to restrict your search to UK sites.

Rather than doing a general search of the Web it is often easier to start at a portal or reference site and just search that. Here are some important portal and reference sites:

www.direct.gov.uk – for all UK Government services

www.ucas.com – for University courses in the UK

www.rdn.ac.uk – the Resource Discovery Network, mainly for degree students but also helpful at A Level

www.biography.com – for biographies of 25,000 people, worldwide

news.google.co.uk – the latest news from hundreds of sources

www.historyworld.net – for historical facts

www.vlib.org.uk - the WWW Virtual Library, for almost anything

www.wikipedia.org – the online encyclopaedia that has been built by its readers.

You should build up your own collection of useful portal sites.

As you gather information you should add notes about it to your list of questions.

You should also give full details of each source, selected from the following lists:

* printed materials – title, author, publisher, date of publication, page reference; you should also note where you saw source and how you can find it again

* other media – name of CD/DVD, title, date and channel of broadcast, title and source of photographs and other images

* experts – name, address, phone, email; you should note how you made the initial contact and how you can contact them again. Before you give their details, you must ask their permission as they may not be happy to have their personal information widely distributed.

* electronic materials – website address, email address.

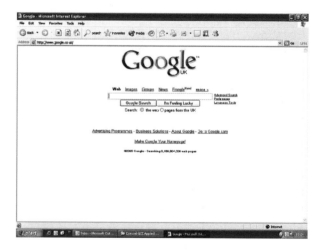

FIGURE 3.5 *The Google search engine*

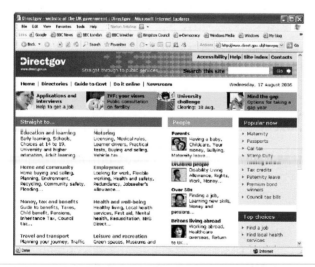

FIGURE 3.4 *DirectGov is the UK Government's portal site for public services*

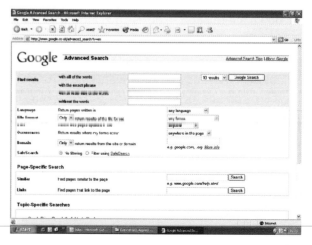

FIGURE 3.6 *The Google advanced search option*

How will I evaluate sources of information to ensure that content is reliable?

You should always ask yourself whether the information you have found, from both primary and secondary sources, is correct. People can give you misleading information either because they want to mislead you, or simply by mistake. You can judge the source of the information as well as the content to decide whether you can rely on it.

Is the information appropriate?

You should check whether the information is appropriate for the problem you are trying to solve. It is easy to be captivated by interesting, but irrelevant facts.

You should check whether the information answers one or more of your questions, even if only partially. You should also try to assess whether it examines the problem in enough depth. You may need to note the source and then continue to look for better sources.

Is the information valid?

You should always check whether the information is a primary or secondary source before deciding whether it is valid. Secondary sources may have interpreted the facts incorrectly, or may not have gone to the right primary sources. You must also be aware that some information is deliberately presented in order to persuade you to take up a point of view, so may not give equal weighting to all the facts.

It is very difficult to decide whether a piece of information is true, even when you do have access to primary sources. If several people witness a crime being committed they will give different accounts in court of the event and may even contradict each other, although they are all trying to tell the truth. The jury has to decide what really happened, and take into account where each person was standing at the time, what they were doing and even their personality.

You need to be aware of these kinds of discrepancies and try to gather as much information as possible so you can cross-check one statement against another.

Is the information current?

You can check whether the information is up to date, by finding out whether a date is given anywhere. Books give the date of original publication plus the date at which it was revised. Newspapers and magazines always give the day or month when they were published. In the case of a webpage you may be able to see when it was last updated.

Of course, old information may still be important and useful, but if you think that later material is available then you should try to find it.

Is the source of the information authentic?

When you buy a copy of a national newspaper, such as The Independent, you can be reasonably sure that you are reading the real thing. But that is not necessarily true of web sites, and a number of scams have been associated with counterfeit sites. A similar problem has occurred in the past with primary historical sources which have turned out to be forgeries.

You can check a website in a number of ways.

* Look at the website address – if it ends with .edu or .ac.uk then you know that it comes from a reputable academic institution in the US or UK. If it ends with .gov.uk then it is a genuine UK governmental organisation.

* Check the Contacts or About Us page – it should give real world contact details, such as an address and phone number. Look for details of the people involved in the site, and do a web search on some of the names for more information about them.

* Do other sites link to the site? You can check this by entering the website address in a search engine (you must put speech marks around it) and see if other sites refer to it. Are they ones that you can trust?

You can check the details of a book or magazine like this:

* look for the name and address of the publisher, and then check the publisher's website (do remember that some people and organisations publish their own material and they will not use a well-known publisher)

* look for the ISBN (International Standard Book Number) allocated to any book published by a genuine publisher. Again, self-published books will probably not have an ISBN, but this does not mean that they are not genuine.

You can check the author or creator of a work several ways.

* Check whether the author's name appears somewhere. If you do not recognise the name then check it out on the Web.

* It is sometimes difficult to know whether the work is created by the named person. In the case of works of art and historical documents an expert in the field may authenticate them.

* You can check whether the item comes from a trusted source. For example, if a web page on the BBC site claims that an article has been written by a named reporter then you can be confident in its authenticity.

3.5 Other factors to consider

Gathering knowledge and resources can contribute greatly to the quality and accuracy of any decisions you make, but there are occasions when information and resources are not enough. Other factors can also have an impact on the way in which you arrive at a decision:

* *Gut feelings* ('I just know that this is the right thing to do'): you have an instinct, something tells you not to do that or not to go a certain place, or not to make a certain purchase. 'Gut feelings' and instinct are often the knowledge we have learned through our past experiences, but which have become so embedded in our minds that we have forgotten how we first learned them.

* *Sentiment* ('what will others think?'): a personal belief or judgment based on feeling or emotion rather than proof or certainty; 'my opinion differs from yours'; 'what are your thoughts on the election?'

* *Emotion* ('I will never forgive myself if I make a risky decision'): how would you feel if you carried out an activity that went wrong? Would you be able to live with yourself? Was the decision against your will – you possibly thought it ethically or morally wrong?

* *Ambition* ('How will this affect my career?'): if I make the right decision, will this improve my prospects for promotion? If I get it wrong, will this harm my career?

* *Lack of knowledge* ('Do I know enough to do this?'): am I ready to make this decision? What if I do not understand something?

Sentiments such as the ones listed at the beginning of this section can play a role in any decisions you must make. You may, for example, decide against a certain course of action in case you upset somebody's feelings, or you may worry about what others may think.

In small groups, discuss an issue that might arise if you were asked to make the following ethical and moral decisions. Would you:

1 Work for a company that carried out testing on animals?

2 Wear leather if you were a vegetarian?

3 Allow a friend to copy your work and pass it off as his or her own?

4 Take the credit for something when you are aware that the credit belonged to somebody else?

5 Own up if you accidentally scratched your neighbour's car?

6 Admit to finding £20 in the school/college canteen?

Ambition can drive decisions: as a knowledge worker you might experiment with ideas to come up with more innovative and creative solutions that could help to advance your career. At the same time, however, you will be aware that the wrong decision may put a halt to any career options you may have.

Gaps in your knowledge might constrain the type of career you choose as a knowledge worker because you do not have the necessary skills or ability. For example, to be a web designer you might need programming skills, flair to design pages and excellent interpersonal skills to communicate with different end-users. The decisions you would need to make to fill in these gaps in your knowledge might include learning to program, attending courses and, possibly, working alongside web designers so that you can learn by watching others doing this job.

3.6 Making a decision

To help you make decisions, you will practise using spreadsheet models. Spreadsheet modelling is useful because data can be extracted from the original data set and placed into a table, used as a basis for further calculations or used

for forecasting and prediction purposes. All of these actions can aid the decision-making process and provide the user with better informed decisions.

The models you create will be checked for correctness and will be evaluated against certain variables to ensure that the information provided meets the specified requirements. These requirements will include such things as cost effectiveness, efficiency and quality issues.

Throughout the modelling process the decisions you take will need to be fully justified and supported by documentation and recommendations. Finally, you will be expected to evaluate the model(s) you have created and to cross-reference your method of solution against the original objectives.

Spreadsheets

Spreadsheets present a clear and consistent way of understanding and interpreting data. Data can be keyed into a spreadsheet and the spreadsheet can be stored as a skeleton template so that further additions and updates can be added when necessary. Provided you have set up formulae on the spreadsheet, new data can be incorporated and updated easily to provide the user with current facts and figures. Spreadsheets can be used as a modelling tool to provide users with a range of features to enable them to:

* produce and display numerical, graphical and statistical data such as:
  - sales forecasts (see Figure 3.7)
  - profits and losses
  - general expenditure (see Figure 3.8)
  - wage and salary information
  - distribution facts
* forecast information
* calculate information
* predict alternative outcomes and behaviour under different conditions
* analyse information
* automate procedures.

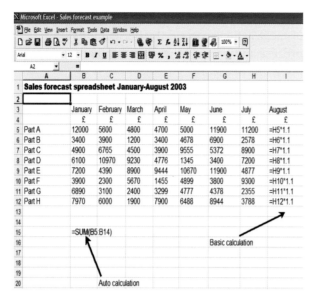

FIGURE 3.7 *Sample spreadsheet to calculate and forecast information*

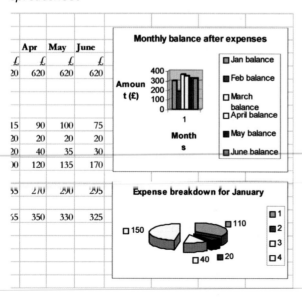

FIGURE 3.8 *Sample monthly expenditure spreadsheet*

FIGURE 3.9 *Examples of the charts and graphs offered by spreadsheets*

Using either a spreadsheet or a database, design a small system to meet one of the following user requirements:

1 A system a hire shop could use to store information about DVDs and videos it has available for hire. Your system should include:

   * customer details

   * details of DVD/video titles

   * rental status.

2 A stock control system template for a vehicle-repair shop that will automatically calculate stock levels and reorder levels. Your system should include:

   * the period January to June

   * stock items (fan belts, spark plugs, wheel nuts, fuses and tyres)

   * a minimum stock level requirement of 60 items

   * an indicator to show when stock items must be reordered

Your designs should be clear and fully functional. All the data you use should come from you and should be substantial enough to demonstrate the functionality of each system.

A spreadsheet that contains large amounts of data may not be easy to interpret. You can, therefore, use the graphical features offered by a spreadsheet to present data in a more visual way. Some spreadsheet applications, for example, have built-in chart and graphic facilities to provide the user with a visual interpretation of the data (see Figure 3.9).

Spreadsheet functions

There are a number of functions that can be used to model spreadsheets. These include:

* SUMIF

* Average

* Count.

	A	B	C	D	E	F	G	H	I	J
1	**Sales and commission for January 2003**									
2										
3		January		Commission 1.5%						
4		£		£						
5	Part A	12,000		180						
6	Part B	3,400		51						
7	Part C	4,900		74						
8	Part D	6,100		92						
9	Part E	7,200		108						
10	Part F	3,900		59						
11	Part G	6,890		10						
12	Part H	7,970		12						
13										
14	Calculated commission for part sales that have exceeded £5,000 in January									£602.40

=SUMIF(B5:B12, "> 5000",D5:D12)

FIGURE 3.10 *SUMIF*

In this section we will look at the SUMIF function. Spreadsheet functions can sometimes be quite complex. However they are quite necessary in order to fully manipulate spreadsheet datasets. In section 3.12 the basics of a spreadsheet are discussed, so you should ensure that you understand how to set up a worksheet and that you can perform basic calculations before you start to use some of the more complex functions.

SUMIF adds up the cells you have selected according to the criteria you have set. SUMIF, therefore, works like this:

SUMIF = range, criteria, sum range

* The *range* is the range of cells that you want to apply the criteria to.
* The *criteria* are used to determine which cells you want to add up. A criterion can be in the form of a number, an expression or text that defines which cells will be added. For example, criteria can be expressed as 40, "40", ">40", "widgets".
* The *sum range* are the cells you want to sum.

The cells in sum range are totalled only if their corresponding cells in the range match the criteria (see Figure 3.10). If sum range is omitted, the cells in the range are totalled.

3.7 Computer modelling

When you practise using spreadsheet models, you must bear in mind that decisions based on these models will only be as good as the models themselves. Before you put your trust in a model, therefore, whether your own or someone else's, you must make sure it is correct:

* is the logic it uses correct
* are the data formats appropriate
* is the syntax of the formulae correct
* are the cell references correct?

It's a good idea to look at a range of existing models; for example, financial models that could illustrate profit, loss and cash flow, and decision models that could perform forecasts for the future based on a given data set and certain rules and conditions. By using different models and evaluating them you can get an overview of a range of tools and techniques that can be used to manipulate spreadsheets. Models can evaluated in a number of ways, for example:

* what processes or scenarios are being modelled
* what does the model actually do
* how well does it do it
* could it be improved
* which variables can be input
* what outputs are identified
* what decisions could be made when using the model?

You work in a large stationery shop. Your role is to help the supervisor with the stock take and the reordering of stationery supplies. Although you are just a trainee at present, it is expected that you will be promoted to a supervisory role within six months.

Part of the supervisor's responsibilities is to try to identify what supplies will be in demand over a four-week period. At certain times of the year it is quite easy to do this – for example, between August and September the demand for 'back to school' stationery is very high. This is also the case in January when students return to school and college after the Christmas break.

In order to assist you in your decision-making process about what stock items should be ordered, the manager of the shop has started to design a spreadsheet based on a budget of £250 (see Figure 3.11).

	B	C	D	E
1		Stock budget		
2				
3	Item	Price	Number	Cost
4	Ring binder	0.79	0.00	0.00
5	A4 Pad	1.25	0.00	0.00
6	A5 Pad	1.05	0.00	0.00
7	Pack 10 clear wallets	2.15	0.00	0.00
8				
9	Pak of 5 folders	1.79	0.00	0.00
10	Pack of 4 pens	0.99	0.00	0.00
11	Stationary set	3.75	0.00	0.00
12	Pack of 3 ruled pads	2.00	0.00	0.00
13				
14	Pack of 3 storage boxes	3.45	0.00	0.00
15				
16				
17	Enter the number of unit stationary items			
18	required to make up the £250 budget			

C4*D4

Formulas need to be added for the cost column

A total column needs to be added to check that the cost falls within the £250 budget

FIGURE 3.11 *Stationery items: sample spreadsheet*

1 Look at the sample spreadsheet and complete the model using various combinations of stationery item quantities.

2 The spreadsheet that has been set up by the manager is incomplete: formulae should be included to total up each stationery item, and a Total Cost needs to be included to check that the items ordered falls within the £250 parameter.

3 Once the spreadsheet has been set up, project the information visually in a graph of your choice.

4 Identify other modelling techniques that can be used with this spreadsheet.

1 What is meant by the term 'spreadsheet model'?

2 Identify a range of spreadsheet models.

3 Why is modelling useful in spreadsheet design and manipulation?

3.8 Using a model to consider alternatives

When you have designed your own model(s), you need to ensure that they are working correctly and that they meet the original design requirements. You may find that, although a solution has been provided, alternatives exist that may be more cost-effective, labour saving or resourceful, for example. Therefore, you will need to devise a system for scrutinising and analysing your model. The system you devise should show that you have addressed, and answered, the following questions:

* Does the decisions I have decided upon produce the best results?

* What alternatives have I looked at?

* What makes the alternatives not as suitable as the solution I have chosen?

* What, if anything, does the model I have chosen *not* take into account – what are its limitations?

* What might be the impact of these limitations or constraints in the short and long term?

Think it over...

Modelling provides a framework on which to base decisions, make prediction and forecasts. What would happen if there were no modelling tools available? How would you be able to make good decisions?

Justifying the decision

Once you have developed and tested your model, you must produce supporting documentation that shows the key features of model and that demonstrates how your design meets the original aims and objectives.

The key features of a model could describe what the model does, how it does it, the benefits and impact of using the model and how it can be adapted in the future. Your model may change over time depending on what your expectations are and how it performs under certain conditions. Your initial aims and objectives may have been met by the model. However, as things change, the model may require updating to accommodate these new requirements.

✳ REMEMBER!

As you work through the decision-making process, keep a record of your processes and results, so that the information will be readily available when you come to write up your report or give a presentation on your decisions and recommendations.

Reporting it to others

You should write a short report that outlines the original problem, aims and objectives, and the final decision you made. This will focus your thoughts in a very structured and systematic way. You could add graphs and charts to the report to provide a visual overview of your model. If the model is quite complex to use, it might also be appropriate to design a user guide to help the reader understand why you have used a particular model and how the model has been created.

Your documentation should also include any recommendations you wish to make. These will help the end-user in understanding and appreciating the complexity of the model. Any recommendations you make should include:

* a summary of the current situation

* your sources and any alternatives you have considered

* other factors that you took into consideration

* the methods you used to reach your decision

* the decision itself

* a justification of your decision, supported by evidence of the decision-making process you went through.

Evaluating a model

To confirm that your model is successful, you must decide whether or not it meets the specified requirements. To do this, you must assess:

* how well your model has performed

* the extent to which the model has helped you in making the right decision

* what else you would like the model to do

* if your model need extending and, if so, how?

To help you in your evaluation, you could use a checklist such as the one shown in Table 3.4, which uses a brief for a toy company as an example.

REQUIREMENTS	MET? YES/NO		
The spreadsheet can display a breakdown of the sales for each toy over a six-month period (monetary and quantity based)			
Average sales can be calculated for each month			
Trends in sales can be identified over the period			
If a new toy was introduced on to the market you would be able to forecast a selling price for the next six-month period based on the average selling price for the month plus 10 per cent			
The spreadsheet can display a breakdown of the sales for each toy over a six-month period (monetary and quantity based)			
Functionality and appearance: * Do the formulae all work? * Are more formulae needed? * Comments:			
Does the model need extending?	Within 6 months	Within a year	Within 1–3 years
Comment on the way in which the model will need extending:			
Final comments:			

TABLE 3.4 *Evaluation checklist*

When you develop a model to meet a user or business requirement, there may be alternative models that you could use that would give you access to different information, or allow you to make different decisions.

For the model that you are developing to meet the requirements of this unit, outline two other models that could be used. Draw up a table to compare your model and the two alternative models in terms of:

* *functionality* – how well will the model work? Compare its features, such as automatic calculations, formulas and functions

* *usability* – how easy and practical are the models

* *practicality* – how useful are the models in terms of aiding the end-user in the decision-making process?

3.9 ICT skills

This section is designed to provide you with an overview of types of application software. You will not be using applications to design and build working models and templates from scratch. However, you may be expected to amend models and templates. This section, therefore, provides you with basics on how to address tasks, and carry out processing activities to enable you to improve initial designs and evaluate their performance. It will also enable you to advance into more complex tasks associated with modelling tools and techniques as identified in section 3.6.

Carrying out spreadsheet modelling tasks

In order to support you in your spreadsheet modelling, you will learn about a range of tools and techniques you can incorporate into your own designs. This section, therefore, provides you with examples and screen shots of some of the more popular tools and techniques used in spreadsheet modelling.

Entering and editing data

Cells in a spreadsheet are identified by a series of letters and numbers. The letters identify the columns and the numbers the rows. To enter data into a spreadsheet, click on the appropriate cell (for example A1, B3, C2, etc.) (Figure 3.12).

In the example in Figure 3.13 you can see that the data entered in cell E5 (1888) also appears in the Formula bar at the top of the screen. If you wanted to change the data for cell E5, you would click on that cell and key in the new data, or key in the data directly on the Formula bar.

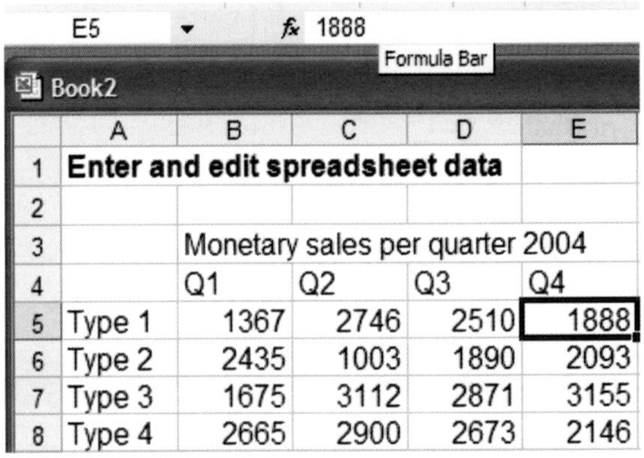

	A	B	C	D	E
1	Enter and edit spreadsheet data				
2					
3		Monetary sales per quarter 2004			
4		Q1	Q2	Q3	Q4
5	Type 1	1367	2746	2510	1888
6	Type 2	2435	1003	1890	2093
7	Type 3	1675	3112	2871	3155
8	Type 4	2665	2900	2673	2146

Revised data can be typed into any one of these two places.

FIGURE 3.12 *Entering and editing data*

Formatting data

In the Formatting menu, there a number of criteria you can select to format your spreadsheet. The examples provided in this section will look at the formatting of cells and conditional formatting features (see Figure 3.13). It is suggested that you experiment with the other format options on your spreadsheet when you do your own modelling.

Formatting cells

You can format individual cells, rows, columns or entire sheets. Here we will focus on the formatting of cells.

Using the **Cells...** option on the **Format** menu drop-down list, **Number** function, it is easy to select data values and set them to two decimal places, as shown in these three easy steps.

Step one (Figure 3.14): enter the data to be formatted.

Step two (Figure 3.15): format the data.

Step three (Figure 3.16): data is formatted.

There are other formatting functions you can use in the Format Cells dialogue box, including

Alignment, Font, Border, Patterns and Protection (Figure 3.17 shows the options available if the **Border** tab is selected).

Conditional formatting

This function allows you to select the type of formatting wish to apply to certain data, and under certain conditions. On the **Menu** bar, select: **Format, Conditional Formatting.**

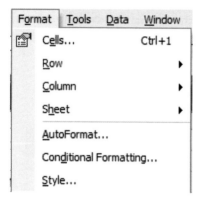

FIGURE 3.13 *Formatting data*

	A	B	C	D	E
1	**Enter and edit spreadsheet data**				
2					
3		Monetary sales per quarter 2004			
4		Q1	Q2	Q3	Q4
5	Type 1	1367	2746	2510	1888
6	Type 2	2435	1003	1890	2093
7	Type 3	1675	3112	2871	3155
8	Type 4	2665	2900	2673	2146

Enter the data to be formatted

FIGURE 3.14 *Entering the data to be formatted*

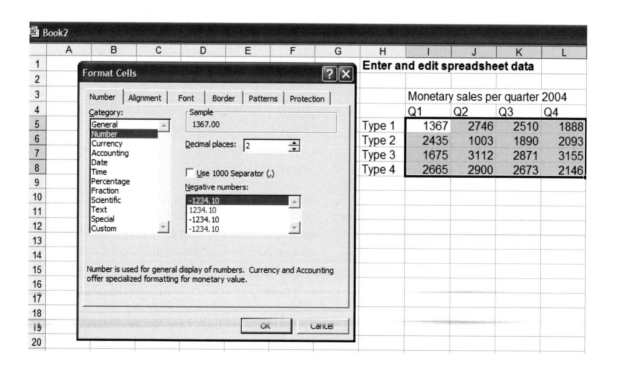

Select 'number' from the format menu, and click up or down for the amount of decimal places – in this e.g. '2'

FIGURE 3.15 *Formatting the data*

	A	B	C	D	E
1	**Enter and edit spreadsheet data**				
2					
3		Monetary sales per quarter 2004			
4		Q1	Q2	Q3	Q4
5	Type 1	1367	2746	2510	1888
6	Type 2	2435	1003	1890	2093
7	Type 3	1675	3112	2871	3155
8	Type 4	2665	2900	2673	2146

Enter the data to be formatted

FIGURE 3.16 *Formatted data*

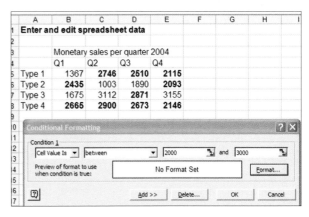

FIGURE 3.18 *Conditional formatting*

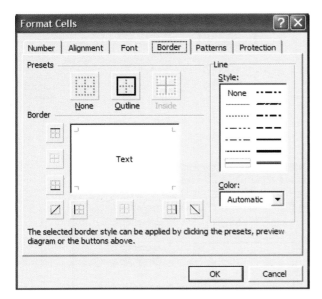

FIGURE 3.17 *Format Cells dialogue box, Border tab selected*

The Conditional Formatting dialogue box is displayed. In the example in Figure 3.18, all data between the value of 2000 and 3000 have been emboldened. To do this, once the conditions have been set in the Conditional Formatting dialogue box, click on: **Format** to display the Format Cells dialogue box where you can chose the required formatting.

Analysing and interpreting data (e.g. filters)

If you apply a filter to a spreadsheet, this will allow you to focus on a particular section of data – screening off the rest of the spreadsheet. On the

Menu bar, select: **Data, Filter, AutoFilter** (Figure 3.19).

By clicking on the down arrow at the side of the Total cell (see Figure 3.20), you can apply a filter to the Total column and therefore select which totals you want to view – in this case those for 8738 relating to Type 1 items.

Sort

The Sort function allows you to sort information in ascending or descending order. On the **Menu** bar, select: **Data, Sort**. The Sort dialogue box is displayed (Figure 3.21). You can select which data you want to sort by clicking on each criteria – **Sort by, Then by, Then by**.

For example, you could sort student enrolment information alphabetically by surname as show in Table 3.5.

Using formulae and functions

Formulae and functions can be used to manipulate data within a spreadsheet and also to take away some of the repetitive tasks involved with calculating and analysing data. Formulae and functions provide you with a ready-made toolkit that will allow you to develop a worksheet into a working financial, statistical, business or decision-based model. Formulae can be set up and then copied to save time and also to reduce errors within the spreadsheet (Figure 3.22). By using cell referencing you can analyse spreadsheet data in almost any way that you may require.

Enter and edit spreadsheet data

Monetary sales per quarter 2004

	Q1	Q2	Q3	Q4		Total
Type 1	1367	2746	2510	2115		8738
Type 2	2435	1003	1890	2093		7421
Type 3	1675	3112	2871	3155		10813
Type 4	2665	2900	2673	2146		10384

FIGURE 3.19 *Applying a filter*

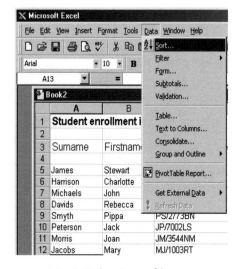

FIGURE 3.20 *Selecting a filter*

FIGURE 3.21 *The Sort dialogue box*

Validating and checking data

There are a number of ways that data can be validated and checked within a spreadsheet. If an incorrect formula has been inserted, an error message may be displayed (Figure 3.23).

If you need to track which variables have been used in a calculation Formula auditing (Figure 3.24) and Trace precedents can be used to map the individual cells. Formulae can also be evaluated using the formula auditing feature to

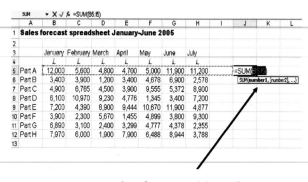

FIGURE 3.22 *Example of a spreadsheet formula*

Unsorted
Student enrolment information

Surname	First name	Enrolment number
James	Stewart	SJ/1267OP
Harrison	Charlotte	CH/5374LP
Michaels	John	JM/2900GL
Davids	Rebecca	RD/6729HN
Smyth	Pippa	PS/2773BN
Peterson	Jack	JP/7002LS
Morris	Joan	JM/3544NM
Jacobs	Mary	MJ/1003RT

Sorted
Student enrolment information

Surname	First name	Enrolment number
Davids	Rebecca	RD/6729HN
Harrison	Charlotte	CH/5374LP
Jacobs	Mary	MJ/1003RT
James	Stewart	SJ/1267OP
Michaels	John	JM/2900GL
Morris	Joan	JM/3544NM
Peterson	Jack	JP/7002LS
Smyth	Pippa	PS/2773BN

TABLE 3.5 *Alphabetically sorted surnames*

identify cells that have been used in any given calculations.

Validation of a spreadsheet model can also include inputting reminders of values to be entered (Figure 3.26).

FIGURE 3.24 *Formula auditing toolbar*

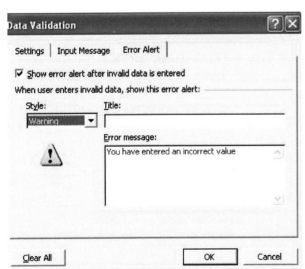

FIGURE 3.23 *Data validation error message*

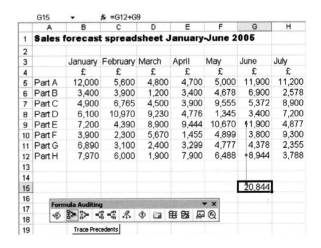

FIGURE 3.25 *An example of formula auditing*

July	Aug
£	£
11,200	16,800
2,578	
8,900	
7,200	
4,877	
9,300	
2,355	
3,788	

Aug sales (Part B)
Use July's figures +25%

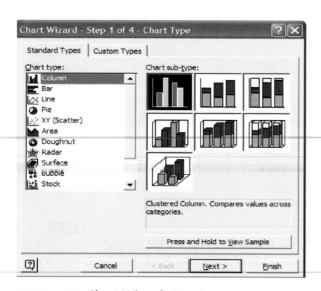

FIGURE 3.26 *Using a reminder*

Presenting information

Graphs and charts provide a more visual overview of any data you have generated in your spreadsheet. If you follow the steps in the Chart Wizard (select: the **Chart Wizard** icon on the Toolbar) (Figure 3.27), there are a number of graphs and charts you can create.

Pie charts

Each segment of the pie chart in Figure 3.28 represents a percentage of games consoles sold for each month from August to January. The smallest segment is 6 per cent for August and the largest is 35 per cent for December.

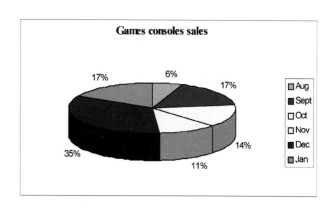

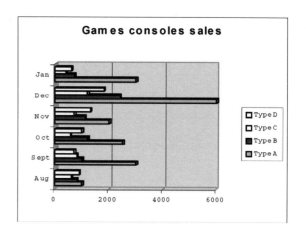

FIGURE 3.27 *Chart Wizard, Step 1*

Bar graphs

Each bar on the bar graph in Figure 3.29 represents a type of games console ranging from A to D. The bar graph identifies how many of each console was sold each month.

FIGURE 3.29 *Bar graph*

Line graph

The line graph in Figure 3.30 clearly plots the sales of each console from August to January. It is evident that Type A console is the best seller and that Type C console is the worst seller. From this graph it is

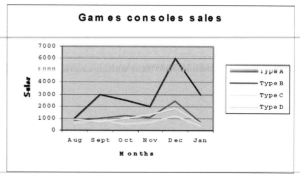

FIGURE 3.30 *Line graph*

also clear that in August, September and January sales were very similar for Types B, C and D.

Scatter graph

Scatter graphs (Figure 3.31) are best used when there is a lot of numerical data that requires plotting to identify a pattern in the data. The scatter graph in Figure 3.31 shows the pattern of sales for each month, 1–6. In August it clearly shows that all four games console types had similar sales figures. However in December these sales are quite different.

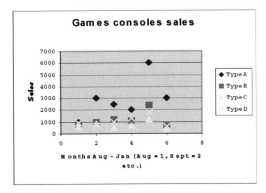

FIGURE 3.31 *Scatter graph*

Modifying spreadsheet models to take account of requirements

Spreadsheet models can be modified to take into account different requirements or needs. For example on a 'sales forecast spreadsheet', a change in the market might impact on the price of an item. Therefore more or less might have to be sold to break-even. By changing a single variable, such as increasing the cost of an item, the entire model will also change and adapt to the new increase.

If a calculation was used to forecast August's sales, based on a 25 per cent increase on July's figures (Figure 3.26), a change in the July forecast figure would then subsequently alter the forecasting for any other months using the July figures as a basis (Figure 3.32).

ICT skills are skills that you acquire, learn and develop when you use certain applications, hardware and software. In terms of software, ICT skills are judged by the competency of the end-user in interacting with the menus and toolbars

	A	B	C	D	E	F	G	H	I
1	Sales forecast spreadsheet January–June 2005								
2									
3		January	February	March	April	May	June	July	Aug
4		£	£	£	£	£	£	£	£
5	Part A	12,000	5,600	4,800	4,700	5,000	11,900	11,200	16,800
6	Part B	3,400	3,900	1,200	3,400	4,678	6,900	2,578	3222.5

FIGURE 3.32 *An example of automatic calculation*

and how the techniques are incorporated into their own designs.

Word processing

Word processing software can support you in the preparation and writing up all sorts of documents. Depending upon the nature of your task, it can be used to:

* import data from other applications

* format documents

* creat document layouts

* check documents.

Importing data from other applications

There are a number of ways that data can be imported from other applications into a word processed document, such as Word. You can, for instance, import a chart created in Excel.

With the Word document open on screen, position the cursor in the document where you want the chart to appear. Now open Excel and open the file that contains the chart. Select the entire chart by clicking in a white space outside the plotted chart area. Click on the **Copy** button and switch back to the Word document by clicking in its button on the taskbar at the bottom of the

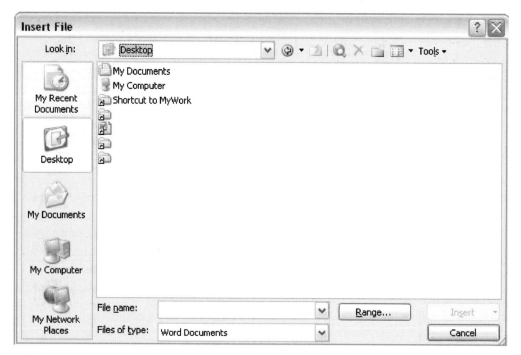

FIGURE 3.34 *Inserting a file*

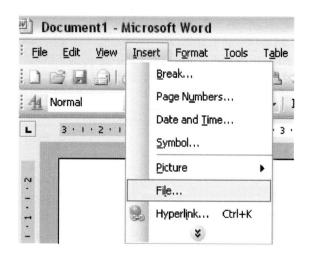

FIGURE 3.35 *Insert File dialogue box*

screen. With the Word document on screen, click on the **Paste** button and the chart will be imported into the document.

You can also insert files into a Word document by selecting **Insert** from the **Menu** bar, then clicking on **File...** (Figure 3.34). This will bring the Insert File dialogue box on screen (Figure 3.35). In the **Look in** box, select the file you want to import (click on the down arrow at the side of this box to view all the files). So that you can view all files

and not just Word files, make sure **All Files** is selected in the **Files of type** box. When you have located the correct file, click on it, then on **Insert.** The file will be imported into the Word document.

Formatting documents that have been imported

There are a number of documents that can be formatted and imported into word processing software such as Word. Documents or files can include:

* tables
* spreadsheets
* graphics
* data sets used for mail merging
* scanned images
* drawings
* downloaded material.

For some documents, the format might have to be changed so that they can be opened into Word format. Layout and sizing changes may also have to be addressed to ensure that it is legible to view or read.

Creating document layouts

You can create tables in Word. To produce a table with a fixed number of columns and rows, on the **Menu** bar, select: **Table, Insert, Table** (Figure 3.36). The Insert Table dialogue box is displayed (Figure 3.37).

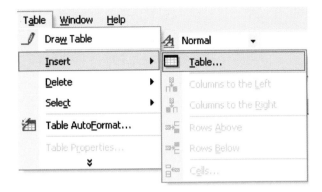

FIGURE 3.36 *Inserting a table*

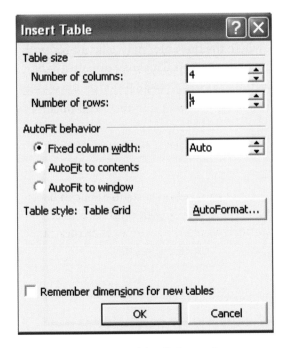

FIGURE 3.37 *Insert Table dialogue box*

Select the number of columns and rows you require in the boxes in the **Table size** pane (the other selections should be left as they are, i.e. **Fixed column width** selected and **Auto** displayed). Now click on **OK**. The table grid will appear in the document. Table 3.6 was produced this way. Once the grid had been created, the entries were added to the cells, and the cells increased in size, when necessary, to accommodate the entries.

If you want to change the appearance of the columns in a Word document, you can arrange these as two, three or four vertical columns. First, highlight the text you want to arrange in columns. Then click on the **Column** icon on the Standard toolbar (Figure 3.38). In the drop-down list, select two, three or four columns, as required.

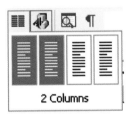

Column icon

FIGURE 3.38 *Selecting columns*

Checking documents

There are a number of standard tools that can be used to check documents in Word, some of these include checking for spelling (**Spell check**), grammar and punctuation. Language checks can also be carried out using the translation tool and text can be converted from English to French or Spanish, for example. In addition, documents can also be previewed and checked prior to printing (**Print preview**).

POLICY NUMBERS	INITIALS	CUSTOMER SINCE	INSURANCE TYPE
ST/01/L/34849	ST	2001	L – Life
RB/02/M/74788	RB	2002	M – Motor
LD/89/H/56337	LD	1989	H – House

TABLE 3.6 *Table created by the Insert Table dialogue box method*

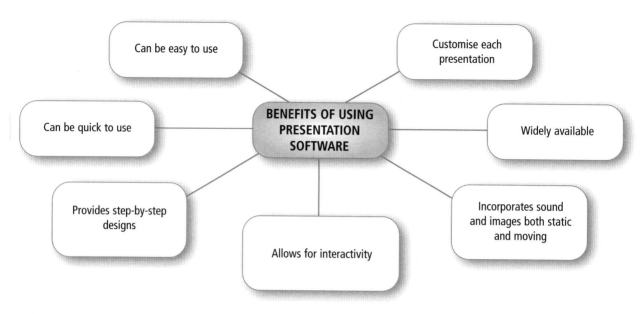

FIGURE 3.39 *Benefits of using presentation software*

Producing presentations

Using presentations

Good presentation skills are essential in all environments; people will have expectations of your ability to present information clearly, cohesively, relevantly and knowledgeably.

Methods and styles of presentations include:

* formal/informal
* use of ICT resources/no ICT resource use
* delivery to a wide audience/to individuals.

Formal and informal presentations

In terms of formality, a presentation will differ depending upon the environment in which it is being delivered and the intended audience. Formal presentations tend to be more structured with more time built into the planning and overall delivery. Formal presentations may also be delivered to an audience that is not known to you. This may be especially true within an organisational environment.

Formal presentations can include:

* providing feedback on a project at work
* representation at a meeting
* press release

* awards ceremony speech.

Informal presentations are more likely to be quite casual, where the presenter may talk 'ad lib' with little or no preparation. This may not always be the case, but informal presentations do encourage 'freestyle' speech.

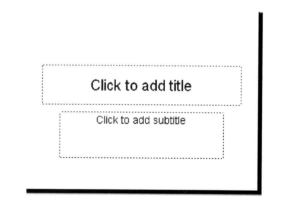

Click to add title

Click to add subtitle

New
🗋 Blank Presentation
🗐 From Design Template
📑 From AutoContent Wizard

Blank presentation

Ways of creating a presentation slide

FIGURE 3.40 *Creating a presentation using PowerPoint®*

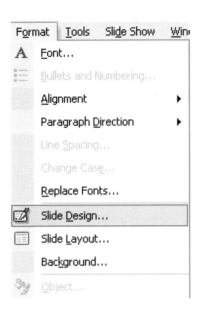

Apply a color scheme:

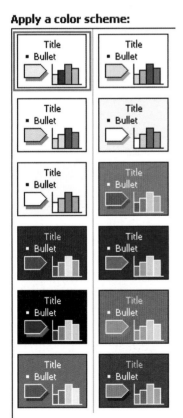

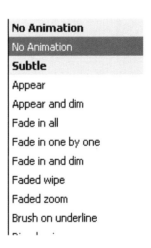

FIGURE 3.41 *Formatting a slide using PowerPoint®*

Informal presentations can include:

* presentation on 'new film releases' as part of your coursework

* recounting events of a holiday to a friend

* thank-you/congratulations speech to friends or family.

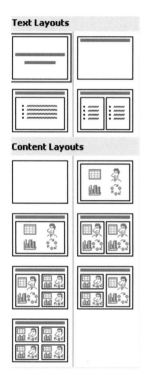

Text Layouts

Content Layouts

FIGURE 3.42 *Text and content layout variations in PowerPoint*

Styles of delivery

Presentations can be delivered in a number of ways, with or without the use of ICT, including:

* reading from cards, sheets, etc.

* free style

* using presentation software

* using aids such as flip charts, overhead transparencies (OHTs), whiteboard, etc.

Some people find it quite difficult to recall large amounts of data and information from memory when giving a presentation. They may, therefore, need a prompt to aid in the recall process. Speakers often use small index cards or a sheet of paper containing a few bullet points as a prompt.

Using ICT to produce presentations

ICT now plays a big role in the way in which presentations are delivered and in the overall quality of presentations. Software applications, such as PowerPoint, can be used for the specific purpose of delivering a professional presentation. Presentation software today can provide a number of benefits as shown in Figure 3.39.
When you use presentation software, you will learn about:

* creating and editing presentations

* formatting slides

* inserting text, pictures and charts

* importing data from other applications

* checking presentations.

Creating and editing presentations

The use of presentation software can allow you to create and edit presentations. Using software such as PowerPoint, for example, you can create professional presentation slides starting from: a **Blank Presentation** slide, a **Design Template,** or from the **AutoContent Wizard** (Figure 3.40).

Formatting slides

There are a number of ways that presentation slides can be formatted using PowerPoint. By selecting: **Format, Slide Design, Design Templates** you can apply or change a design template; choose **Colour Schemes** to apply or change the colour scheme, and **Animation Schemes** to apply or change an animation (Figure 3.41).
In addition, by selecting Format, Slide Layout, the slide can be formatted to include a variety of Text Layouts and Content Layouts (Figure 3.42).
By selecting: **Slide Show, Slide Transition,** you can customise your slide show to:

* control the speed of each slide

* determine the way in which the slide appears on the screen (for example, dissolving in)

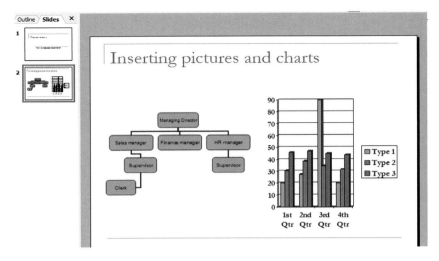

FIGURE 3.43 *Using a Text and Content Layout to insert content using PowerPoint®*

* automatically time the length of each slide
* decide how the slides are advanced.

You can also include a link to other applications on the Internet.

Inserting text, pictures and charts

Inserting text, pictures and charts on a slide can easily be achieved in PowerPoint using **Text Layouts** or **Content Layouts.** Select the layout you want to use for the slide, then click on the relevant icon to add the content you require (Figure 3.43).

Importing data from other applications

Importing data from other applications can also be carried out quite easily using a PowerPoint® presentation and selecting: Insert from the toolbar. Graphs, charts, pictures or other applications such as spreadsheets can all be integrated into a slide show (Figure 3.44).

Checking presentations

When you have completed your presentation slides, it is a good idea to check through the content to make sure that there are no spelling or grammatical errors. In addition, check that the graphics and any imported files, charts, pictures, etc. are positioned correctly. If you have used any special features, such as timings or animations, also ensure that they have been

set up appropriately. When using animation and sound, make sure that these do not distract your audience from the content of the presentation.

Run through your complete presentation a least a couple of times before presenting it to your target audience

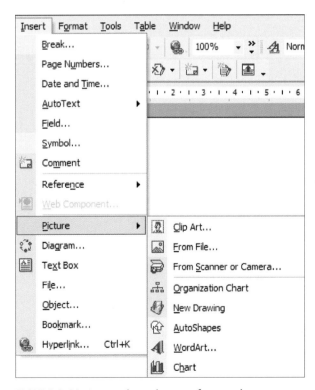

FIGURE 3.44 *Importing pictures from other applications using PowerPoint®*

1 Create a short presentation using six slides. The presentation theme should be based on mobile phone technologies.

2 Within your presentation, use at least one graphic and one table or chart.

3 Use at least two formatting features to enhance your presentation.

4 Print your presentation out six slides to a page.

Presentation software is an excellent way for a knowledge worker to visually communicate their thoughts and ideas.

1 Give three examples or scenarios showing when and how a knowledge worker could use presentation software.

2 What are the benefits of communicating information in a visual format?

UNIT 4

System design and installation

Introduction

This unit is about the personal computer, its hardware and software, which are used to ensure that it operates as a home and business system. You will develop an understanding of how systems are designed and how differing systems have various technical requirements. You will learn how to communicate with ICT users using non-technical language to gain information about their requirements and produce specifications to meet their needs.

What you need to learn

In completing this unit, you should achieve these learning outcomes:

* Know the hardware and software requirements of computer systems
* Produce system specifications that meet users' requirements
* Analyse users' needs
* Evaluate and investigate many different computer systems
* Select and combine appropriate system components.

Resource toolkit

To complete this unit you need these essential resources:

* access to computer hardware including a printer
* access to computer software, in particular, a current version of Windows® operating system to install and Microsoft Office®
* access to the Internet
* access to old/spare computer components to investigate.

This practitioner-focused unit is internally assessed. Page VII explains what this means.

There are three assessment objectives:

AO1 Carry out a needs analysis and produce a system specification for a specified client (assessment evidence a and b)

AO2 Install and test a computer system and configure system settings for a specified client/purpose (assessment evidence c and d)

AO3 Evaluate the system (assessment evidence e).

To demonstrate your coverage of these assessment objectives, you will produce an e-portfolio of evidence, showing what you have learnt and what you can do:

(a) You will produce a needs analysis for a specified client with complex needs, including a description and detailed evaluation of two existing systems that meet similar needs.

(b) You will complete a detailed system specification which:

* fully meets the needs of the client

* is presented effectively in simple, non-technical language

* includes a full justification for the choice of computer system components

* gives some consideration to ergonomics

* demonstrates consideration of the audience (client).

(c) You will provide evidence of installation and configuration of a fully functional system, optimised for a specified client/purpose.

(d) You will provide evidence of testing to ensure that the system's configuration functions correctly.

(e) You will complete a comprehensive evaluation of the performance of the system, as well as your own performance on this unit.

Your e-portfolio will contain all the evidence on which your performance will be judged. Some **Assessment activities** can be used towards your e-portfolio. These will contain **Assessment hints** on what you can do to pass (✓), gain a better mark (✓✓) or top marks (✓✓✓). For example, when providing a 'needs analysis' for a specified client with complex requirements, it must be detailed, including a comprehensive description and evaluation of at least two existing systems that meet similar needs.

The system specification has to be comprehensive, but in simple, non-technical language that the client can understand. You must ensure it fully meets the needs of the client. You should justify your choice of computer components, and give reasonable consideration to ergonomics and the client who will be using the system.

You must provide proof that you have installed and configured this system to meet the user's needs and have covered every task systematically. The testing of this system must be comprehensive and must prove that it is working effectively.

Why not keep a log of the time you take to complete this unit? Devise for a blank form that you could use to record the time that you spend on this course.

4.1 Needs analysis

When planning and implementing a new computer system, an ICT practitioner must work closely with the client to analyse his or her needs and agree the specification of the system. This will ensure that the new system will be fit for purpose and will meet the client's own 'personal' requirements.

In this section, you will learn how to investigate a client's requirements by carrying out a detailed needs analysis, covering the client's requirements, what technique to use, and using your knowledge to see how a client's needs can be met best. This involves:

* establishing how the current system (either a manual system or an existing computer system) works

* identifying the problems/limitations of the current system and therefore any user dissatisfaction

* identifying the requirements for a new system in terms of functionality, costs and timescales.

You will use a range of different investigative/ analytical techniques in order to find out what you need to know, including:

* interviews
* questionnaires
* face-to-face meetings
* observation
* document analysis
* data analysis.

Once you have a clear picture of a client's needs, you can consider how they can best be met. It is almost a certainty that there will be an existing system in use that fulfils a similar need. You will learn how to evaluate existing systems, looking at features such as:

* components (both hardware and software)
* effectiveness
* usability
* drawbacks and limitations.

By looking carefully at these systems, you may get an idea of what might be appropriate for your client, what alternatives there are and what drawbacks you may need to consider.

✱ REMEMBER!

This unit also looks at the lifeblood of the ICT industry – the client. As an ICT practitioner, you will depend on clients for the work you receive and, therefore, your income. The way you treat the client is therefore of paramount importance.

If you work for a company, your manner will reflect on your employees and their reputation. It goes without saying, therefore, that your manner should always be professional and you should show respect for every client, regardless of their level of technical knowledge.

The client's requirements

Establishing how the current system works

To analyse a client's requirements, you must first establish how their current system works. You may encounter clients who have not adopted computerisation as a solution to their business or personal needs. In countries like the United Kingdom, most people under the age of 35 see computers as an everyday part of life, but there is also a much larger (and generally older) part of the population who have a varied and often limited experience of computer systems. It is worth noting that, in our global economy, there are also clients from developing nations who may be using computer technology for the first time.

When dealing with a client for the first time, you will need to find out which of these situations applies:

* whether they have an existing manual system, which requires *converting* to computer technology

* whether they have an existing but old computer system, which requires *upgrading*.

In a later section (pages 159–162), you will learn about a variety of tools that will enable you to establish what the client's existing system is and how you may be able to improve it. You have to spend time with the client and establish:

* how the current system operates
* what the sources of information are
* who needs the information
* what software may be required to enable the task to be completed
* what computer hardware may be required to ensure that the task is completed reliably and effectively
* how, and to what level, does the client require training on the new system and software.

Identifying the problems/limitations of the current system

If a person or an organisation is looking to change an existing system, whether by changing from a manual to a computer system or upgrading the existing computer system, there has to be some sense of dissatisfaction with the current system.

This may arise from recognition that the current system no longer meets people's demands or expectations, or from a desire to improve the current system so it can support others more effectively. In some cases, the motive to change arises from the client's wish to have the latest technology, rather than a real need for it.

In looking at the current problems and limitations, you will need to find out any faults that are occurring and any problems as perceived by the client. In describing faults and problems, the client is likely to use non-technical language and you may need to prompt him or her to find out the information you need. You may have to ask questions such as:

* Is the system too slow for your current business or personal need?
* Is the system too small for your current business or personal need?

Identifying the requirements for a new system

In the technical society of today, the functionality of any system is essential. If you are using a system that has problems with its functionality, it can make people's work harder, mistakes may be made, and it tends to be unpopular as it is not as easy to use as it should be.

Functionality

Improving functionality is essential as this will increase the acceptance of the system by all involved, especially if there have previously been problems. Better acceptance improves:

* the use and therefore the popularity of the system

* efficiency and accuracy through the assumed correct use of the system

* sales (this is important if you are the manufacturer of the system).

Costs

Cost is an important factor in much of our daily life, as well as in the ICT sector. When making a purchasing decision, it is normal to think about:

* how much it costs

* whether it is too expensive and whether you can afford it

* if it costs more that you can afford, whether you really need or want it

* if it costs more that you can afford, where will the additional money come from – by saving, by cutting back elsewhere

* whether it will soon be out of date, and if so, will it be worth paying the price quoted.

If you ask yourself such detailed questions when making your own purchases, consider that others making buying decisions ask themselves similar questions, whether they are buying computer equipment for their own personal needs or for business purposes.

The cost needs to be reasonable to the person or organisation involved as well as reasonable for the task required (see Table 4.1). Buying the latest,

LEVEL OF SYSTEM	WHO MAY USE THE SYSTEM (GUIDE ONLY)	TECHNICAL SPECIFICATION
Entry	Home users, office staff, Internet users	The lowest specification processor and memory available at the time; most hard drives will suffice; a general purpose operating system
Intermediate or 'power user'	General programmers, web and system developers	Anything up to the best specification memory and processor; a larger hard drive may be required
Advanced	Games developers, graphical artists, engineers, architects and animators	The best specification processor and memory available; the size of the hard drive and quality of the sound/graphical systems are also important

TABLE 4.1 *Reasonable personal computer specifications*

'hottest' PC for straightforward word processing is simply absurd, but it may be exactly what is required for a graphics or gaming system.

Timescale

Throughout much of our lives, we experience constant pressure due to lack of time; this can cause problems personally as well as at work. Respecting and appreciating timescales is an essential factor of your professional experience. You will discover that timescales may affect:

* the attitude of the client, who may need the system urgently

* your prices, due to the costs of delivery

* the desired speed of servicing and repair in relation to the urgent nature of the problem

* your ability to secure work, as someone else may be able to deliver faster.

Getting the timescale right – in terms of the original quoted timescale as well as delivering within that timescale – means that you will be perceived as reliable, and therefore may obtain more work from the same client in the future. Keeping to your own estimated timescales also means you are more likely to make a profit, as taking longer than planned will affect your profitability. Taking too long or being too slow is seldom good for anybody's business.

Most Internet retailers rely on the client not needing the resources immediately, whereas high street retailers can often provide what is required on demand, based on their having stock in store. This is why internet retailers often offer highly competitive prices – they don't have to maintain the same stock levels and service staff as high street retailers. You expect to pay more if you want something quickly.

The timescale involved in the service and repair of equipment is often agreed through a 'service level agreement'.

UK law provides us with a one-year warranty automatically, but you can pay for up to five years in some cases. However, for computer equipment the normal warranty is for three years as most equipment is considered redundant after this time.

Analyse the problem using different techniques

Often you have a client who needs a new computer system to replace a manual system or an older computer system. They know that 'things need improving' but sometimes cannot actually explain in detail what they want. For you to find out what they need, you will have to use a range of different investigative and analytical techniques, including:

* interviews

* questionnaires

* face-to-face meetings
* observation
* document and data analysis.

Interviews

Taking the time to sit with, listen to and interview the client is essential. It will help the client to trust you, but a properly planned interview will also help you to understand the system at all levels. You must identify who you are going to speak to (for example, technical directors, managers, technical professionals, as well as the most important of all – the people who are going to use the system), and the questions you will ask each group. You need to ensure that your questions are appropriate to the level, experience and responsibility of the person being interviewed. For example, asking an ICT user a technical question is as invalid and irrelevant as asking an ICT professional how they feel about the colour of the interface.

In the course of all the interviews, you would expect to ask questions about:

* the amount that the organisation or individual wishes to spend on the system
* timescale expectations, i.e. how soon the system is required
* how they expect the system to be used
* what is the anticipated functionality
* how the new system is expected to supersede the existing system
* what are the personal or business requirements for the new system
* what training may be required or desired on the new systems.

How you conduct the interview is very important. For some employees, the prospect of a new system will invoke fear, while for many there will be anxiety. They may be unsure if it will make their job redundant, or they may be worried that they will lose their job if they can't cope with the new system. Your manner has to be encouraging, reassuring them that they will be supported in the transition to the new system.

During the interview, you will need to take notes or record the conversations (with the express permission of the interviewees) but once the interview process has been completed, you will need to collate and analyse all of the responses. This will form part of your proposal for the new system.

Assessment activity

Interview one of the following 'clients': your employer, your teacher, a member of your family or a friend. Make sure that you have planned the questions and base the purpose of the interview around 'ordering a new computer, to replace an older system'.

An interview can be completed in any environment, so long as you have the attention of the client. The importance of interviews becomes apparent when you have to analyse the results. Better questions will yield better responses and give you better results to analyse. If you have interviewed more than one person regarding the same system, you will need to create a collation sheet which will contain a comparison of all the answers.

Think it over...

What methods would you use to interview the staff at your centre if, as a student, you had to implement a new system? Consider the fact that many of them are more experienced than you and you would have to put them at ease.

Questionnaires

Some organisations are simply too large for you to interview everyone. An alternative information gathering technique is the questionnaire. A questionnaire ensures that you will be able to 'ask the right questions' of many more people as well as collate their responses successfully.

(A questionnaire can also used to collect information *after* the job, to discover client satisfaction and to improve services as appropriate.)

A well-designed questionnaire will make the collation process easier. Although it seems easy to ask clients to write paragraphs of information in answer to your questions on the questionnaire, it will be easier for you to collate all their responses if you design questions with a scale of importance (like 1 to 5), as shown in Figure 4.1. (This will also probably be quicker for the clients to complete.) Many computer mark systems will scan in a scaled questionnaire for you and collate the results, which is ideal for a large-scale survey.

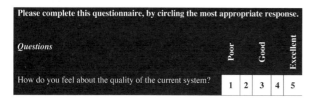

FIGURE 4.1 *An example of a question from a scaled questionnaire*

Face-to-face meetings

Like an interview, a face-to-face meeting is a more personal way of finding out information from a client about a proposed system. An interview tends to be a 'staged' method of finding out information about a given subject from many people, whereas a well managed face-to-face meeting allows for an informal dialogue to take place between all parties concerned with the new system.

A meeting will require a purpose (sometimes called a stated objective) along with an agenda, which will list all the subjects being discussed. The agenda is circulated and agreed before the meeting, and each point may be led by a different member of the meeting. Each point is discussed, agreed and recorded; the record of the meeting is often referred to as the 'minutes'. The chairperson – and this may be you – will run the meeting, to ensure that it proceeds smoothly and keeps to the agreed agenda; he or she may need to exert their authority to bring the meeting 'back to order' if it goes off course.

Observation

Watching people at work is invaluable. What you see may be different from what you have been told. Your observations on what is actually happening may bring fresh insights into a situation that is often so familiar to those involved that they don't see things clearly. You may need to observe those who are using the system or those who manage and develop various elements within the system.

Document and data analysis

Like observation, your independent view arising from analysis of documents and data can often reveal areas for improvement. Document and data analysis involve looking at:

* the documents and information that go into the system from external sources

* the way information and documentation is stored in the system

* how the information is released from the system and the format that the documentation takes, i.e. whether it is in printed or electronic form.

It is critical that you understand who the client is for any documentation. Developers sometimes forget that the information is for others as well as themselves.

Using your knowledge

Client's needs

Once you have a clear picture of a client's needs, you may consider how they can best be met. Almost certainly, there will be an existing system that fulfils a similar need. If not, you may have to recommend the creation of a bespoke system. You will learn how to evaluate existing systems, by looking at features such as:

* hardware – the technical requirements of the new system

* software – the applications that will support the business needs of the client

* the operating system, which will ensure that the hardware and the applications will work together and provide the access and functionality required by the client.

Key term

Bespoke describes something made for individual use or to meet individual requirements. In this context, it means to create a custom-made computer system. The term was originally used by tailors who would create custom-made suits for those wealthy enough to afford them.

A bespoke system will require more detailed planning than an 'off the shelf' system. It may be that you need to specify the system hardware to ensure that the new system will support the business or technical load required, whereas having bespoke software will involve the commissioning of an experienced team of programmers and developers. Most web-based solutions tend to have a bespoke nature due to the newness of the industry and the specific needs of most of the clients.

✱ REMEMBER!

You can have new hardware devices created as a bespoke solution. Although this is a worthwhile technical discipline, it can be extremely awkward for anyone commissioning a computer system.

Components: hardware and software

The hardware and software components for a computer system can easily be sourced from any computer retailer. If the system is reasonably common, you should have no difficulty in specifying a system. If you are sourcing the full system, you will find that sourcing each element separately will cost less than buying a complete 'off the shelf' solution from many high street retailers.

Effectiveness

In the ICT sector, a system is considered effective (usable) if:

* it is reliable and has little or no down time

* it does not add to the daily work of an individual or organisation

* it allows the work of the organisation or individual to be improved through its use.

To measure the effectiveness of any system, you have to look carefully at the performance of the client before the system was implemented and compare this to how the client performs after the system is implemented. (This will need to be covered in any questions you will ask during interviews, etc.) All new systems take some time to establish themselves; it may be two to three months before you may see any discernable improvement.

The effectiveness of a system may also relate to the quality of the work produced. For example, the multimedia and graphics we now enjoy are of a much higher quality than those of previous years, and they are produced by newer more powerful – effective – computer systems.

Think it over...

If you were to upgrade a computer system at home or at college, how would you expect your work to become more effective? How would this expectation affect what and how you might upgrade? How and when would you make the comparison?

Table 4.2 lists the range of components which you may expect to obtain for a commonplace entry level system. Using the criteria and descriptions given, copy and compete the table, to specify a standard system with a £500 overall limit. Visit websites such as www.ebuyer.co.uk and www.dabs.com to find accurate and up-to-date information to cost the computer and complete the table. Follow the links from www.heinemann.co.uk/hotlinks (express code 2016P). Any terms you are not familiar with in the table will be explained later in this chapter and on the websites concerned.

COMPONENT	SPECIFICATION	COST	MANUFACTURER
ATX case for the computer	Find the lowest price		
Motherboard	Must support an AMD processor and have onboard AGP, MODEM, sound and network card		
Processor	With an AMD Athlon or Sempron (or whatever the current equivalent product is) at the lowest possible speed available		
Memory	Must be at least 512 MB and be compatible with the motherboard		
DVD-ROM	Obtain the lowest cost device		
CD writer	Obtain the lowest cost device		
Floppy disk drive	There is only one type		
Hard disk drive	Must be IDE and have largest capacity for less than £60		
Monitor	Must be a 17 inch CRT and cost less than £80		
Speakers or headphones	Must cost no more than £5		
Mouse	Must be a standard ball mouse and have a scrolling wheel and cost less than £2		
Keyboard	Standard 105 key and cost less than £4		
Operating system	Linux related	Most should be free to download	
Office application	OpenOffice.org	Should be free to download and compatible with MS Office®	
	Total cost		

TABLE 4.2 *Essential components shopping list*

Usability

The usability of the system is an extension of its functionality. This could be how the system is used physically, as well as the design of the software's user interface.

The physical layout of the system, often referred to as part of the system ergonomics (see page 146), looks at layout, comfort, access and the creation of a working environment that is productive, allowing the client to work effectively. Good posture and habits at the computer are important in terms of being able to maintain this sort of work for any length of time, and preventing repetitive strain injury, or RSI.

(see page 146)

Key term

In general terms, *RSI* is an injury caused by a repetitive action in a limited range of movement (for example, playing tennis or the guitar). In terms of computer use, it can arise from poor typing technique and posture when typing.

Think it over...

Consider the layout of your computer desk and how it is designed for your individual comfort. Are frequently used items within easy reach, or do you have to stretch or twist to access them? Do you 'put up with' things that don't suit you, or do you change them to make your work environment more comfortable?

The layout and design of the software, through the development of the graphical user interface (GUI) and the human computer interface (HCI), is a branch of technology in its own right. Consider the development of the Windows operating system. At the time of writing, the current version is Windows XP; it is designed for ease of use and accessibility for the technical as well as the non-technical user. Applications like Flash MX (see Figure 4.2), which are complex development platforms, have 'docking' windows, which appear and disappear as required.

Key terms

The *graphical user interface (GUI)* is what the user sees in order to be able to use the computer system.

The *human computer interface (HCI)* is a term used to describe all the software/hardware systems used to cable or use a computer system.

Flash is an application used to develop animations and interactive applications for websites.

Drawbacks and limitations

All systems have some drawbacks or limitations. It is important you know how these can be managed or overcome. Likely issues include:

* the speed of the system
* the network communication speed
* the Internet communication speed
* the overall size of the storage available
* the quality of the graphics.

Technology constantly improves, so most existing limitations soon become a feature of the past (although new limitations are created at the same time). Less than 10 years ago networks operated at 10 MBps, but now we have systems that can exceed 1000 MBps and the average is 100 MBps.

Key term

MBps stands for megabits per second; it is a measurement which indicates how quickly data is transferred on a normal Ethernet network system.

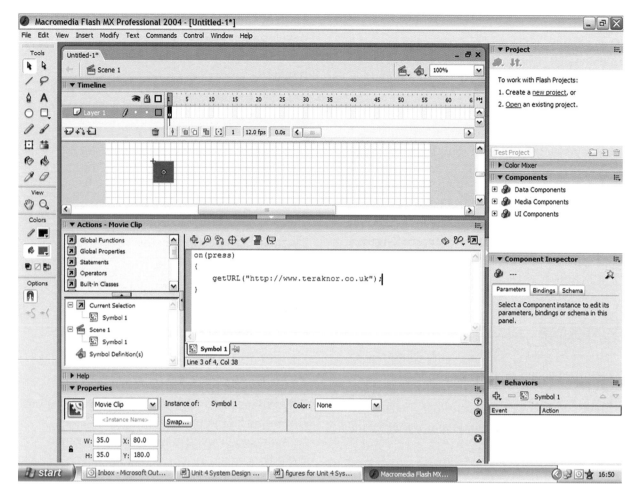

FIGURE 4.2 *Flash MX*

Signposting for e-portfolio evidence

Save this work in your e-portfolio. It could contribute towards covering evidence (a).

4.2 Application software

You must also be able to select appropriate types of application software either for your own use or for a client, choosing between the different packages available. To do this effectively, you should know about and have practical, hands-on experience of as wide a range of software as possible, including:

✱ word processing software

✱ spreadsheet software

✱ database software

✱ website software

✱ artwork and imaging software

✱ presentation software

✱ specialist software, such as:

– accounts applications

– logistics and project management applications

– computer-aided design applications

– digital video editing

– music composition and editing.

The choice of software will be affected by a number of factors. These include:

✱ the client's budget

✱ the ICT competence of the intended user

✱ the training requirements and therefore the costs and implications

✱ the availability of training materials

✱ the availability of product support

✱ compatibility with other software used by others with whom the client will communicate electronically (for example friends, colleagues, clients and employers)

✱ the advantages and disadvantages of open source software

✱ the creation of bespoke software, or ensuring new software created is compatible with existing systems.

Word processing software

The Word application from the Microsoft Office® suite dominates the word processor market. Many documents (including the manuscript for this book) are now produced as a result of this extensive and versatile application. The word processor allows you to edit and reshape documents as you wish, in a way that gives you a 'virtual' view of the piece of paper you are about to print. Applications like Word have revolutionised our ability to produce material of a professional standard and appearance.

Most word processing packages can now do much more than produce a letter or plain typed text. They can also be used as:

* a database integration tool for the production of mail shots, i.e. sending letters to many customers
* a mini publisher application for leaflets and posters for adverts and promotions
* a web development tool.

> **Think it over...**
>
> If Microsoft Word® can be used as a multi-faceted tool, consider what applications it is replacing and how this may replace many other office applications.

Spreadsheet software

A spreadsheet is a numerical analysis tool; it is used for the management of accounts as well as the analysis of scientific or technical data. The power of a spreadsheet is that it can handle large and multiple quantities of data, yet allow you to summarise the information using a variety of numerical or graphical techniques, for example, by displaying lots of tabulated data in easy-to-interpret graphs using categories such as age ranges, population or sales figures.

As part of the Microsoft Office® suite of applications, Excel is an excellent example of an easy-to-use spreadsheet application. It has a wide range of mathematical functions (for example,

sine, square root, binary to decimal, as well as a Visual Basic extension.

> **Key term**
>
> *Visual basic extension* means the data can be linked to a variety of other computer, software and operating systems.

> **Theory into practice**
>
> Produce a wide range of different graphs (bar, line, pie) using data already provided from a spreadsheet.

Database software

A database is a computer-based information storage, retrieval and management system. There are many powerful database systems. A relational database system provided by Oracle is considered among the best commercial options as it can manage immense quantities of information. For smaller systems, Microsoft Access® is an ideal database system, because of its flexibility.

> **Key term**
>
> A *relational database* is a database which uses a system of tables and links (called relationships) to store and manage large quantities of data.

Website software

Whether an application is an appropriate website application depends on the technical requirements you, your employer or your client place on a particular website.

There are purists who insist that HTML coded in Notepad is still the best method of web design as this is the original language (Figure 4.3). Some website designers prefer FrontPage® by Microsoft for its ease of use; technical web designers (who have programming skills) prefer Dreamweaver by www.teraknor.co[1] - Notepad

File Edit Format View Help

```
<html>
<head>
<link href="teraknor.css" rel="stylesheet" type="text/css">
</head>
<body>
<div align="center">
  <table width="724"  border="0" cellspacing="0" cellpadding="0">
    <tr>
      <td colspan="3"><div align="center"></div>
           <div align="center">
        <hr width="100%" size="3" noshade color="#000000">
      </div>
      <div align="center"></div></td>
    </tr>
    <tr>
      <td colspan="3"><div align="center"></div>        <div
align="center"><img src="images/banner.jpg" width="750" height="75">
      </div>        <div align="center"></div></td>
    </tr>
    <tr>
      <td colspan="3"><div align="center"></div>        <div
align="center">
        <hr width="100%" size="3" noshade color="#000000">
      </div>        <div align="center"></div></td>
    </tr>
    <tr>
      <th width="22%" bgcolor="#CCCCFF" class="teraknor"><div
align="left">General</div></th>
      <td colspan="2" rowspan="35" align="right" valign="top"><div
align="right">
        <iframe src="myiframe.html" name="myiframe" align="middle"
scrolling="yes" frameborder="0" height="400" width="580">if you see this
i've forgotten to do something!</iframe>
      </div></td>
    </tr>
    <tr>
```

FIGURE 4.3 *HTML coding*

Macromedia which includes a specialist HTML editor (Figure 4.4). Artistic web designers prefer Fireworks by Macromedia. For inexperienced web designers, there are many options including Microsoft Word® and Publisher. Table 4.3 summarises different website applications and users who might find them appropriate.

Theory into practice

Visit a web page of your own choice. When you 'right click' on the web page text, you should see an option which allows you to view the source code. Do this and see the HTML which makes up the web page.

Key term

HTML stands for hypertext markup language, which is the code used to create all web pages. This language is regulated by the World Wide Web Consortium (W3C) who can be found at www.w3.org. Follow the links from www.heinemann.co.uk/hotlinks (express code 2016P).

Key term

The *source code* is a term for the original programming code used in the development of a web page or an application.

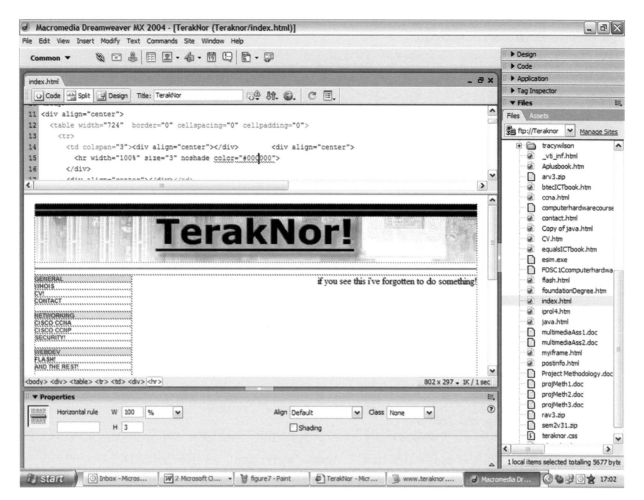

FIGURE 4.4 *Dreamweaver*

WEBSITE APPLICATION	LIKELY USER	ADVANTAGES	DISADVANTAGES
HTML Editor	Programmer	No extra 'unwanted code'	Harder, time-consuming to learn
FrontPage	User	Ease of use	Technical incompatibilities, requires specialist web servers
Dreamweaver	Web developer	Enables access to many web programming systems	More technical
Fireworks	Artistic web developer	Produces visually appealing websites	Requires artistic skill to use
Microsoft Word®	Beginner	Simple to use	Websites lack complexity
Microsoft Publisher®	Beginner	Simple to use and artistic	Websites lack complexity

TABLE 4.3 *Website applications*

Artwork and imaging software

The manipulation of images using computer technology is a key feature of many professions. The ability to create, improve, adapt and merge images electronically is now considered an artistic skill in its own right. Artists, graphic designers and web designers working for any communications-based media (for example, publishers, printers, marketing and advertising agencies, will use such technology). You may have already used artwork and imaging software in the creation or manipulation of an image for a piece of coursework.

Applications like Microsoft Paint® offer very basic image creation and manipulation features. It is for amateur rather than professional use. PaintShopPro allows you to work with images from your family's digital camera or from a camera on a mobile phone. Images that are digitally stored are commonly referred to as bitmaps. Software such as Photoshop by Adobe and Fireworks by Macromedia are used for the manipulation of bitmap images. Applications like QuarkXPress are used for the creation of professional publications. Some applications will manage images as vectors. A popular vector application is Flash by Macromedia, which is used for 'media rich' web applications and images.

Table 4.4 summarises different imaging packages and their relative advantages/disadvantages.

Presentation software

Presentation software is used by teachers, lecturers, and public speakers to visually support the information that they are giving to an audience. Applications like PowerPoint® by Microsoft and Flash MX Professional by Macromedia are used in the delivery of professional presentations. Generally, presentation software will display images and easy-to-read statements supporting the speaker's script. A number of visual and aural enhancements are also available.

IMAGING SOFTWARE	LIKELY USER	ADVANTAGES/DISADVANTAGES OF APPLICATION
Paint	Beginner	Simple, does very little image manipulation
PaintShopPro	Semi-skilled	Has some useful image alteration and improvement tools but is not ideal for commercial image manipulation
Photoshop	Graphic artist	Useful for professionals
Fireworks	Web developer	Useful for web development
QuarkXpress	Graphic designer	Is used in the production of professional publications
Flash	Multimedia developer	Used primarily in the use of interactive websites

TABLE 4.4 *Imaging software*

Specialist software

Many industries use applications which have been designed for a specific task.

Accounts applications

Microsoft Excel® may be used for simple account keeping on a small scale. But book-keeping is a specialist skill, so a specific application such as Sage Accounts is better suited to corporate financial management, especially for small to medium enterprises like many local businesses and retailers.

Logistics and project management applications

Microsoft Project is used in the planning and management of large, long-term projects. It is used by business managers, software project managers and the construction industry. Microsoft Project® allows the project manager to create a feasible plan, identify critical areas and manage the project during its lifecycle. Stages can be linked, and dependencies identified (i.e. where one stage is dependent on another), so that 'knock-on' effects of delays can be evaluated. Some smaller projects can be planned using Excel or Word, but these lack the analytical features offered by Microsoft Project®.

Computer-aided design applications

The design of buildings and engineering components, whether simple like a widget or complex like an airline, can be done using computer-aided design (CAD) applications. Companies like AutoDesk have created AutoCAD to be used by engineers and architects alike.

Digital video editing

Both the television professional and the home movie enthusiast need to edit 'raw' video. Professional applications can blend, merge and fade each scene as well as allow material to be reordered, new material to be added and unwanted material to be removed. Adobe Premiere is an example of a mid-range video editing application. Windows Movie Maker, which is included in Windows XP® is an example of a good, entry level video editing application. Table 4.5 lists the advantages and disadvantages of some common video editing applications.

VIDEO EDITING APPLICATION	LIKELY USER	ADVANTAGES/DISADVANTAGES OF APPLICATION
Adobe Premiere	Video editing professional	Can be used for television, computer movie editing
Windows Movie Maker	Home user	Ideal for short, family movies

TABLE 4.5 *Video editing applications*

Music composition and editing

There are a range of applications which you can use to edit music you have created. CuBase by Steinberg allows you to include any form of music you have created along with an extensive library of pre-programmed samples. With practice, you may be able to use CuBase to create a 'chart topping' track with no direct involvement by others, simply by mixing different pieces of music.

The client's budget

When working with the client to evaluate their needs and requirements, you must understand that they will have an ICT budget to work within. Many clients do not want the latest, biggest or best technology, and will be happy with something which meets their current and likely future needs.

It is important that you specify the system based on what *they need*, rather than what *you want* them to have. If the computer is used for general office work, then the required level of

---

✱ REMEMBER!

In the dot.com boom of the mid-1990s, many ICT clients wanted the biggest and the best technology that their money could buy, regardless of what they actually *needed.* This meant they often bought the wrong equipment – equipment that was too powerful or technology that ended up in a store room gathering dust – and wasted their money.

Theory into practice

What sort of computer system would you like to have? Find out how much it would cost.

A standard computer system has the components listed in Table 4.2. Now visit www.yellowstone.co.uk/calc (follow the links on www.heinemann.co.uk/hotlinks (express code 2016P)) and identify how much a standard computer system would cost. Compare this to one you would prefer to have. Are the extra features of your preferred computer worth the extra money?

---

technology will be basic. However, if the computer is being used for graphical or engineering design, then the required size of memory and type of graphics card will be greater.

The ICT competence of the intended user

Although they might be *capable* ICT users, some users are not as *skilled* as they might believe, mainly due to their lack of experience on a range of applications. When commissioning a new computer for any user, you need to ensure they will be able to use all the components of the system – hardware as well as software.

Training requirements
Costs and implications

If an ICT user is unable to use either the system or an application essential to the use of the system, then the cost of implementing the system will increase, due to:

✱ the actual cost of training the ICT user (i.e. the cost of a trainer or a manual)

✱ the time taken by the user in training (i.e. the time they spend training and 'not working')

✱ the cost to the company of the user's lack of productivity while they learn how to use the system.

It is important that the client is aware of any such indirect costs before they purchase a new system, as any problems in this area may have a negative impact on your 'relationship' with the client.

Availability of training materials

For users who are sufficiently competent, training manuals may be an appropriate (and cheaper) alternative to training consultants. There are many books and guides for the majority of popular applications. Often the manufacturer includes such materials as part of their website support, and the Internet contains many free or low cost guides for a diverse range of applications.

Availability of product support

The availability of product support is very important to some clients. 'Product support' may be help on getting started and how to use the application, or assistance with 'troubleshooting' when an issue arises. Most applications, for example Windows®, have an 'inline' help application. Many software manufacturers also offer free help via the Internet, through their website, or via e-mail (sometimes clients pay extra for this support). Some companies still offer phone help and will offer support contracts to send in technical specialists if required.

Compatibility with other software

For a system or an application to be effective, it generally needs to be compatible with other applications. For most applications, a technology called OLE operates, allowing them to share resources.

When you copy a picture from a web page and paste it directly into another Windows® application you are using OLE technology. This is similar for network and database technologies, where LDAP will allow your login and password to work on a variety of different systems.

Open source software

Many applications provided by commercial software manufacturers are good, but they may cost too much for some clients. Many institutions and organisations (for example charities, schools, colleges, and voluntary organisations) as well as organisations in developing countries, have to consider every cost carefully.

To assist this, there is an unofficial international movement among technical experts to provide open source software, free or at a low cost (as for some parts of the Linux operating system). This means that the programming code is made available and the user can adapt this if they wish or use it unchanged. Any user of open source software should follow the courtesy of ensuring credit is given to the original creator of the software.

Applications such as OpenOffice.org offer a spreadsheet, database and word processing solution as a free alternative to the Microsoft® suite of applications. And operating systems such as

Linux offer an alternative to other well known systems for running your computer.

Creating bespoke software

Some companies and organisations, whether artistic, governmental, engineering, or a research organisation, have such specialist software requirements that they cannot perform efficiently using 'off the shelf' software – they need software developed for their specific and individual purposes. The options are for creating bespoke software are limited only by time, money and the current technology. The process of creating bespoke software is time-consuming and costly, but it is ideal when there is no alternative available or when the software meets an essential business need.

Knowledge check

1 What are the types of applications in use? Who are likely users?

2 How they may be configured for use at home, college or in the workplace?

3 What types of computer systems are available?

4.3 Operating system software

The operating system is specific software which enables any user to access and manage the technology (the computer system). There are many types of operating system, depending on technology and purpose.

* Single-user disk operating systems (for example, Windows®) are used primarily for file and device management and user access.

* Real time operating systems are used for defence and control-based systems like a fire alarm console.

* Network operating systems provide services to many other computers or users across a network.

* Cluster operating systems concentrate on sharing the processing power of several computers (sometimes referred to as grid computing).

* Multi-user operating systems focus on many users sharing the processing power of one resource.

* Dedicated operating systems are used by personal digital assistants and mobile phones.

Microsoft Windows® is not the only operating system product for which there are many systems and many versions available. Common operating systems currently used include:

* Windows XP® for home or professional use

* Windows® 2000 and 2003 server products

* Windows® CE for personal digital assistants

* the Novell, NetWare server product family

* Linux (there are many versions, each with its own advantages)

* Unix for multi-user systems

* Sun Microsystems, Solaris 9

* Mac OS X, for the Apple platform

* QNX for dedicated real time systems.

Theory into practice

1 Go to www.linux.org, and find out how many versions of Linux are available and what they offer.

2 Visit www.novell.com and www.microsoft.com/windowsserver2003 and compare the NetWare and Windows 2003 operating systems.

3 Knoppix is an excellent example of open source software in action. Visit www.knoppix.net. Download a copy of the operating system and follow the instructions to burn it on to CD and boot up your computer using Knoppix. You will find that Knoppix has available in a CD image the same type of application software as Windows. Follow the links on www.heinemann.co.uk/hotlinks, using express code 2016P to access these sites.

As an ICT professional, you must know about operating system software and be able to assess features, including:

* the installation of an operating system
* the need to customise an operating system
* supporting connectivity of portable media
* security, stability and reliability of the operating system
* ease of management and associated utilities
* cost of the operating system and support for the user.

Considering all this information will help you to select the appropriate operating system for your client to fulfil their needs.

Installing an operating system

As part of your AS studies, you will install an operating system from a prepared installation CD/DVD. In early computer technology, installation of an operating system could be a complex procedure, but it is a much simpler, automated process now. For example, when installing the Windows operating system, the user simply inserts the installation CD and on-screen instructions guide them through the installation process. Refer to pages 156–157 for detailed information about installing an operating system.

Customising an operating system

Not all clients have the same requirements. When installing an operating system you must ensure that it suits the needs of that particular client. You may need to configure the operating system *during* installation, setting hardware or network properties. Or you may need to configure the operating system *after* installation, especially in the installation of the client's personal software or desktop settings.

Supporting connectivity of portable media

Portable media enable us to move data from one computer system to another. They include:

* a floppy disk
* a rewritable CD or DVD
* a memory stick or memory card.

Most memory cards will work on personal digital organisers, mobile phones, MP3 players and digital cameras. Computers are generally able to recognise these formats and treat them as an additional storage device. Newer computers include a memory card reader as a standard drive.

Flash card reader

Flash card

Flash card reader

Security, stability and reliability of the operating system

Protecting your computer system and ensuring that it does not fail is of considerable personal and commercial importance to everyone who uses a computer. Consider how costly to your time it would be if someone gained unauthorised access to your computer, corrupted your data and you lost all your coursework.

Having a secure operating system includes:

* using a firewall to prevent others from trying to access your computer via the Internet

* ensuring that other users on the computer system cannot access your files, passwords or privileges

* preventing viruses, worms, trojans (see Unit 6, pages 251–254) or spyware from causing damage to your software or files.

Sometimes, there are problems with new versions of operating systems. Occasionally, these problems delay the release of the operating system (as the manufacturer rectifies the problems prior to release), and sometimes the problems are fixed after the release, by means of downloaded patches from the manufacturer's website. Microsoft® has experienced and dealt with a range of such problems.

The manufacturer of an operating system will ensure that security issues are controlled as part of their operating system. But individual ICT users should not be complacent, and need to follow good practice. It is your responsibility to ensure that your computer has a firewall if you use the Internet and that you have installed the latest anti-virus software.

Both Windows® and Linux enable you to keep the security of your operating system up to date. They both allow your computer to automatically receive daily updates from your anti-virus application (this is now the normal level of security expected for the home broadband user).

Key term

Broadband: a term for a higher speed Internet connection for the home or small office user. The connection speed varies from 128 kbps to more than 3 Mbps, depending on the service provider. The speed is constantly increasing as technology improves; soon home Internet access will be of a comparable speed to the speed of the average corporate network ten years ago.

Key terms

Firewall: hardware or software that filters incoming Internet traffic. It prevents applications from accessing data on the PC it protects.

Virus: a file which will inflict some form of damage to your computer system; like a medical virus, it can self-replicate, infiltrating your computer from another infected computer.

Spyware: covert or hidden software, which sends information on your computer habits and activities to others.

Ease of management and associated utilities

It is important that the ICT user can manage their operating system with little effort. They need to ensure that the hardware is working, that the applications are in order, and that any networking functions are working properly. In the early 1990s, when Windows® 3.1 was introduced, it featured the control panel, the operating system's management function. The control panel has been included in all subsequent versions of Windows® (see Figure 4.5).

For power users, Windows® also has a computer management tool to assist in the management of the system (Figure 4.6). The computer management tool includes disk management tools like the disk defragmenter, which tidies up the way information is stored on the hard drive. There are other utilities like MSCONFIG (Figure 4.7) and REGEDIT (Figure 4.8), which are used to manage the way the system database (the registry) is configured.

FIGURE 4.5 *Windows® control panel*

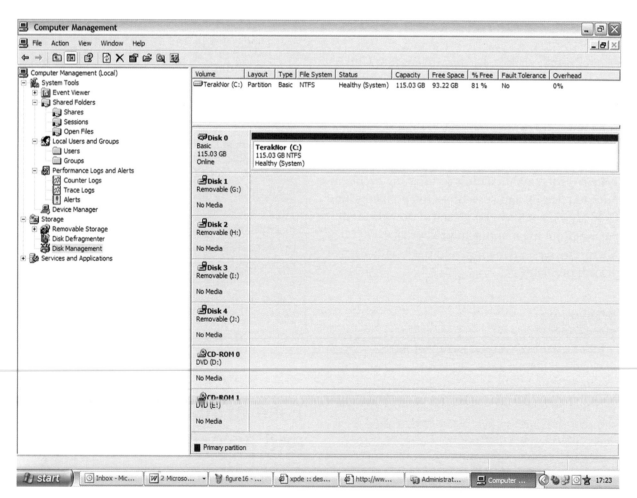

FIGURE 4.6 *Windows® computer management*

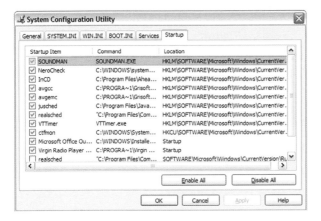

FIGURE 4.7 *Windows® MSCONFIG*

FIGURE 4.8 *Windows® REGEDIT*

Cost of the operating system and support for the user

The cost of the operating system alone governs the choices made by most clients, as it can add over £80 to the cost of the computer system. If money is limited, Linux is a very accessible operating system offering value for money spent at purchase. However, as many users are not familiar with the way Linux operates, there can be considerable costs attached to the training and support such users will need before they can use the system effectively. (Linux is becoming increasingly popular, so these additional indirect costs might be less of an issue in the future.)

The Windows® operating system has been hugely successful since the early 1990s, and many users have used Windows® on computers at home, school, college or work. The current

operating system (Windows XP® Home and Professional) combines the best features of Windows® 98 and 2000. Windows® offers extensive support on new versions of its operating systems, and there are also many good books and web guides for reference.

Types of operating systems

The Home and Professional editions of Windows XP® are known as single user operating systems as they are designed to be used by one person at any given time.

Windows® 2003 is a server operating system. By definition, it is a multi-user operating system as it is designed for many users to access the server's resources simultaneously. You are likely to find Windows® 2003 being used in the following multi-user contexts:

* shared Internet access for multiple users

* website management and e-commerce

* the management of many printers for a college, school or corporate network

* the shared and managed access to a common file system

* e-mail systems

* commercial database systems.

Selecting an operating system for a user

Your knowledge of the different operating systems available, and the different advantages they offer (ease of management, configuration issues, etc.), and your understanding of the client's needs (along with any limiting factors such as existing hardware or software, cost of implementation, and competence of users) will enable you to select the operating system that is appropriate to that client.

Theory into practice

Find out from www.microsoft.com what the minimum hardware specification is for Windows XP. Compare this with the specification for Knoppix, which is a version of Linux, by visiting www.knopper.net/knoppix-info/index-en.html. (Follow the links on www.heinemann.co.uk/hotlinks (express code 2016P).)

Knowledge check

1 How is the operating system an integral part of the computer system?

2 How can the operating system be installed?

3 How can you configure operating systems to suit the needs of the user?

4 What types of operating systems are available? In which context is each likely to be used?

4.4 System hardware

Before you can design the hardware specification for a system, you need to understand the range of ICT components and their purposes, including:

✱ motherboards

✱ processors

✱ heat-sinks and fans

✱ media devices such as graphics cards, sound cards, TV cards

✱ multimedia devices, such as scanners, digital still and video cameras

✱ network interface cards

✱ hard disks

✱ optical drives

✱ main memory

✱ other storage media

✱ input and output devices

✱ ports.

Motherboard

The motherboard is the main circuit board of a microcomputer; it contains the connectors for attaching additional boards. It can be likened to the chassis of a car, or the skeleton of a human. Typically, the motherboard contains the CPU, BIOS, memory, control chips, mass storage interfaces, serial and parallel ports, expansion slots, and all the controllers required to control standard devices, such as the display screen, keyboard and disk drive. Collectively, all the chips residing on the motherboard are known as the 'motherboard's chipset'.

Key terms

The *motherboard* is the body of the computer, supporting all the components that run in the computer system.

The *CPU* is the central processing unit, and is the technical term for the processor than runs the computer.

BIOS stands for 'basic input output systems'; it is a computer chip which controls the computer startup process.

Most modern motherboards are designed to allow the addition of extra cards to the computer, so it is easy to upgrade a system. This is part of a system called the system bus, which contains a wide range of interfaces (connections) for video, data and additional components.

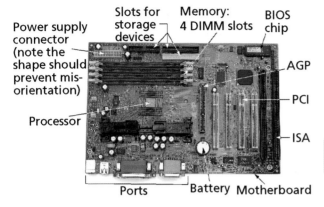

Power supply connector (note the shape should prevent mis-orientation)

Slots for storage devices

Memory: 4 DIMM slots

BIOS chip

AGP

PCI

ISA

Processor

Ports

Battery

Motherboard

A motherboard

Processors

The central processor is the heart of the computer; without a central processor, effectively, you have no computer. The central processor is a highly complex integration of semi-conductor circuits. Each circuit forms a junction called a gate (transistor). Millions of gates will operate together to carry out a basic command or task.

The speed and capacity of a central processor is identified by its:

* clock rate
* bit type
* cache size.

The clock rate is the number of command cycles that can be carried out per second. It is measured in megahertz (MHz) or gigahertz (GHz). (Mega is a prefix meaning 1 million, and giga is a prefix meaning 1 billion.) So a 3.2 GHz central processor operates at 3.2 billion cycles per second.

The Pentium series of processors manufactured by Intel is currently 32-bit, which means there are 2^{32} (4 294 967 296) possible commands. The AMD Athlon 64 operates at 2^{64} (18 446 744 073 709 551 616) possible command units.

The cache is a small local memory, which speeds up the performance of the processor. Memory is measured in bytes. A low quality (small) cache is 256 KB (kilobytes), whereas bigger (better, faster) caches are 512 KB to 1 MB (megabytes). The larger the cache, the better the performance of the processor; it is like having extra memory on hand for exams.

A central processor

Heat-sinks and fans

The electrical activity caused by the millions of transistors inside a processor generates heat inside the processor. The heat generated needs to be controlled; otherwise, the overheating processor will slow down and possibly become damaged or the system will 'crash'. With the speed and power of today's processors, it is essential that the temperature be kept to below 40°C. To help control the temperature, all processors must have a heat-sink, to dissipate the heat, and a fan attached to extract the hot air, to ensure that the processor stays cool.

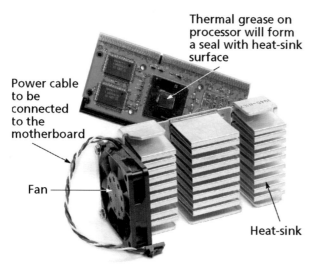

Thermal grease on processor will form a seal with heat-sink surface

Power cable to be connected to the motherboard

Fan

Heat-sink

Heat-sink and fan

Multimedia devices

Multimedia devices include the various types of hardware used to experience interactive programs. These include graphics and sound cards, CD players, scanners, digital still and digital video cameras. To experience a multimedia product or program, you also need appropriate software, for example Microsoft Word®, PowerPoint® or Flash!

Key term

Multimedia computer technology integrates images (video, graphics, text) and sound to produce interactive and entertaining products.

Since the advent of modern computer technology in the 1940s, there has been continual improvement in the quality of audio and visual devices. Most of the work carried out on a computer is based on visual information, so the display monitor is an essential component of any computer system. The system needs a video card (also called a graphics card or adapter) to drive the monitor. The video card converts the information stored digitally by the computer system to the analogue information which is seen onscreen.

Key terms

Digital: this signifies the data of the computer systems as binary 0s and 1s, or as ON/OFF electrical pulses.

Analogue: a physical form of information; radio waves for your FM radio are analogue.

All current graphics cards use a data connection called AGP (accelerated graphics port), which enables high speed communication between the processor and the display monitor. All graphics cards have memory to improve their performance. At the time of writing, the standard graphics card has about 64 MB of memory and a 'gamers' graphics cards have 512 MB of memory.

The TV card is an adaptation of the graphics card. It enables your computer to receive the standard terrestrial UHF signal, allowing you to connect your computer to various TV channels and video players.

Graphic controller chip

AGP graphics card

Graphic connecter to monitor

AGP slot

A graphics card

Key term

UHF stands for ultra high frequency, a method of describing the way the television signal is carried.

Sound cards are a simpler technology than video cards as their signal range is more limited. All computers now have audio out and in (microphone) capability. The majority of computers use 16-bit (2^{16} = 65 536) sound cards, which is adequate for the average user. Musicians and multimedia developers use better sound cards as their more specialist work requires a higher sound quality.

Other multimedia devices

The scanner is a component that allows you to electronically capture an image. It works like a photocopier, passing a light source across the image and using a light sensor to read the image into a digital encoder, which sends the data to your computer. Most computer centres and many homes have scanners. With accompanying software, a scanner allows you to:

* scan in text from a book and convert it to a format recognised by applications such as Microsoft Word®

* scan in a photo or other 'professional image' and convert it to a digital format

* selectively scan an image, especially from a book or magazine, and enhance, adapt or alter that image.

Digital still and video cameras are constantly improving in quality and decreasing in price (relative to the features provided). The resolution of the images stored by a digital camera is always improving, so the images you see on a camera today will be sharper, more detailed and with better colour than those from a camera even a year or two old.

Key term

Resolution is the number of pixels (image units) per image; the resolution offered by an average digital camera is 1024 × 768.

Think it over...

Have a close-up look at an image on your display monitor or on a TV screen. You should be able to see the individual pixels.

A digital camera works by capturing an image using an array of light sensitive cells. All digital cameras store the images on internal flash memory, which means that it is stored permanently, whereas traditional memory loses its information when there is no power available. To manipulate or print the images, you need to upload them to your computer. Most new digital cameras have a removable memory card, which can be inserted into a reader on a computer. The conventional image is saved in a jpg format which is recognised by all applications and operating systems.

Digital video cameras operate in the same manner as digital still cameras, but there are some important differences:

* The digital video camera requires much more memory to store the image.

* The digital video camera stores the image in an MPEG format, as this makes it easier to use on a computer system.

Key terms

JPG (pronounced jay-peg) is the term for the image format devised by the Joint Photographic Engineers Group. (The E was dropped for historical operating system reasons.)

MPEG (pronounced em-peg) is the digital moving image format developed by the Movie Players Engineers Group.

Network interface cards

The network interface card (NIC) is the device on your computer which allows it to connect to a network, whether at work, school or college. Many home computers use a network card to link directly to the Internet via a cable modem.

> **Key term**
>
> A *modem* is an abbreviation for modulation/ demodulation; it converts the signals that the computer creates into one that can be sent along the telephone line (this is called modulation), and then back again at the receiving end (called demodulation).

Network interface cards may communicate by fibre optics, wireless radio-based systems or electrical cables. If you have a laptop, you may have a wireless network card. Bluetooth is a different type of wireless computer network connection which can be made available on mobile phones. See page 149 for more information about Bluetooth technology.

A network card

Hard disks

The hard disk is the principal information storage device of a computer. This is where the operating system, applications, system data, files, games, music and movies are stored. A hard disk is a complex magnetic medium, based on an airtight platter (circular disc) spinning at a high speed, while data is being read and written to it.

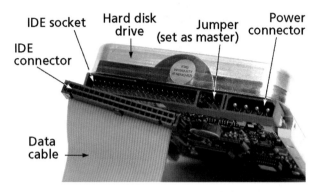

Hard disk drive

The hard disk storage is measured in gigabytes (GB, billions of bytes of information). Older computers generally have smaller storage facilities. At the time of writing, the smallest hard drive is about 80 GB (this costs less than £40); the minimum size will continue to increase, with newer larger products being released constantly.

Data lines

A specialist data line connects the hard disk to the computer system. There are a number of these data connections, including SCSI, IDE and Serial ATA.

> **Key terms**
>
> *SCSI* stands for small computer serial interface; it is a standard device used for higher speed systems, such as file and web servers. Some systems can support up to 15 hard drives.
>
> *IDE* stands for integrated drive electronics; the current standard technology for transmitting data from the hard drive, it can support up to two drives per cable. Most computers have two IDE cables so they can support four devices.
>
> *Serial ATA* or SATA stands for serial advanced technology attachment, which is a high speed technology now used for the transfer of hard drive data. Most newer, larger hard drives use SATA connections.

Optical drives

Compact disk (CD) and digital versatile disk (DVD) media use optical technology. They both use disks that reflect light on to a reader, which has a laser which can read the 'marks' on the disk. CD and DVD writers (often called 'burners') have a laser that can have multiple settings and can 'burn' new data on to the light-sensitive disk. A CD can only hold 800 MB of data, whereas current DVD technology supports at least 4.7 GB. Technically, the maximum capacity of a DVD can be increased to 17 GB, but the technology has not yet reached this capacity.

Main memory

The main memory of a computer is only used when the computer is switched on (i.e. has power); when the computer is switched off, all information is lost. The memory will store any document or file you are working on, anything you have copied for pasting, the operating system, applications running and any specialist services such as anti-virus software.

Memory now comes in quantities of 256 MB, and 512 MB of memory for a computer system is commonplace and will increase. Some systems support up to 4 GB of memory which is useful for gamers and graphical media experts.

See Unit 6, page 235 for information on adding memory.

Other storage media

Apart from hard drives and optical media, there are two other types of storage media you are likely to meet as an ICT user and ICT professional. These are tape media and flash memory.

Tapes

Early computer systems used tapes as a way of storing data. Although it may seem old-fashioned, tape is an excellent medium for ensuring that a computer system has a safe backup copy of data. Tapes are used commercially to complete automated nightly back-ups of network servers as they can hold considerable quantities of data in sets of up to one terabyte (1 TB).

Flash memory

Unlike main memory, flash memory can store information permanently. It is, however, proportionally more expensive than main memory and has a considerably slower access time. It is commonly used as boot memory for specialist devices like routers which connect networks, and portable storage for MP3 players, digital cameras and personal assistants.

Input and output devices

An input device is a piece of technology that allows information to *enter* the computer system as it is created. An output device allows information to *leave* the computer system; sometimes this happens when the information is created and sometimes it is when it is required. The output device converts electronic information into a format that the ICT user can use. Output devices include display monitors, graphics cards and printers, while scanners, keyboards, mice and game controllers are input devices. Sound cards are both.

Printers

There are many types of printer, but the three most common are the laser printer, the ink-jet printer, and the dot-matrix printer. The main differences between these are listed in Table 4.6.

Laser printers

Initially, laser printers were very expensive, and were used only when high quality output was required. Laser printers are now much cheaper – a basic black and white laser printer can be bought for less than £200, and a colour printer for £800. The laser printer is very popular in business and large institutions due to the quality and speed of the printed output. You have probably used one at school or college.

A laser printer uses a laser beam to produce an image on a drum. The light of the laser alters the electrical charge on the drum wherever it hits. The drum is then rolled through a reservoir of toner, which is picked up by the charged portions of the drum. Finally, the toner is transferred to the paper through a combination of heat and pressure. (This is also the way photocopiers work.)

Laser printers are very good at printing graphics. And they can produce any text font, because the computer's operating system treats text as an 'image'.

Ink-jet printers

In-jet printers can retail for £30 to £1000 depending on quality and speed. The ink-jet printer is slower than a laser printer, but some ink-jet printers are capable of producing high quality print approaching that produced by laser printers (called photo quality).

Most ink-jet printers use thermal technology where heat is used to fire ink on to the paper. They work by spraying liquid ionised ink at a sheet of paper. Using electronic information from the computer, magnetised plates in the ink's path direct the ink on to the paper in the desired shapes.

The operation of an ink-jet printer is easy to visualise.

* Liquid ink in various colours (cyan, magenta, yellow and black) is squirted at the paper to build up an image.

* A print head scans the page in horizontal strips, using a motor assembly to move it from left to right and back, as another motor assembly rolls the paper in vertical steps. A strip of the image is printed, and then the paper moves on, ready for the next strip.

* To speed things up, the print head doesn't print just a single row of pixels in each pass, but a vertical column of pixels at a time.

Dot-matrix printers

Dot-matrix printers do not produce high-quality output and are relatively expensive (although difficult to cost accurately because they are generally not sold individually, but as part of an overall specialist package). However, they can print multiple copies of a page simultaneously (i.e. like carbon copies), something laser and ink-jet printers cannot do (they print multiple copies

PRINTER	ADVANTAGES	DISADVANTAGES
Laser	High quality printing; speed of printing	Cost of toner
Ink-jet	Low cost	Lower quality than laser
Dot-matrix	Impact printing allows for printing to be completed on multiple copies simultaneously	Slow and noisy

TABLE 4.6 *Different types of printer*

continuously). They can do this because of their technology is more mechanical: pins strike against an ink ribbon to print closely spaced dots in the appropriate shape.

The speed of a dot-matrix printer can vary from about 50 characters per second (cps) to more than 500 cps. The quality of the printed output is determined by the number of pins (the mechanisms that print the dots), and can vary from 9 to 24. The best dot-matrix printers (24 pins) can produce near letter-quality type, although you can still see a difference if you look closely.

Ports

The photo below shows the ports at the rear of a computer. A port is a computing term for a specialist plug/socket array for a specific task. At the back of a computer, you are likely to find ports for:

* PS/2: to the keyboard

* PS/2: to the mouse

* serial: to older mice and other external devices which use a slow connection

* parallel: to printers (and now rarely other devices which require a higher speed connection)

* USB: universal serial bus for a wide range of devices which will benefit from a higher speed connection

* 15-pin, D type video port: for the connection to your monitor.

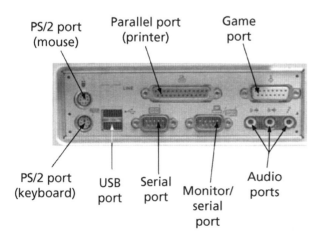

PS/2 port (mouse) Parallel port (printer) Game port

PS/2 port (keyboard) USB port Serial port Monitor/serial port Audio ports

The rear of a computer

Theory into practice

It is important for all clients to budget their computer purchases, especially if they are looking to obtain multiple systems. Use Table 4.2 to consider a solution which includes:

* the discount you may receive for bulk purchases

* the time it will take to install the system, therefore cost of labour

* the cost of managing the system.

Assessment activity

Carefully open up a computer and identify all of the components described in this section. Then create a plan for:

* how the computer may be upgraded

* what options are available

* whether the options are essential or 'nice to have'

* what the cost implications are for the client

* how this will affect the client's budget.

You will also need to consider issues of compatibility (hardware and software).

Knowledge check

1 What is the purpose of each hardware component of a computer system?

2 How is computer hardware improving?

3 How do system components interact with each other?

4.5 Mobile technology

The advent of mobile technology has allowed many computing devices to become portable, revolutionising the way people live and the technologies people use. This section explores:

* note-book/laptop computers
* personal digital assistants
* mobile phones
* wireless data links
* Bluetooth.

Note-books and laptop computers

A note-book or laptop computer is essentially a smaller, more mobile version of the personal computer (PC). Note-book and laptop computers have exactly the same technology as a standard PC, but they are relatively more expensive than a PC of equivalent specification. You pay more for the feature of portability, which enables you to have access to a wider range of ICT resources than you might have had.

Theory into practice

Visit an online computer retailer. Find a note-book and a PC of equivalent specification, and compare their prices. Now find a note-book and PC of similar price and compare their specifications. Which do you feel offers better value?

Personal digital assistants

A personal digital assistant (PDA) is a small hand-held computer. Like the note-book computer, it is a smaller version of a standard computer system, but the PDA has some important features and benefits, including:

* its small size and compact nature
* its ability to offer a wireless network connection
* data is input via a stylus and handwriting sensitive interface

* it will synchronise with your other computer(s) and offer personal management features such as a diary, as well as standard features (word processing, etc.).

Key terms

Wireless is a radio-based communication system which can reach up to 100 metres.

Synchronise means that two devices will ensure that they are holding the same common data.

The price of PDAs varies from £100 for a basic system through to £400 for a comprehensive system.

A personal digital assistant

Theory into practice

Visit your local computer retailer or an online store. Compare prices and types of PDAs on offer.

Mobile phones

Most people in the UK now have a mobile phone, and mobile phone technology is constantly changing, with more facilities and services being offered. At the time of writing, third generation (3G) mobile phones offer the following range of functions: video, games, e-mail, camera. 4G phones offer communications technology, and broadband mobile telecommunications are in development. Developers have created a combination of PDA and mobile phone (for example the XDA from O2). Mobile phones can also communicate using Bluetooth technology (see below).

Wireless data links

Networking technology is largely the same, regardless of the method of communication. Wireless data links use a standard called 802.11, which covers wireless network connections of up to 3 km away and at a speed of up to 104 MBps. The wireless technology used by mobile devices like a PDA has a range of 100 metres, which means you can access your PC or laptop if it has a wireless network card and is within range. Most wireless systems require a central point called a wireless access point to which provides the physical connection to a network or the Internet.

Bluetooth

Bluetooth is a new development in technology that is available in many portable systems, from mobile phones to wireless computer keyboards. Bluetooth uses an ultra high frequency spread-spectrum signal. This means that the wavelength is over 2.4 GHz and Bluetooth uses a range of frequencies and techniques to send data. The purpose of Bluetooth is to create mobile short-range networking for all small devices.

* Users with mobile phones which have Bluetooth can send pictures and documents to each other on a one-to-one basis.

* Laptop computers with Bluetooth can connect to each other, creating a small local network.

* Bluetooth allows a PDA to connect to a computer or a mobile phone without any cables or software.

Theory into practice

Bluetooth is still being developed. Visit www.bluetooth.com and list all the applications of the technology. (Follow the links on www.heinemann.co.uk/hotlinks (express code 2016P)).

Knowledge check

1 What enables a mobile device to be portable?

2 What are the limitations of mobile devices?

3 What developments are current in mobile communications?

4.6   Ergonomics

Ergonomics is the scientific study of the design and arrangement of equipment and systems that enable users to interact with them in a comfortable, healthy and efficient manner. When designing and installing computer systems, you will need to think about ergonomic issues relating to:

* hardware and software

* workstation layout

* furniture.

Hardware and software

Important hardware and software factors you will need to consider are:

* the layout and design of the keyboard

* the design and grip of mouse

* the accessibility of graphical user interfaces for applications.

The design of the keyboard

The keyboard that is commonly used is the 105-key QWERTY keyboard. The original design which this is based on, developed in the nineteenth century, was designed to slow down the typists who could type faster than the mechanical hammers of the typewriter. New keyboards are now designed for speed and ease of use. Some are specifically designed for comfort; a common keyboard is the 'natural' keyboard, which is physically shaped to reflect your hand shape and arm reach. Many keyboards come with wrist rests that provide support while you are typing. This design feature is aimed at preventing repetitive strain injury (RSI). There are also specialist keyboards for individuals with physical disabilities.

A natural keyboard

Mouse

A modern, well designed mouse is designed to fit the shape of the hand as it sits over the top. Some users consider the weight of the mouse, while others look at the number of buttons. Some mice are designed for left-handed users, while others

Think it over...

Look closely at your mouse and see how it is shaped. Is it symmetrical? If you are right-handed, pick it up in your left hand and see how it feels. Compare this with the 'comfort' it offers when in the right hand.

are designed for people who are ambidextrous (use both hands).

Graphical user interface

The graphical user interface (more commonly known as its abbreviation, GUI) is what the user sees in order to use most computer or technical systems. The design of the GUI is based on the need to make the user environment accessible. Some older, poorer designs may make the user uncomfortable when using the system; continued discomfort can cause physical problems with pain in the wrist or fingers, so any problems should be addressed as early as possible.

Most current operating systems allow you to improve the accessibility of the operating system by modifying the user environment. This can be done by:

* showing the user how to improve their use of the mouse

* using the mouse keyboard settings, which turns the numerical keypad into the mouse controller

* setting the screen display so that the mouse cursor is larger or has trails

* adding sounds and additional user assisting features (locators for the cursor).

Workstation layout

It is important to create an environment which is comfortable and safe for the user to work in. Using ergonomic principles, you can position a computer to suit the user. You can use yourself as the test subject in positioning the computer, but you should make sure the intended user is present to ensure the set-up suits their personal requirements. When installing a computer at someone's desk, you need to consider all the factors described in Figure 4.9. You should ensure:

* the monitor is at the right height (at eye level) and distance from the user

* that an appropriately designed keyboard is at the right height

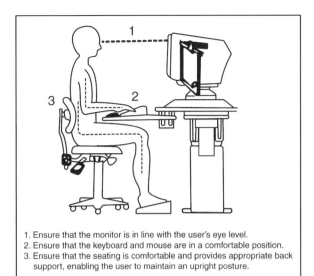

1. Ensure that the monitor is in line with the user's eye level.
2. Ensure that the keyboard and mouse are in a comfortable position.
3. Ensure that the seating is comfortable and provides appropriate back support, enabling the user to maintain an upright posture.

FIGURE 4.9 *An ergonomic workstation*

* that the mouse is comfortable and there is adequate space for its use

* there is adequate desk space for the tasks the user is likely to perform

* there is seating that encourages appropriate posture and can be adjusted to suit the individual requirements of the user.

If these general principles are followed, the user should be protected from RSI, joint issues or back injury.

Monitor glare

Monitor glare is the single greatest cause of frustration and eye strain, making the screen harder to read and therefore harder to use. You can prevent this by ensuring that the monitor screen is positioned away from windows or a strong light source. The light-reflecting glass screen of a CRT monitor is a major source of monitor glare. Newer TFT monitors have a resin screen which can reduce the amount of glare.

> **Key terms**
>
> *CRT* (cathode ray tube) is the type of monitor that uses the same technology as your family television.
>
> *TFT* (thin film transistor) is the technology used in new flat panel and note-book computer displays.

Multi-use monitors

Many monitors are not for solo or individual use, especially if they are a public access terminal, a demonstration station or in an environment where it is likely that more than one person may wish to view the screen at any given time. In such instances, it is unhelpful to have the monitor cramped in a corner or turned at an angle away from the viewer. When installing any computer equipment, you must find out who and how many may be using the system, and discuss with the user(s) what the ideal arrangement may be.

Laptops

Laptop users can adjust the angle of their monitor to improve their viewing of the screen. Some laptops are very uncomfortable to use over long periods of time (especially for continuous typing), so some users will plug a standard keyboard into the laptop. For those who use a laptop as their 'permanent' desktop computer, it is also worth considering raising the unit so that the monitor is at the correct height for the user (so they don't have to keep looking down at it, putting undue strain on the neck and shoulders).

Furniture

The type and design of the furniture used by the ICT user is also a major factor that contributes to the ergonomics of the system. You need to consider the type of seating used, and the layout of the desk.

Seating

The posture of an ICT user as they sit at the computer is very important. Poor seating encourages poor posture, and this can cause long-term damage to the user's back. Some seating is adequate only for the short-term or occasional user. Longer-term users must be able to customise their furniture to suit their individual physical requirements (i.e. height, build, reach, vision). Such flexibility in seating arrangements may be more expensive but are usually worth the investment in the long term.

Desk

In establishing an ergonomic desk arrangement you need to think about the following questions:

✳ Can the seat and desk be arranged so that the keyboard is at the correct height for the user?

✳ Is the monitor at a comfortable height?

✳ Is the base unit for the CD/DVD technology easy to reach?

✳ Can the user reach the printer easily?

Think it over...

The arrangement of the workspace may vary according to location and personal preference. Discuss how the following locations may affect the set-up:

✳ a bedroom

✳ a family study or sitting room

✳ a busy office

✳ a manager's or director's office.

Knowledge check

1 What is the potential impact of poor ergonomics on an ICT user?

2 What ergonomic factors should you consider when designing a computer system?

3 What are the design requirements for an operating system?

4 How can other technologies improve ergonomics?

5 How can the layout of the computer system affect an ICT user?

4.7 System specification

When specifying a system for a client, it is important to consider whether a particular component of a computer system is essential or optional. You will have to bear in mind the client's requirements and the implications for their budget. (Look back at pages 116–120 for more detail about establishing the client's needs.) The client will expect you to explain and justify your proposal, convincing them that it is the solution that best suits their requirements and budget.

You should present the proposed system specification to the client in simple, non-technical language, and will need to identify:

✳ the hardware and software components to be used (see pages 127–146 for more detail)

✳ any special equipment (if appropriate), such as mice, keyboard, speech input/output, screen magnifiers, etc.

✳ alternatives that may be appropriate (for example processor speed, backup options with DVD burners, etc.) but with a full justification for your choice

✳ a possible upgrade path if they want to modify the system at a later date (bearing in mind that most systems lose their upgrade route after 18 months and become obsolete within three years)

✳ workstation layout and furniture (see pages 150–151 for more detail)

✳ recommended security measures, such as anti-virus software and firewalls (see pages 251–254 for more detail)

✳ a test plan (see page 162 for detailed information about the test plan)

✳ a training schedule, specifying method, cost and time implications

✳ the cost of any follow-up support and warranty.

The proposal needs to be clear and comprehensive. This will ensure that the client fully understands and accepts the system you are recommending, and should prevent later problems arising from any misunderstanding.

Hardware and software components

It is important that you check the compatibility of the hardware components chosen with one another and with software you have selected. You will need to read the manufacturer's guidelines and possibly carry out some technical research on the Internet. For example, many motherboards are only compatible with specific processor and memory types. You have to ensure that the motherboard will support your intended processor; otherwise, the system will not work. At the same time, you need to ensure that memory speed is compatible with the motherboard's requirements; otherwise, the system will run slower than expected.

Theory into practice

Refer back to page 124 where you specified a new system for a client who has a maximum budget of £500 (including the operating system). Follow the links on www.heinemann.co.uk and visit www.ebuyer.co.uk and www.yellowstone.co.uk/calc, and consider how the cost may change if:

* you change the monitor to a TFT monitor

* the client also needs a DVD rewriter

* your operating system was unusual

* the client wants the fastest processor available

* the client now needs the largest possible memory or hard drive.

Assessment activity

In non-technical language, propose a system specification for a client, taking into account all their needs, budget and timescale. If appropriate, refine your analysis of the client's requirements. Specify hardware, software and the operating system, describing alternatives and justifying your choices. You will need to take into account ergonomic considerations, and any user-specific requirements.

Assessment hint

✓ Produce an outline system specification.

✓✓ Produce a detailed system specification.

✓✓✓ Produce a detailed system specification with full justification for choices made.

Signposting for e-portfolio evidence

Save this work in your e-portfolio. It could contribute towards covering evidence (a) and (b).

Knowledge check

1 When specifying a system for a client, what hardware costs do you need to consider?

2 When specifying a system for a client, what software and operating system costs do you need to consider?

3 When specifying a system for a client, what labour costs might be involved?

4.8 System installation

This section describes the procedures involved in installing a new system, and emphasises the need to work in a safe, controlled environment. In class, you may gain practical experience of installation by setting up a stand-alone computer system. You will learn how to connect and set-up equipment, such as a monitor, keyboard, mouse, audio technology and install components, such as a graphics card, sound card, CD/DVD drive. You will also learn about installing and configuring software, including operating system software, and applications software.

This section covers the building of a stand-alone computer system from individual components, and the setting up of a system that has come 'fresh' from the box. Once the components are assembled, you will then install the operating system.

Building a computer system from components

The process of building (installing) computer systems is generally the same. Before you start, check that you have these standard tools:

✓ size 1 Phillips screwdriver (the crosshead variety)

✓ anti-static mat and wristband earthed, so that you discharge any static electricity you may generate

✓ a torx screwdriver (6 spokes, used rarely but sometimes required).

Once you have the tools and the components, you can build the system. Building a computer is a step-by-step process which must be done carefully. Any failure, like a processor not working because you have been too rough, means that you may need to replace the component, possibly affecting the time and budget allowed for the installation.

> **✷ REMEMBER!**
>
> For safety, you must wear an anti-static wristband at all times and the computer should always be on an anti-static mat.

Step 1 Unpacking components

Remove the computer case from the box and remove the outer cover. You will find at least three screws on the back. Make sure that you have safely stored the screws. Most organisations require that you keep the packaging until the computer is installed. Then you should dispose of the waste in an environmentally sound manner.

(Many companies will supply a carton to assist with this disposal.)

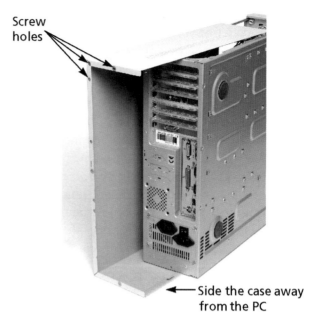

Screw holes

← Side the case away from the PC

Case with lid removed

Step 2 Connecting and setting up equipment

Connect the motherboard to the computer. You must be careful to ensure that the support struts are correctly installed, and that you do not over-tighten the screws on the motherboard. Most causes of motherboard failure at this stage are because the motherboard makes contact with the case or because the screws are so tight that they cause the motherboard to bend.

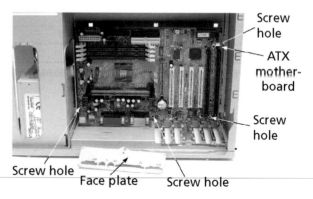

Screw hole

ATX mother-board

Screw hole

Screw hole   Face plate   Screw hole

Case with lid removed and motherboard installed

Step 3 Unpacking and inserting the processor

Remove the processor's packaging and carefully insert the processor in the ZIF socket. Do not use any force to do this. Check that the pins are correctly lined up before inserting the processor. The motherboard manual will indicate what jumpers need to be set, according to the processor that you have installed (voltage and clock speed).

> **Key terms**
>
> *ZIF* stands for 'zero insertion force'; it is a no-strain connector for a processor on a motherboard.
>
> A *jumper* is a small switch used to configure the hardware.

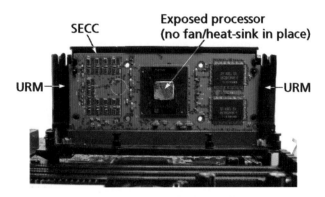

SECC

Exposed processor (no fan/heat-sink in place)

URM → ← URM

Processor inserted

Step 4 Installing components

Add the memory to the motherboard. The number of slots you need to use will depend on the quantity purchased. The motherboard manual will indicate which slot is zero, and this will be the first that you must use.

See Unit 6, pages 235–236 for information on installing memory.

Step 5 Insert AGP card

If you do not have an onboard graphics card and you have decided to have an independent AGP (accelerated graphics port) card, gently insert the card into the AGP slot now.

Step 6 Test the system

You now need to make your first system test. Connect the ATX power plug from the power supply to the motherboard. Connect the monitor to the graphics card and connect all the external power cables.

> **Key term**
>
> *ATX*: AT is an old IBM computer that became the standard for computer cases and power supplies; ATX is an extension of the AT standard.

Start the computer, and complete a simple POST (power on self test) of the computer. Everything is working properly if:

* there is a display
* the computer has completed a memory test, indicated by a simple message.

Normally the boot (startup of the computer) process will stop at either keyboard or hard drive failure. This is to be expected as you haven't installed them yet.

Likely problems are:

* no display: this can be caused by motherboard, graphics card or processor issues
* no memory check: this means there are memory issues.

Refer to the motherboard manual to identify any BIOS beep codes and find out what errors and failures they signify.

Step 7 Connecting storage devices

You now need to connect the storage devices; each has a supporting slot in the case and a connection in the motherboard. The primary hard drive from where you will boot the operating system is normally the master on the primary IDE. The BIOS will automatically detect these devices. Note: if you are using components that are over three years old, you can use an older BIOS to search for the hard drive.

When installing storage devices, you will need to follow these steps (they may vary, depending on the manufacturer).

1 Install the floppy disk drive in the case.

2 Connect the floppy disk drive to the 34-pin connector on the motherboard and the drive, ensuring that the red stripe is at pin 1.

3 Connect the power supply to the floppy disk drive.

4 Check that the jumper on the hard drive is set to master before installing it into the case.

5 Connect the primary hard drive to IDE 1 (or 0 as numbered on the motherboard) ensuring that the red stripe is at pin 1.

6 Connect the power supply to the hard drive.

7 Connect the DVD/CD-ROM or CD-RW drives to the case.

8 If you have more than one storage device then the first will be the slave on IDE 1 (or 0) and the next the master on IDE 2 (or 1) and so on.

9 Connect the power supply to the DVD/CD-ROM or CD-RW drives.

10 Check that the SATA connectors do not visibly show signs of damage.

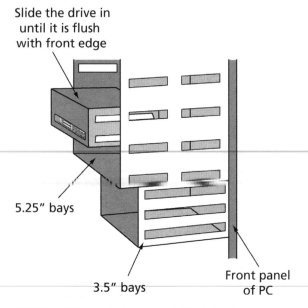

Slide the drive in until it is flush with front edge

5.25" bays

3.5" bays

Front panel of PC

FIGURE 4.10 *Hard drives and CD drive in case*

> ### Key terms
>
> The *master* is the storage device which is in control; in your computer this is the hard drive, which is used to start your operating system.
>
> The *slave* is any additional storage device which resides in your computer system.

Step 8 Connecting other elements

At this point, you will connect the enclosure connectors following the guidelines in the motherboard manual.

> ### Key term
>
> *Enclosure connector*: a cable from the case to the motherboard for the reset button and various lights.

Step 9 Connecting and testing

Now you can check that it all works. Connect all the computer components to the mains and add the keyboard and mouse. Switch the computer on. If all is well then the computer will go through the entire POST boot process until it discovers that there is no operating system installed and then wait. If there are any problems, check if any storage devices from step 7 are faulty or connected incorrectly.

Step 10 Installing the operating system

Now you will install the operating system. You may install the operating system from CD. Your educational institution may have specific policies on how you are to do this.

Installing from CD

To install from CD you will need to set the boot features in the BIOS. In the advanced menu, the boot order is normally:

1 hard drive

2 floppy drive

3 CD.

Change this so that the CD is the first device.

Insert the CD and restart the computer. For the installation of any operating system (including Microsoft Windows®) you will be provided with comprehensive instructions. To ensure that this is completed successfully, you will need to have:

✻ the serial number of the licensed operating system

✻ the name of the workstation that will be used by your educational institution

✻ any workgroup or network addressing details (you must obtain this from someone in a supervisor position, though normally these will be in guidance documentation).

The operating system will detect all hardware and where appropriate will ask for the manufacturer's driver disk. Insert this as instructed by the installation display. The computer will reboot, and the operating system will start. You will need to localise the system and configure the following elements:

✻ screen resolution

✻ colour depth

✻ keyboard locale

✻ local time

✻ local language (UK/US, etc.).

For more information about customising the system, refer to pages 158–162.

Installing a pre-built computer

It is essential that you know how to build a computer system from individual components. However, you will rarely have to do this as most organisations buy pre-built computers in bulk. A pre-built computer will already have the specified operating system and software installed. If a company buys more than 100 computers at a time, they can save up to 25 per cent of normal retail price.

When installing a pre-built computer you will have the following hardware components:

✻ a monitor

✻ a keyboard

✻ a mouse

✻ power cables

✻ the processor base unit

✻ speakers and/or sound cables.

In addition to connecting components, you will need to test the system (refer to pages 162–164 for more detail about testing).

Step 1 Removing the packaging
Carefully remove any packaging, polystyrene baffles and any bags. If the computer or monitor is in a box, open the top of the box and carefully turn it upside down; ease the item out using its weight to slide out of the box.

Step 2 Assembling the components
The following steps describe how to connect the different components. Refer to section 4.6 (pages 149–152) for specific detail on setting up a computer and workspace ergonomically.

Placing the base unit
Put the base unit in an appropriate location. If it is a tower unit, which stands upright, you will normally position this on the floor. If it is a

desktop unit, you must ensure that wherever you place the unit, there is adequate space for the keyboard and the user can comfortably view the monitor. The base unit must be near any network ports and in easy reach of a mains outlet. If this is not enough the rear of the base unit must have adequate ventilation space so that the system can be kept as cool as possible.

Connecting the monitor
Connect the monitor to the mains as well as the base unit. The monitor must be positioned at eye level height so they user can see it easily. If you are connecting a CRT monitor, ensure that the back of the monitor is not covered; otherwise, the monitor may overheat.

Connecting keyboard and mouse
When connecting the keyboard and mouse, check that they are in easy reach of the user. Don't forget the user may be left-handed; make sure that they are comfortable.

Customise the operating system
The operating system will be installed by the individual who has built the computer system, but you must configure the operating system to the requirements of the customer. You may need to:

* calibrate the mouse
* set the keyboard speed
* adjust the screen resolution/colour depth
* set locale, ensuring that your system is in the right country/region
* install any applications that the user requires
* configure any additional user features (disability settings, etc.)
* apply the organisation's security policies, user login, etc.

Creating directory/folder structures
You will also need to ensure the folders for applications and files are correct, by checking that all system folders like C:\windows and C:\documents and settings are installed as expected.

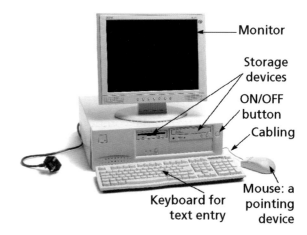

The assembled computer

> **Knowledge check**

1 What steps are involved in the building of a computer system?

2 How is installing a computer system that has come to you pre-boxed different from building a computer system from individual components?

3 What must you consider in setting up the installed system to suit the needs of the client?

4.9 System configuration

After setting up a computer and installing a system for a client, you may have to customise the system to suit the client's specific needs. This may involve altering the configuration of the operating system or application software or both. You may need to:

* access the BIOS and make suitable and safe changes, such as setting a BIOS password to prevent unauthorised access, etc
* edit anti-virus configurations
* edit the desktop – icon size, font size, colour, background, icon choice, etc.
* create startup options
* set file sharing/permissions
* create and reconfigure application toolbars.

Accessing the BIOS

The BIOS has a simple and interactive menu sub-system, which is used to configure the computer's startup and hardware settings (Figure 4.11). If an unauthorised or inexperienced user gains access to this element, they can cause considerable damage to the computer system. The BIOS has a password facility to prevent any such unauthorised access to either the BIOS or the computer.

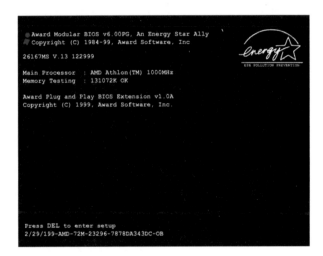

FIGURE 4.11 *BIOS setup utility*

Sometimes the supervisor and user password are not known or forgotten. (This can be due to poor management processes or because of malicious intervention on the part of an unhappy employee.) The presence of any BIOS passwords on a computer system is a considerable issue of commercial concern because no one can access the data on the computer system unless they know the password.

To overcome this, you can open up a computer and temporarily remove the battery from the motherboard, before re-inserting it. This battery provides the back-up power for all the BIOS settings, so the temporary loss of power will wipe all password settings. It will also remove all other settings from the computer system, so you will have to reconfigure the BIOS.

Editing anti-virus configurations

Anti-virus software is used to protect a computer against unwanted attacks and malicious damage. Only an ICT expert should change the settings on an anti-virus system as changing settings may render a computer vulnerable. With Windows XP®, Service Pack 2, Windows can automatically monitor the state of the anti-virus software (Figure 4.12), so intervention should not be necessary. If you have an operating system that doesn't do this automatically, you may need to make changes to ensure the system completes a daily check of all files, and updates the anti-virus database daily; this will depend on the anti-virus system installed.

Editing the desktop

Editing the desktop involves changing the look and display of the desktop for the comfort and personal preference of the user. It may involve changing icon choice and size, font size, colour, background, etc. Sometimes, features are edited to improve accessibility (for example if the user has impaired vision). In many cases, however,

FIGURE 4.12 *Microsoft® Security Center*

the user edits the desktop to customise the appearance of the operating system, placing their personal stamp on their work environment.

Creating startup options

Creating a startup option such as a shortcut is quick and easy. For example, you might want to create a shortcut to additional applications at startup. If you press **Start/All programs/Startup** you will see that there is a folder for any application you may wish to use. Creating a shortcut to a file is also straightforward. Right-click on any file icon and you will have the option to create a shortcut. Create a shortcut to the files in your My Documents folder and drag them onto the desktop.

Theory into practice

Create a shortcut to your favourite website. Right-click on your desktop and choose the *Create Shortcut* option. Then type in the address of your favourite website, remembering to precede it with http://

Now copy it to the *Startup* folder. Restart your computer and you will see that this website is now loaded on login.

Setting file sharing/permissions

There is a fine balance to be achieved between maintaining secure computer systems, data and files, and obtaining improved efficiency by sharing files between relevant ICT users. If you right-click on a file you can enable it to be shared and accessed by others using the same network (Figure 4.13). You can elect for the file to be read only or full access.

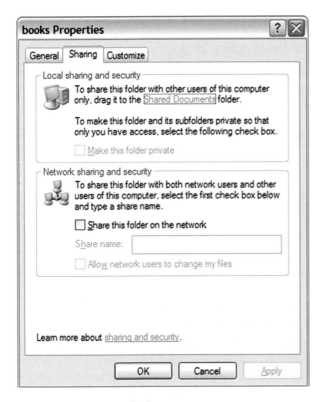

FIGURE 4.13 *Network sharing*

On any computer, there is a shared folder that is common to all users; copying files into this location will make them accessible to all.

Creating and reconfiguring application toolbars

Most applications (for example, Microsoft Word®), provide many more features than can easily be accommodated on the toolbar. So, the application will be provided with the 'standard' toolbar, showing the options and commands that are most commonly used. But, if you are a specialist user who needs frequent access to any of the 'non-standard' functions, you can customise the standard toolbar by adding and removing buttons (Figure 4.14). For example, a mathematician might frequently use the 'superscript' function (which allows you to convert highlighted text to small raised text like the 'th' in 'Friday the 4th' or the 2, in 10^2). To do this you go to the **Tools** menu, select **Customize**, and thenselect the **Commands** tab. From the **Categories** menu choose **Format**, and from the list of buttons under the **Commands** menu on the right select the superscript button (x^2) and drag the button icon onto your toolbar.

FIGURE 4.14 *Customising in Microsoft Word®*

Signposting for e-portfolio evidence

Save this work in your e-portfolio. It could contribute towards covering evidence (c).

4.10 Testing

It is essential that the system you design and build for a client has been thoroughly tested. You need to plan and conduct effective testing to make sure that everything works as it should. As part of any installation of a new system, or during a maintenance check or investigation of any problems or issues of an existing system, you will need to test a variety of components to ensure that they are working to specification (for a new system), still working according to specification (for a current system) or to troubleshoot a perceived issue.

Test documentation

ICT professionals use two essential documents when testing computer hardware and software: the test plan and the test report. This section shows you how to plan the test for a computer system and provide the appropriate record of the results.

The test plan

The test plan is a document that outlines the strategy that you will take when investigating a problem or when you are testing a computer for performance (this is often seen as preventive maintenance). Many problems or performance tests are reasonably common, so you may find that there are appropriate test plans already available that you can follow.

A test plan will have the following information:

* a description of the problem or test type

* any other possible symptoms and other tests that may need to be performed

* likely causes

* tools and other resources that may be required

* steps that must be taken to identify causes with possible solutions

* checks to ensure that the fix has not become the cause of other problems.

The test report

The test report provides all involved (you, your successor, the client/user and your supervisor) with a comprehensive breakdown of the work you have completed and the issues you may have discovered.

Most organisations use test reports to:

* communicate issues or sometimes the lack of issues (i.e. everything is fine)

* identify commonly recurring faults

* provide evidence in the case of legal action, pursuit of warranty (where a supplier has to provide a replacement) or provision of support for a user that may be causing the issue.

The test report is read by many people and can be used in a legal situation, so you have to be careful when writing your opinion of the problem as well as the solution you have provided. Inappropriate and offensive statements are unprofessional and can damage your relationship (and that of your company) with the client. When there are genuine issues, try to frame the problem/solution in a positive way, turning issues into concerns that need to be addressed, and problems into potential business opportunities, for example:

* The user may appreciate some specialist training and support on the use of the system.

* The equipment is faulty and may need to be referred to the manufacturer.

* The equipment appears to be incompatible with a specific element of our system.

* The technology has now been superseded and a suitable replacement is required.

For most organisations, the test report will have the following important information:

* date/time of test

* who performed the test

* which computer the test was carried out on

* what the test was and why it was required

* the results of the test, including a description of any faults

* description of the solution provided, if required

* resources used.

Figure 4.15 is an example of a test report.

Computer/System tested	Finance/Ms Jayne Parr
Date	30/01/2004
Time	14:50
Name of tester	Bill S Spear
Signature	*Will Spear*

Fault/issue as reported by client
Computer not starting

Tests carried out
POST check
Power check
Monitor Check

Results and likely outcomes
Monitor faulty, no power, no display

Recommendations/Solution
Monitor replaced, faulty monitor sent for warranty repair

Reported to	Mr Marr

Resources required
Monitor taken from stores

FIGURE 4.15 *A test report*

Theory into practice

Use the example shown in Figure 4.15 to create test reports for:

* identifying if a computer has a virus infection

* checking hard drive performance

* dealing with a possible keyboard fault.

Each test report must be comprehensive and provide someone else with an understanding of the work you have done.

Conducting the test

There are many components in a computer system, all of which need to be tested. Overlooking the test of an item can be the weak link in the system that eventually leads to failure. You must be prepared to be systematic and methodical, even though it might seem boring.

You will need to test several elements when testing any new installation.

* Check that all connectors are correctly connected, internally and externally, by checking each device that is connected and that there is a mains connection to the computer system.

* Check that the display is working correctly, where the resolution is adequate for the monitor and the applications that are going to be used on the system. You also need to check that the colour depth is correct, as some systems may need 32-bit rather than 24-bit colour quality.

* Check that the processor and memory are performing adequately, i.e. all the memory is available (apart from that which is reserved for system tasks) and the processor is able to offer optimal performance.

* Check that the hard drive is performing adequately and there are no issues with the storage media.

* Check that the operating system is performing as expected and there are no issues that prevent the user from being able to successfully use the system.

* Check that all applications installed are working as expected, where the user is able to carry out work as required on the system.

* Check that default folder settings, like My Documents, Documents and Settings, Program Files, Windows are all present, unless you have elected to make a specific change to the system.

* Ensuring that desktop shortcuts, like My Computer, work is essential, as users need to access various system features easily. (Note: Windows XP® has a new desktop version, which eliminates all of the desktop shortcuts except the Recycle bin. So a lack of icons on the desktop doesn't indicate there is a problem! Windows XP® also runs a desktop clean-up wizard every 30–60 days, which will place all unused icons in a separate folder on your desktop.)

* Having the correct drivers for each system device is essential, otherwise it will not work (or in some cases operate incorrectly). Windows and other operating systems require that you install the drivers (often supplied on disk) when you install a new device. In some cases, if the device is commonplace, the operating system will automatically detect the device and install the required drivers for you. You can look in the system settings and check the validity of any device and its drivers.

* In printing, having an application with incorrect paper settings is frustrating. You may find that the default setting is 'legal', whereas you may need to set the default to A4, or that all printouts are set to 'portrait' when you need them to be landscape. Applications such as Microsoft Word® and Excel® allow you to change the print settings in **Tools/Options** as well as **File/Print**.

* Application and operating system menus are often set as standard for any system. In Windows®, you may wish to customise the appearance of any application menus by dragging and dropping various options. When you do this, you must consider if and how other users may access the system as well as yourself.

* Setting the date and time, by clicking on the time icon in the bottom right of the screen, is straightforward. With Windows®, you can synchronise the system with an Internet time server which will ensure that your computer's time is constantly accurate.

* When setting up any system, you must ensure the system is safe and that cables do not present a hazard. Any trailing cables will pose a risk which will be an issue in any workplace. It is important that you use cable tidies, cable ties or racks to keep all the cables together, tidy and out of reach.

Other system checks

There are many methods that can be employed to check that the system you have installed is working correctly. Likely tasks that you may have to complete on installation include:

* file check
* registry check
* anti-virus scan
* disk scan
* system tune-up or benchmarking.

File check

Most operating systems 'won't work' if any important files are missing. Therefore it is essential to complete a file check. Many organisations require that you install system special files that allow the system to work effectively within the organisation. This may include document templates, system files, small applications or utilities, etc. You can use Windows® Explorer to ensure that all is in order with an operating system such as Microsoft Windows®, and check the following folders (which contain essential operating system files) exist:

* C:\Windows
* C:\Windows\system
* C:\I386 (for Window® 2000 and XP)
* C:\program files.

Registry check

The Windows® registry is a database (of sorts) used by Windows® to record the settings for all system hardware and software. Once the system is installed to your satisfaction, you can perform a simple test called the registry check to see that the registry is intact. Click on **Start** and choose **Run**, then enter 'scanregw'. If there are any faults with the registry, it will notify you, and then attempt to repair the registry keys.

Key term

A *registry key* is a unique reference to a device or driver in the operating system.

Anti-virus security

Anti-virus security is of paramount importance, so completing an anti-virus scan on installation and of the installation media is essential. Many operating systems are configured to meet an organisation's needs and the customisation process could have allowed a virus in. As soon as a new operating system installation is connected to a network, it will 'broadcast' its presence. This is an open invitation for network-based trojans and worms to infect an unprotected system.

Key term

Broadcast: a network message that is sent to everyone on the system that is listening.

To adequately protect the computer from viruses and other threats to the computer's security, you must ensure that it has a firewall before you install and run an anti-virus application. Windows XP® now runs a firewall as a standard feature, and will warn you if it has been disabled

Disk scan

Running a hard disk scan at installation will not improve the performance of the computer. There is little software on the system, and as the system is new, there will be no fragmentation issues with the hard drive arising from prolonged use, compared to what you are likely to find when you do preventive maintenance on an existing computer system.

The sole reason for completing a disk scan at installation is to identify if there are any faults with the surface of the hard drive. To achieve this you need to use the Scandisk and Defrag applications.

System tune-up

In operating systems like Windows® 2000 and XP, the system tune-up is continuous as it is completed by the system on boot as well as during operation.

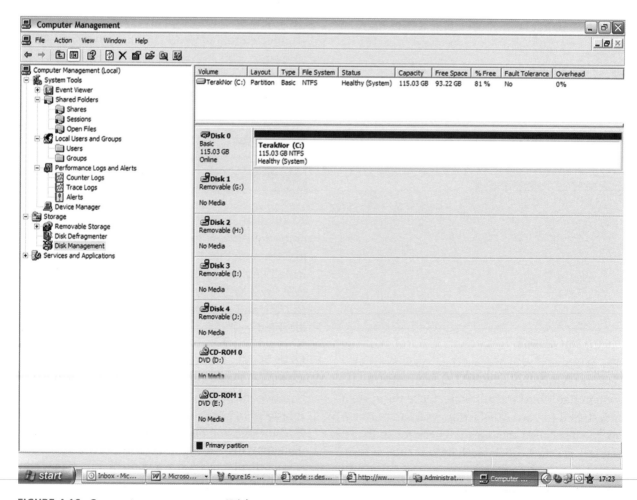

FIGURE 4.16 *Computer management/Disk management*

Signposting for e-portfolio evidence

Save this work in your e-portfolio. It could contribute towards covering evidence (d).

4.11 ICT skills

As you are working with clients in a technical capacity, it is essential that you develop working skills which support a strong troubleshooting and diagnostic ethos. In most cases, when the client calls you, it's because they have a problem with their computer which you will have to resolve using all the skills you have developed in the course of this unit. You will be able to use your skills to:

* install a stand-alone PC

* install operating system software

* install application software

* configure hardware and software according to a client's needs

* prepare and implement test procedures for any computer system that has an issue.

For more detail on these skills, including 'how to...' instructions where appropriate, refer to the relevant sections in this unit.

When you install a stand-alone PC, you need to consider the client's needs and the working environment at all times. Do not be distracted by thinking about 'how clever' the technology is. You must remember that most clients are intelligent, but not necessarily technical. They will probably use this computer for at least three years and they will want it to cause minimal trouble. You must remember what layout will work best for the computer system as well as the client. Poor ergonomics often leads to users working inefficiently and unproductively.

> *** REMEMBER!**
>
> Many clients will not need the latest technological wonder. The computer needs to be fit for purpose – if it is used only for word processing, it doesn't need to support the latest gaming and multimedia technology.

You must ensure the specification of the computer system is able to support the operating system proposed. (The operating system is likely to be the current version provided by Microsoft®.) You will need to consider the installation of the operating system and how this will benefit the client. Once it is installed, you may need to adapt various features of the operating system to ensure the client is able to use the system most effectively. This may involve adapting the appearance of the screen display or including additional features to ensure the system is accessible to those with varied physical needs.

The installation of application software should be a straightforward process so long as you remember to consider the following questions.

* Is it the application needed by the client (as identified by your initial needs analysis)?

* Can the computer system support the specification of the application? (This is often particularly relevant for games and media based applications.)

* Is the licensing of the application suitable? Might it cause any legal issues?

Once the system is installed or you have completed an upgrade/further installation, you will need to test the system. Changes to the system which will necessitate testing include:

* the installation of a new hardware component such as an additional card

* any changes to the operating system such as a service pack or a vendor update

* the installation of a new application.

You will also need to test the system if the client reports any faults or problems.

UNIT ASSESSMENT

To complete this unit and ensure that you submit evidence of the work you have done, you have completed the assessments in this unit and prepared appropriate documentation. You will have:

* analysed the complex needs of a client

* described and evaluated two existing systems that meet similar needs

* specified a suitable system that meets the client's needs

* installed the computer system as required by the client

* specified, installed and configured an operating system which is suitable for the computer system as well as the needs of the client

* recommended and installed applications as required, appreciating the differing needs of the client and the capacity of the system

* recommended and implemented appropriate changes to the system such as configuring the system for the user's needs

* planned and implemented a variety of tests, which will ensure the system is 'functioning' normally.

Having completed these tasks, you finally need to evaluate the performance of the computer system, as well as your own performance on this unit.

Assessment hint

✓ Make simple evaluative comments.

✓✓ Evaluate performance of both system and self, incorporating feedback from others and recommend improvements.

✓✓✓ Fully evaluate performance of both system and self, incorporating feedback from others and recommend realistic improvements.

 ### Signposting for e-portfolio evidence

Save this work in your e-portfolio. It could contribute towards covering evidence (e).

Web development

Introduction

Increasingly, people use the web to find information about products and services. It is therefore increasingly important for businesses and organisations to have an online presence, promoting themselves and their products and services on the web. Even if you are not planning a career as a web developer or designer, as a future ICT practitioner who will be advising clients about their online needs, you need to know how to develop and build a website, and the principles underlying good website design.

In this unit, you will design and produce a static 'brochure' website for a specified business client. Static websites are those that are not linked to dynamic structures such as databases that enable customers to set up accounts and to place orders. In setting up a brochure website, you will need to promote the products or services of your client, but do not need to offer the facility for online purchases. You are not expected to upload the website that you produce to a web server; indeed, no credit will be given for doing so in this unit.

You will also learn how to conduct appropriate testing of the website, and to propose ways of enhancing the functionality of the website to support online trading.

What you need to learn

In completing this unit, you should achieve these learning outcomes:

* Know how to plan, design and build simple static websites
* Differentiate between clients and end users (customers)
* Work effectively with both clients and end-users to produce websites that are fit for purpose and suitable for their target audience
* Be able to evaluate a website and make proposals to enhance its functionality

* Have an understanding of the importance of conducting end-user acceptance tests to make sure a site is fully functional, easy to use and accessible to disabled users.

Resource toolkit

To complete this unit, you need these essential resources:

* access to appropriate computer hardware and software facilities, including web authoring software and word processing software
* access to the internet
* wide range of information sources, such as books, trade journals of the IT industry, newspapers
* contacts working within the IT industry, especially professional web designers.

How you will be assessed

This practitioner-focused unit is internally assessed. Page VII explains what this means.

There are four assessment objectives:

AO1 Plan and manage a project to build a static website for a specified client (assessment evidence a)

AO2 design, build and test the website (assessment evidence b and c)

AO3 evaluate the website and recommend an improvement (assessment evidence d)

AO4 produce a proposal for enhancing the functionality of the site to support e-commerce (assessment evidence e).

To demonstrate your coverage of these assessment objectives, you will produce an e-portfolio of evidence, showing what you have learnt and what you can do:

(a) You will produce a project plan for the development of a static website for a specified client. This will show the tasks (broken down into subtasks) to be carried out, the time allocated to each task, the order in which they should be completed, and any factors which might cause delays. You should include evidence to show that you used the plan to monitor progress.

(b) You will generate design documentation for a 'brochure' website reflecting the requirements of the client, consisting of: storyboards, a structure diagram and a flowchart. Your website will include a menu system or navigation buttons providing easy access to a number of linked pages.

(c) You will use an iterative approach to website development to create a fully functional static website. You will use prototyping to refine the initial design, and include the results of any testing that you have carried out, as well as proof of your management of the site.

(d) You will evaluate the finished website, assessing how well it meets the client's requirements.

(e) You will make proposals for enhancing the functionality of the site to support e-commerce.

In your e-portfolio, you will correctly use technical terms that have specialised meanings in this area of study.

How high can you aim?

Your e-portfolio will contain all the evidence on which your performance will be judged. Some **Assessment activities** can be used towards your e-portfolio. These will contain **Assessment hints** on what you can do to pass (✓), gain a better mark (✓✓) or top marks (✓✓✓). For example, how well you design and create your website will determine the maximum number of marks that you can earn: the more detailed your plan and the more clearly identified the tasks that you decide to do, the higher the marks you might be awarded.

Having planned your website, the documentation of your design can earn you more marks. Your approach to developing the website will also determine the maximum marks available to you. The highest marks are available to students who show a sound awareness of the audience and fully meet the needs of the client.

Having developed your website, you will evaluate it – and earn more marks if you seek feedback from your client and incorporate changes that may be recommended.

Finally, you will consider how your site might be enhanced to support e-commerce, and present a report to your client in simple non-technical language. The quality of your report – and the number of alternatives that you present – will determine your marks.

Ready to start?

This unit should take you about 60 hours to complete. Why not keep a log of your time? Devise a blank form that you could use to record the time that you spend on this course.

5.1 Software development lifecycle

In developing your website, you must use an iterative approach.

Key term

An *iterative* approach involves revisiting your design over and over again as necessary, so that it evolves through time, each time getting closer to what your client wants.

You will need to work closely with the client and with end-users of the website, to develop and refine successive versions of your site until you and your client are satisfied that it meets all the specified requirements. You both need to be satisfied that, if the website were uploaded to the Internet, it would also meet the needs of the end-users.

✳ REMEMBER!

There are two sets of needs to be considered in developing and building a website: those of the client (whose company/products/services are promoted by the website), and those of the end user or visitor who goes to the website for information about that company/products/services.

Like the development of any other software product, building a website for a client involves a number of activities and follows the traditional software development cycle (Figure 5.1), although,

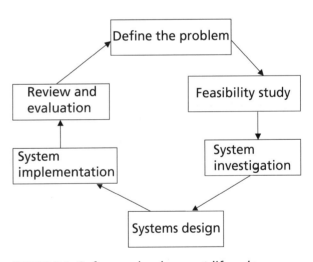

FIGURE 5.1 *Software development lifecycle*

for the purposes of this course, the activities are identified as:

✳ requirements analysis

✳ design

✳ prototyping

✳ user evaluation

✳ testing.

The stage of analysing requirements determines the scope of your project, setting targets – both in terms of functionality and time deadlines – and must be completed through negotiation with your client. This will include your estimating the costs involved and obtaining approval from your client of a budget for the completion of the project. This therefore replaces the standard stages of defining the problem, carrying out a feasibility study and the systems investigation.

Design involves matching your knowledge of the client's requirements to the features of web authoring software – and presenting a 'solution' to your client using design tools such as storyboards and flowcharts. In the light of subsequent negotiations with your client, you may need to refine your design to better meet their requirements.

Prototyping is a development technique which allows the client to see what you propose – rather than read a report that describes what you propose. The prototype gives the client a better 'feel' for the end product, before you start on the detailed developmental work. It can be used to present alternatives to a client – such as colour themes – so that your client can be guided towards a final choice of design. The prototyping stage allows the systems design stage of the systems life cycle to include more input from the user, and should mean that the design more closely matches the user's needs. It also takes the system through to the implementation stage.

User evaluation is essential. You may produce a website that seems to meet your client's needs but, to be absolutely sure and to obtain acceptance – and payment – from your client, you need to ensure that he or she completes a full evaluation of your product. This evaluation should focus on the extent to which it is fit for purpose (i.e. meets your client's requirements) and meets the needs of the intended end users (i.e. visitors to the website).

Although testing is mentioned last here, you should review progress and test your website at various stages during the development cycle, as well as at the very end, just before you would upload the website for use on the internet. Refer to pages 162–163 for further information on testing strategies.

Notice that, with the exception of requirements analysis which is done at the start, all the other activities are interlinked and – in line with the iterative nature of development – will need to be revisited over and over again until you are satisfied with your completed website. So, as with the standard life cycle, an iterative approach is essential.

Knowledge check

1 What is meant by the term 'iterative approach'?

2 List the main stages of the software development cycle.

3 Outline what is involved in the requirements analysis stage of a project.

4 What is meant by prototyping?

5 Why is user evaluation essential?

6 Distinguish between the needs of the client and those of the visitor to the client's website.

5.2 Project planning

Before you begin to build a website, you need to consider how you might plan your project, and how you can use this plan to manage your progress during development.

'If you fail to prepare, be prepared to fail.' This sound advice applies as well to website development as to any other venture. Before you start to work on your website – or any project – time spent planning what you will do is well spent. It may save you much wasted time later.

Your first step is to draw up a project plan. This plan should identify important generic aspects:

* What tasks – broken down into subtasks – need to be carried out?

* How much time should you allocate to each task and subtask?

* In what order should the tasks be completed?

* What are the key milestones for this project?

* What factors might cause a delay in the completion of your project?

The tasks that are needed for your particular project may seem obvious when you first start a project. However, as time goes on and you learn more about your client's needs, you may need to review your task list and refine it.

There are two main purposes of the project plan.

✳ *Before you start:* you need to think about what will be involved, how much time this might take you, and how you are going to manage to complete everything before the deadline.

✳ *While you are working on the project:* you can use the plan to help you to identify if everything is going well, i.e. managing the progress of the project. If, for example, you are slipping behind schedule, you need to know soon enough to be able to revise your plan or to spend extra time to catch up. This may involve reducing the scope of the project and/or negotiating an extension of the deadline.

It makes sense to use the computer to help you to produce your plan – and to monitor progress during the project. Although there are a number of sophisticated project management software packages available, you can plan your project using simpler electronic alternatives.

You could use standard software such as a word processor to create a straightforward numbered list (Figure 5.2). At later stages of the project, you might amend this list, add more detail and, maybe, reorder the tasks.

PROJECT PLAN: Develop a website

1. Talk to the client. Find out what he wants. Collect samples of proposed content.
2. Draft a design – storyboard creation.
3. Think about themes, basic template.
4. Set up initial prototype: home page (based on main template) + menu structure + 2 or 3 other pages.
5. Go back to client. Check he is happy with prototype.
6. Collect content. Finalise content plan and site plan.
7. Develop prototype to show navigation links – to dummy pages.
8. Go back to client. Check he is happy with prototype.
9. Further development to complete the content.
10. Go back to client. Check he is happy with content/layout.

FIGURE 5.2 *A numbered list*

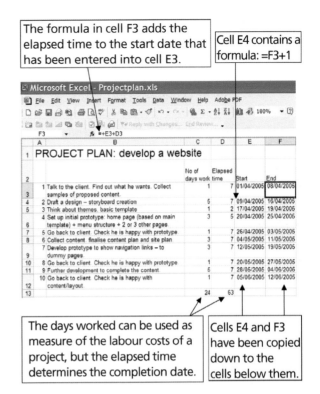

The formula in cell F3 adds the elapsed time to the start date that has been entered into cell E3.

Cell E4 contains a formula: =F3+1

The days worked can be used as measure of the labour costs of a project, but the elapsed time determines the completion date.

Cells E4 and F3 have been copied down to the cells below them.

FIGURE 5.3 *Using formulae in a spreadsheet to link stages of a project*

Or you could use spreadsheet software to record important stages in your project, and link these so that any delay early in the project automatically affects the expected completion date. In Figure 5.3, the two formulae that you need to use to automatically calculate the end date are in cells F3 (+E3+D3) and E4 (+F3+1). The start date is entered into E3, and then E4 and F3 are copied down the columns. Notice that the formulae rely on elapsed time – not the actual number of days' work a stage is expected to take. This builds in some 'breathing room' – not least for weekends.

✳ REMEMBER!

When planning any project, it is a good idea to build in some contingency or 'buffer' time, in case you are prevented from working on the project as and when you planned, or in case things actually go wrong in the project. But you don't want to allow so much of this time that it makes you seem like a slow project manager!

If you feel you have the skills to do so, you could use spreadsheet software to produce a Gantt chart to provide a graphical representation of your plan.

The original schedule contained some buffer time; it showed an end date of 12 June 2005, which was unacceptable to the client. So, in Figure 5.4, the stages have been slid (using cut and paste from the original generous schedule) so that some of them overlap. The line between rows 35 and 36 shows a cut-off point. Approval by the client is considered essential here, before further progress can be made.

The end date has been improved; it has now moved back to 17 May 2005.

Until you list all the tasks and subtasks and estimate the time each step might take to complete, you cannot predict how long the total project will take. You may need to build in stop points for approval, or you may have to suspend work on the project due to other commitments – or illness – or non-availability of the client, or resources. It is important therefore to review progress regularly, for example each Monday morning, to check that you are on target and to amend the schedule if necessary. Some renegotiation of deadlines may be necessary, and it is far better to do this 10 days before the deadline than the day before.

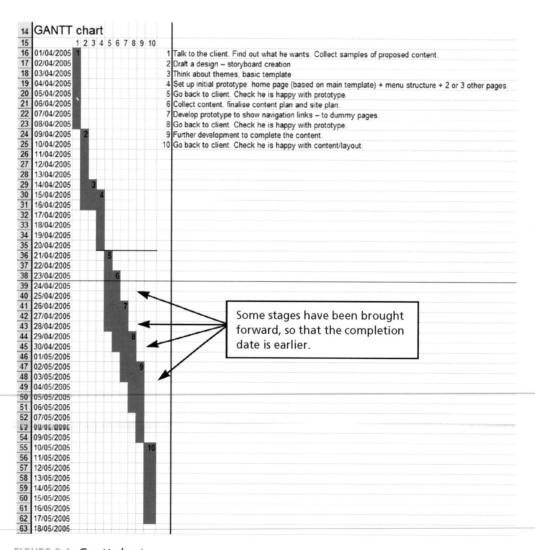

FIGURE 5.4 *Gantt chart*

Signposting for e-portfolio evidence

Save this work in your e-portfolio. It could contribute towards covering evidence (a).

5.3 Requirements analysis

In designing the website, you cannot just dream up whatever suits you or catches your imagination. The website needs to meet the needs of a client and you must identify these needs by carrying out a requirements analysis.

Ask the right questions

There will be questions to ask and information to collect. Your client's idea of what the ideal website contains may be similar to what is seen on many other sites, but you need to collect precise details before you can be sure of meeting your client's needs precisely.

Your client will expect the website to reflect a consistent corporate look, so you need to collect information about the company logo, preferred colours, preferred fonts, and so on. Some organisations publish a house style as a guide for suppliers of stationery and web designers.

You will need to obtain accurate information about the company's contact details. These should be displayed somewhere on the site, maybe running across the bottom of each screen, or on a special screen entitled Contact Us. Many websites include a facility for a visitor to contact the company direct from the site: a Contact Us button. Although the site may display a contact telephone number, for some visitors, the option to communicate via e-mail may be preferred. Once the visitor has chosen this route, the communication software (for example, Outlook Express®) should automatically load with the To: field in a new e-mail being automatically completed for the visitor. For visitors that would prefer to write the e-mail address down, the communication software should include the text of the e-mail address.

You will be producing a brochure website, so you need to obtain full details of the company's products. This may include the product name, a short description, size information, pricing, delivery arrangements and maybe an image of the product. You may also need to incorporate multi-media elements such as video or a voice-over. If your client provides a service rather than selling a product (for example, a hairdresser), you will need to include different

information, such as salon location, opening hours, rates for different services, discounts if appropriate, etc.

There are two main ways of organising the navigation through a website, so that the visitor can access all pages: a vertical menu bar or a horizontal menu bar. Your client may have ideas as to how potential visitors would use the site and preferences as to how hotlinks to other pages should appear.

Key term

A *hotlink* is text or an image which, when clicked on, takes you to another page within a website or to another website altogether.

FIGURE 5.5 *Edexcel download option for the exam specification*

Some clients may want the website to offer visitors downloadable material such as an order form. You would need to obtain a copy of any such material in a format that allows the majority of visitors to access it. Providing Adobe Acrobat files in the PDF format is a popular choice (Figure 5.5), not least because the page

layout is maintained during the download. This may not be the case for other formats.

Regardless of the format you use, you should also provide a link to the software manufacturer's website so a user can easily download any software if they need it.

Your client may choose to have a site map (Figure 5.6) to help visitors to find their way around the website. This lists the sections within the website and provides links to each one. There are a number of ready-made applets that you might incorporate into your website. For example, your client may be interested in including a banner or a hit counter (Figure 5.7).

> **Key term**
>
> *PDF* stands for portable data format. Documents in PDF format always retain the pagination and layout when you download them. This is not true of other formats, such as the .doc files created in Microsoft Word®.

FIGURE 5.6 *Edexcel site map*

(a)

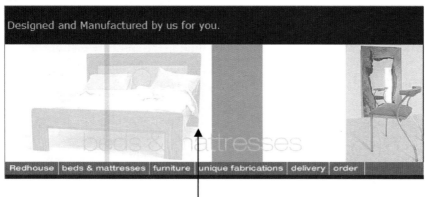

Designed and Manufactured by us for you.

Redhouse | beds & mattresses | furniture | unique fabrications | delivery | order

A series of images travel across this banner, some from right to left, and others from left to right.

(b)

Latest In The Forums

	New Topics	Poster	Views	Replies	Last Poster
	firewalls	morrigan	14	2	morrigan Mar 02, 2005 at 19:05:56
	Be Fair	goldengirl	111	7	morrigan Mar 02, 2005 at 19:03:35
	Hellfire, son of RM's Hellfire	meganr	1643	286	karjon Mar 02, 2005 at 19:03:11
	Rewrites	scampmeister	2	0	scampmeister Mar 02, 2005 at 19:02:40
	Days? Times?	ZoeK	52	10	kittyred Mar 02, 2005 at 19:01:17

Topics: **1891** | Posts: **11567** | Views: **91793** | Replies: **9762** | Members: **507**
[Goto Forum]   [Search]

The writers' Dock website attracts members and visitors, and the counters give an indication of the amount of traffic on the site.

FIGURE 5.7 *Extra features available as applets: (a) redhouse banner and (b) Writers' Dock counters*

Key terms

Applet is short for application and describes a very short program, i.e. a piece of code, written for use on the world wide web.

A *hit counter* records the number of hits, i.e. the number of visitors to the site to date.

A *banner* is an image link that is used to advertise a sponsor of a website; it usually runs across the web page, for example across the top of the page.

Your client may not understand all terminology related to website development – and has no need to do so if you present visual

Think it over...

Discuss with others in your group, what are the benefits of including a hit counter. What are the drawbacks?

examples of what he or she might like to have incorporated into the site.

Theory into practice

1   The redhouse website presents information about the products that they manufacture and sell. Follow the links from www.heinemann.co.uk/hotlinks (express code 2016P) and visit the redhouse site. Explore the

site and make notes on what you like about it. Note also anything that you think you would want to change or avoid.

2 Gerry Baptist's website shows samples of his work and invites prospective clients to contact him to discuss their requirements. Follow the links from www.heinemann.co.uk and visit Gerry Baptist's site. Explore this site in the same way, making notes about what works and what you would like to change.

3 Visit two other sites of your own choosing and make further notes on features that you admire, and those that you would avoid in any site that you were to design. Look in particular for evidence of sponsors. Take screen grabs to illustrate your findings. Compare notes with others in your group.

4 Bookmark some web pages which illustrate features that your client may want to consider, such as sponsors and counters. To help you in your presentation to your client, rename these bookmarks, for example Counter on Writers' Dock website.

Establish what the client needs

Initial discussions with your client should focus your client's mind on exactly what is required. Your goal, through these discussions and other techniques that you might use to collect information, is to establish the requirements of your client.

✳ What is the purpose of the client's website? Is it just a showcase for products? Or will the client need to offer visitors the option to purchase online at some later stage in the development of the site?

✳ Who is the target audience? Who might be most interested in your client's products or services? What age group would be most likely to visit the site? Do your client's products only appeal to a small specialist group, such as actors or ballerinas, sailors or teachers?

✳ What information will the website provide to visitors? Who will supply this information to you (or to whomever is responsible for maintaining the site after you have completed the development of the site)?

✳ What features, such as a hit counter, are be provided? Some of these features cannot be tested until the site is online, but you might still decide to incorporate them.

✳ What level of user interaction is required? For example, are downloads to be made available to visitors? Will the site need an order form that can be completed?

✳ Is there any information to be collected about visitors to the site? Is a cookie to be placed on the computer of each visitor?

Think it over...

With others in your group, discuss the benefits of cookies. Do cookies cause any problems?

Theory into practice

1 Working in a pair, select four different websites and, for each one, decide the purpose of the site. Try to identify who might be the target audience, based on the look and feel of the site.

2 Swap sites with another pair and repeat the exercise. Then compare notes and see how closely you agree.

3 Draw up a list of ways in which sites try to appeal to particular audiences.

There are other practical and 'administrative' issues which need to be considered before development starts.

* How will your client access the site (for example what hardware, software, and connection method will be used)?

* What plans does your client have for maintaining and updating the site once it is up and running? Who will be responsible for this?

* How are security requirements to be addressed? It will be important to address these issues during the design of the site, so that it is protected from attack.

* What legal requirements need to be addressed? Your client should be aware of codes of conduct in putting information on to the Internet.

When you communicate with your client, bear in mind that he or she may have no understanding of the process of website development. Equally, you may have little understanding of the product or the service that the website is being developed to promote. However, it is your responsibility to bridge any gaps in understanding which will impact on your ability to develop a website that meets the client's requirements.

* Ask questions to clarify any terms that your client uses and that you do not understand.

* Avoid using technical terms unnecessarily; speak in plain English. Do not expect your client to understand the technical terms that you do use, or to attempt to learn them.

* Use images of other sites to demonstrate the features you are proposing. You could do this using screen grabs but it would be more effective to show them online.

* Make extensive notes during each meeting or telephone conversation.

* Collect samples of relevant documents and annotate these so that you can remember their purpose and where they fit into the overall system.

You cannot be sure that you have a completely accurate understanding of what your client needs until you have taken all the information you have collected and put together a design that your client can look at. You need to be prepared to rethink some aspects if it turns out that you had not understood something that the client told you, or if they change their mind once they see their ideas 'mapped out'. The objective throughout this process is to arrive at a mutually understood description of your client's needs and what you intend to supply to meet those needs. Having completed the requirements analysis stage, the next step towards arriving at such an agreement is your design.

Knowledge check

1 What is meant by 'house style'? Why is it an important consideration when developing a website?

2 What is a hotlink? What is its purpose?

3 Explain these terms: applet, hit counter, banner, cookie.

4 How might a company use information obtained from hit counters and cookies?

Assessment activity

1 Through discussion, establish the purpose of the website that you will develop for your client.

2 Find out the intended audience and what distinguishes them from people who are not expected to visit the site: their age, gender, how they spend their time, their interests and so on.

3 Through discussion, discover the needs of your client and list these. Identify implications for the development of the website.

4 Obtain all information that you need: company contact details, any information regarding company house style, for example the company logo, product details and any material that the website visitor may be offered for downloading.

📁 Signposting for e-portfolio evidence

Save this work in your e-portfolio. It could contribute towards covering evidence (b).

5.4 Design

The design stage involves the creation of an idea that meets your client's needs (and budget) within the constraints of your skills and the resources that you have at your disposal. This idea then has to be written up in some way to explain it to your client, and so that someone – probably you – can implement it. This section looks at the features of a good design and how you can present your design to your client.

Design criteria

A well-designed website meets several criteria.

* The site establishes an identity/brand by the clever and consistent use of logos, colour schemes and layout.

* The site is structured to facilitate navigation so that it is easy for visitors to find what they want on the site. Hyperlinks should be intuitive and there should be no dead ends, i.e. links that lead nowhere.

* The site provides the right balance of information on each page. Cluttered pages may look daunting and deter visitors, yet if each page offers little more than the previous page, the number of clicks needed to navigate

through pages to find information required may also drive visitors away.

* The site is responsive (speedy) and secure.

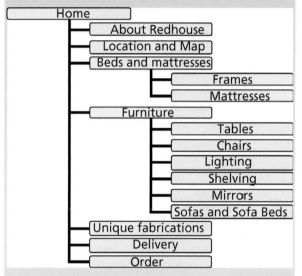

Design documentation

To convey to your client exactly what you propose, you will need to produce detailed designs covering every aspect of the website. Your client needs to understand the proposed layout and structure of the site, i.e. what will appear on each page, and how each page will look.

You can use a storyboard (Figure 5.9) to present your design ideas to the client.

Having established the overall structure of the website, you will need to explain the navigation routes, what action controls you expect to include and the navigation aids that you propose to give. For example, what icons do you intend to use on your menu bars? What style of text will be used to denote internal links? Your storyboard and electronic prototype should show your client all the major routes through the site and the links that you intend to set up.

Alternatively, a flowchart (Figure 5.10) might be used to show all the pathways through your website.

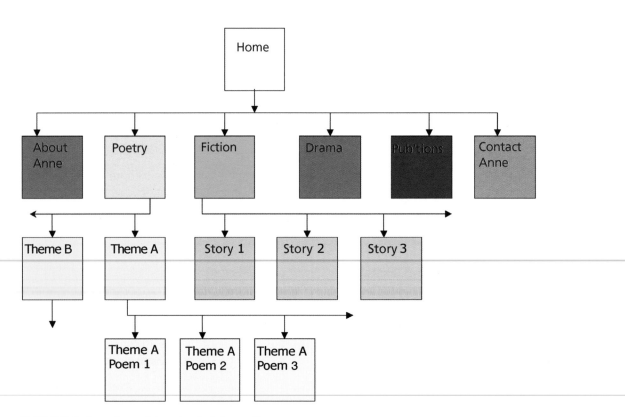

FIGURE 5.9 *Storyboard for the Rainbow site*

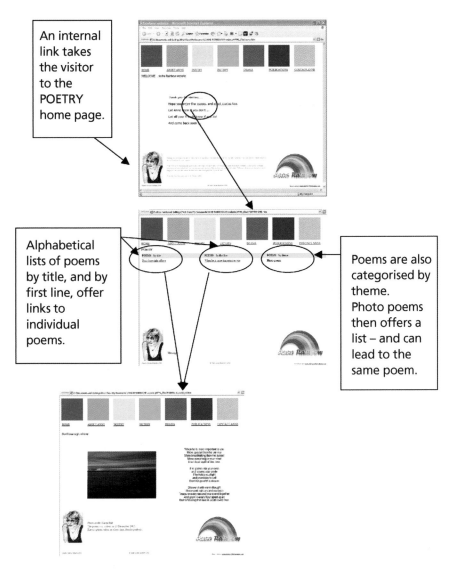

An internal link takes the visitor to the POETRY home page.

Alphabetical lists of poems by title, and by first line, offer links to individual poems.

Poems are also categorised by theme. Photo poems then offers a list – and can lead to the same poem.

FIGURE 5.10 *Flowchart for the Rainbow site*

Once the overall website plan is agreed, you need to focus on the detailed design of the page content and layout. You will need to decide exactly what is to appear on each page, and then to lay it out suitably. This could be presented to the client using storyboards, but it may be better presented using a structure chart.

Interactive features also need to be designed and presented to the client for approval. Finally, you should consider what accessibility options (Figure 5.11) to incorporate for disabled visitors.

There are three main paper-based techniques available for communicating your design ideas to your client:

* storyboards to map out the layout and content of each screen

Think it over...

Within a small group, discuss how a site could be made more accessible to a partially sighted visitor. A site may be viewed from anywhere in the world; your site will be written in English. How could it be made more accessible for those for whom English is not their first language?

* structure charts to show how content is organised
* flowcharts to describe the user interaction and pathways through the website.

You will need to adopt a consistent style and format for the site. However, this may best be demonstrated to the client using the prototype.

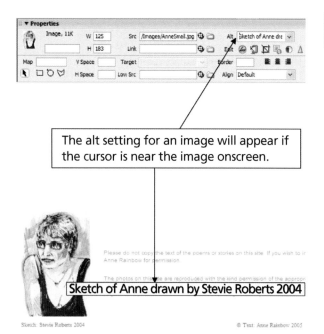

The alt setting for an image will appear if the cursor is near the image onscreen.

Please do not copy the text of the poems or stories on this site. If you wish to in Anne Rainbow for permission.

The photos on this site are reproduced with the kind permission of the appropr

Sketch of Anne drawn by Stevie Roberts 2004

Sketch: Stevie Roberts 2004

© Text: Anne Rainbow 2005

FIGURE 5.11 *Accessibility options*

 Signposting for e-portfolio evidence

Save this work in your e-portfolio. It could contribute towards covering evidence (b).

5.5 Implementation

Having agreed an outline design for the website with your client, through the use of storyboards and flowcharts, you need to start to prepare a prototype of the website. This will help your client to see even more clearly what you intend.

Web authoring software

In this unit, you are expected to use dedicated web authoring software to build your website. If you have never used such software before, do not worry. It may seem complicated at first sight, but there are very few functions that you need to use at the start, and lots of what you already know about other software will prove useful to you.

❋ Like word processing software, web authoring software is mostly WYSIWYG: what you see is what you get. So, what appears on your screen is what any visitor to the website will see.

❋ Web authoring software shares the approach of some database software in that you can look at what the visitor will see, and then switch to see the coding or design which is creating this effect for the visitor. But, as you will soon realise, you do not have to spend time looking at code. The software takes care of that for you.

* Web authoring software is, in some ways, similar to DTP software in that it adopts a paged-layout approach. Text is dealt with separately from images, and you can create space for each of them.

* Web authoring software adopts many of the simplest techniques that you will have met in other software packages. For example, it offers a drag and drop approach to building web pages, which makes it easy to create each page.

Theory into practice

1 Using a web authoring package, find out how to do the simplest things: create a new page, insert some text, insert an image. Do not worry about what is on your web page. Take this opportunity to learn about the tools the software offers.

2 Explore the menus to see what features the software offers. Some terms will be new to you. Use the Help feature to find out what some of them mean. Share what you find with others in your group.

3 Watch any tutorials to find out how to do more complex things like incorporating links from one page to another. Try to resist launching into creating your website until you have had time to become familiar with the software you will use.

4 If you have access to a second web authoring package, repeat Questions 1–3 and compare the two packages. Discuss what you found with others in your group.

Development through prototyping

In implementing your website design, you are advised to use web authoring software to create a series of prototypes, each one bringing your client closer to accepting the final design. For each prototype, you will produce a number of differently designed web pages.

* Your first prototype should establish the main navigation of the site. You should create menus and hyperlinks and other interactive components such as buttons, hotspots and rollovers.

* Early on, you should decide on a colour scheme and style for your web pages.

* In developing each page, you will use tables to present page content, including multimedia content and simple animations.

* Somewhere on the site, you should incorporate some ready-made applets, for example a banner or a hit counter.

* In line with your client's requirements, you will incorporate a form for the visitor to complete. This may be an order form, or it may be a comments form requesting feedback on the site.

* Finally, you will adapt your web pages using replacement text for visually disabled access.

Assessment activity

1 Review your storyboards and other documentation to decide how you will fit these two features within the website: a ready-made applet such as a banner or counter, and a form for the visitor to download.

2 Review where you plan to place the content of your website, so that you know what text goes on each page.

(continued)

3 Focus on how you might source images for your site and where they might appear. You might consider including animations and videos as well as static images. Make notes.

4 Review your project plan and refine it to include subtasks such as 'incorporate a counter on page 7'.

5 Review the overall timetable to check that it is feasible, and consider reordering tasks.

6 Write an evaluation of how you consider the project has gone so far.

 Signposting for e-portfolio evidence

Save this work in your e-portfolio. It could contribute towards covering evidence (a), (b) and (d).

Web page creation and development skills

This section focuses on the skills you need to acquire to create your prototype and develop that into a fully functional website. You will use web authoring software such as Dreamweaver (Figure 5.12).

Before creating any web pages, it makes sense to set up one or more templates on which all other pages will be based (Figure 5.13). The template will establish the theme – or basic colour scheme – that you plan to adopt for your website.

Setting up the basic template may involve, for example, changing the background colour of the page (Figure 5.14). You can then create each new

---

Dreamweaver is one of several web authoring software packages.

The **Workspace** is divided into two areas for the web designer: one in which the pages are created, and one for the panels.

The **Files panel** is in the same group as the Assets panel. They appear together or not at all.

A **Site** needs to be set up, and subfolders created within that site: HTML, Images and Library.

FIGURE 5.12 *The workspace in Dreamweaver*

The main template of the Anne Rainbow website is based on a table with 6 rows and 7 columns.

The columns are all equal width - and the main navigation bar runs across the first two rows.

The rows are of varied depths to create a layout that will suit all pages.

The cells in this row have been merged into one large area.

Some individual cells of the table are merged to create larger areas.

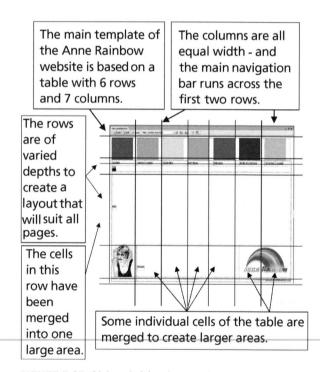

FIGURE 5.13 *Using tables to create a structure for a template*

---

page based on the template and insert text, tables and images according to your planned content.

Tables – apart from being used to create the basic structure of a page – may be used to present web page content in rows and columns. This also

Having moved the cursor so that it is in the area you want to control, clicking on the table tab <tr> selects the whole row of the table.

The Bg field controls the background colour.

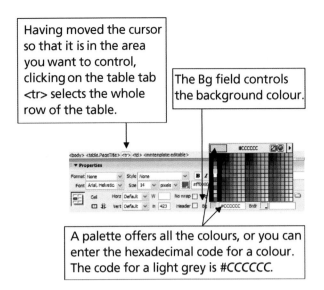

A palette offers all the colours, or you can enter the hexadecimal code for a colour. The code for a light grey is #CCCCCC.

FIGURE 5.14 *Changing the background colour using Dreamweaver*

imposes a meaningful structure on the page, and can aid sight-impaired visitors who will find it easier to interpret tabulated content.

The available space on a page is measured in pixels, but the software will let you specify the percentage of the width of the screen that the table is to fill (Figure 5.15).

Specify the number of rows and columns that you need.

Select the table width as 100% if you want it to fill the whole web page. You could also specify the width in pixels.

A border thickness of 0 pixels results in no visible borders.

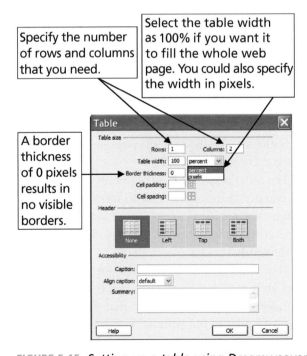

FIGURE 5.15 *Setting up a table using Dreamweaver*

Knowing the number of pixels available within the width of a column (Figure 5.16) is important when you want to fit an image into the space (Figure 5.17).

This table was created with 4 rows and 6 columns. The widths of the columns were then changed to produce this layout of cells.

The table was created to fill 100% of the width of the webpage. This is equivalent to 1066 pixels.

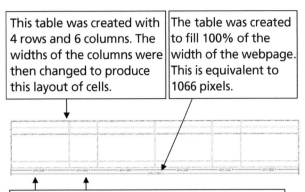

When each cell width is increased or reduced the new percentage, and the number of pixels this represent is shown.

FIGURE 5.16 *Sizing a table using Dreamweaver*

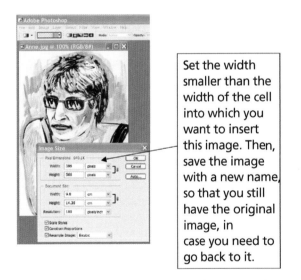

Set the width smaller than the width of the cell into which you want to insert this image. Then, save the image with a new name, so that you still have the original image, in case you need to go back to it.

FIGURE 5.17 *Sizing an image to fit into a cell, using Dreamweaver*

Resizing the image so that it is just the right size will reduce its file storage size; it is also important for the image file be stored in a compressed format so that the download time is minimised.

Formatting of text is possible using tags (Figure 5.18) but for consistency reasons, you would be advised to use style sheets (Figure 5.19). To help visitors, especially when they want to bookmark the site, you should choose effective and useful page titles (Figure 5.20); this will also

In Dreamweaver, tags are shown in blue; content appears in black.

Each tag appears within triangular brackets. <b> turns bold on; </b> turns it off.

This web page code was created using Save As Web Page from Word. Notice how many lines of code are generated!

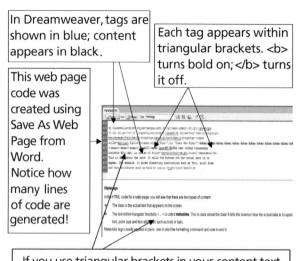

If you use triangular brackets in your content text, these appear as codes which start with a &.

FIGURE 5.18 *HTML code example 1: tags*

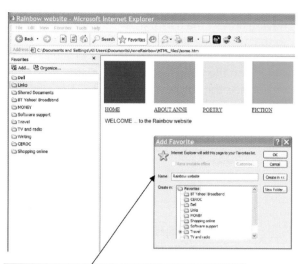

The entry in the <title> tag is offered as a default name for the web page.

FIGURE 5.20 *Title for a web page*

Dreamweaver lets you view the HTML code at the same time as a WYSIWYG version of your web page.

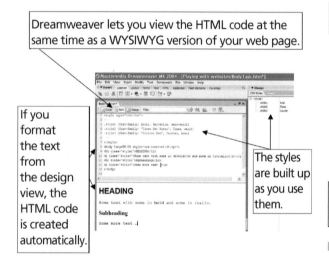

If you format the text from the design view, the HTML code is created automatically.

The styles are built up as you use them.

FIGURE 5.19 *HTML code example 2: styles*

Links appear in blue and are underlined - avoid using these styles for other text on your web page.

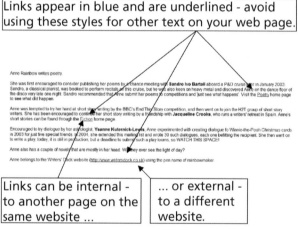

Links can be internal - to another page on the same website ...

... or external - to a different website.

FIGURE 5.21 *Linking conventions*

act as an aid to search engines.

One of the main features of website is its connectivity to other pages within the same website and to other websites. This connectivity is

achieved using hotlinks (Figure 5.21).

Links may be made within the same web page, using anchors (Figure 5.22).

The most important or commonly used links are usually grouped together to form the main navigation bar. This can be placed across the screen (horizontally) or down the screen, probably on the left-hand side (vertically).

There may also be other links, for example, to send an e-mail. It is important that the e-mail link includes the e-mail address, so that the visitor may take note of the address, rather than having to click on the link to discover the address when it appears in the To: field of the automatically

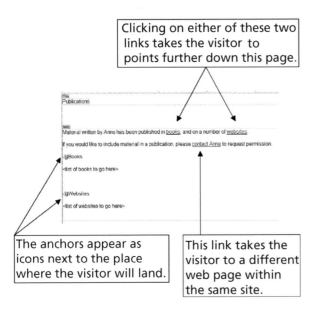

Clicking on either of these two links takes the visitor to points further down this page.

The anchors appear as icons next to the place where the visitor will land.

This link takes the visitor to a different web page within the same site.

FIGURE 5.22 *Links to named anchors*

Theory into practice

1 Visit some sites and check what the pages are called. How helpful is this?

2 Visit a site and look especially at the use of anchors and other navigational aids. Share your findings with others in your group.

Assessment activity

1 Develop your design further and produce a prototype showing the main navigational routes through the website. You may produce additional documentation such as a structure diagram and/or flowchart to explain your design.

2 Decide on two or three design styles/themes that you think would appeal to your client. Apply them to your prototype, and present these to your client.

3 Obtain agreement with your client as to which theme to apply and of the overall design of the website, so that you can proceed to the next stage of detailed development of the site.

4 Review your progress against your plan. Are you on target? Do you need to revise your plan to take into account recent discussions with your client?

Assessment hint

✓✓ Use your prototype effectively, to refine your initial website design.

✓✓✓ Listen carefully to your client and aim to fully meet your client's needs.

 Signposting for e-portfolio evidence

You can start testing your website as soon as you have started creating your first page. Save this work in your e-portfolio. It could contribute towards covering evidence (b) and (c).

generated e-mail.

Optional extras

To make your website more functional – and maybe more exciting for the visitor – there are a number of add-ons that you might consider (Figure 5.23).

Applets such as a counter or a banner (as shown in Figure 5.7 on page 178) may be offered by your web authoring software (Figure 5.24). If not, you will need to obtain the coding from a third-party source. In such instances, these are known as 'third-party components' because they come ready-made,

FIGURE 5.23 *Add-ons*

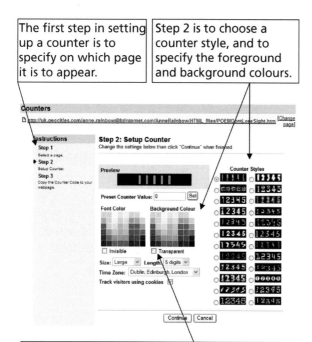

The first step in setting up a counter is to specify on which page it is to appear.

Step 2 is to choose a counter style, and to specify the foreground and background colours.

If you choose a transparent background colour, the numbers will appear without any 'boxing'.

FIGURE 5.24 *Incorporating a counter*

provided by a source external to the parties involved in the development of the website.

The coding for a counter may be something like: <IMG SRC=http://visit.geocities.com/counter.gif ALT="Counter">. This describes an image which displays the counter, once your website is on the internet (Figure 5.25); it will not show while you are just testing locally.

A banner could be created in image editing software such as Photoshop. You might also want to include an animation similar to the one seen on

the redhouse website. For this coding, you might choose special software such as Flash.

Enhancements such as scrolling marquees catch the eye and are useful for advertising. However, too much movement on a screen can become irritating and distract the visitor from other important content. It may also cause problems for visitors who suffer from epilepsy, so excessive amounts of flashing images should be avoided.

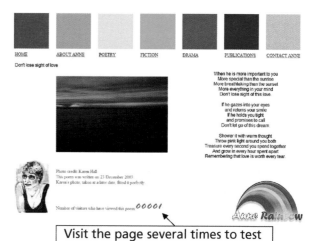

Visit the page several times to test that the counter is working.

FIGURE 5.25 *A counter of the visitors to a web page*

3 If time allows, incorporate at least one third-party component: a counter, an animation or a banner. Search the internet for the code that you should include.

4 If time allows, enhance your site by incorporating a scrolling marquee.

Assessment hint

✓ Make sure that your website works, at least as far as you have developed it.

✓✓✓ Provide evidence to show you are using your plan to monitor your progress.

 ### Signposting for e-portfolio evidence

Continue to test your website as it develops. Save this work in your e-portfolio. It could contribute towards covering evidence (a), (b) and (c).

Editing HTML code

Web pages are written in HTML code. This language was invented so that text and images could be displayed through a browser on the internet. The HTML code specifies how the content is to be formatted: its position and appearance on the screen.

Key term

HTML stands for hypertext mark-up language.

This qualification requires you to show that you are able to edit this HTML code, even though you don't need to be able to write the code from scratch. You need to know how to make simple edits to pages, and two such edits are discussed here: adding

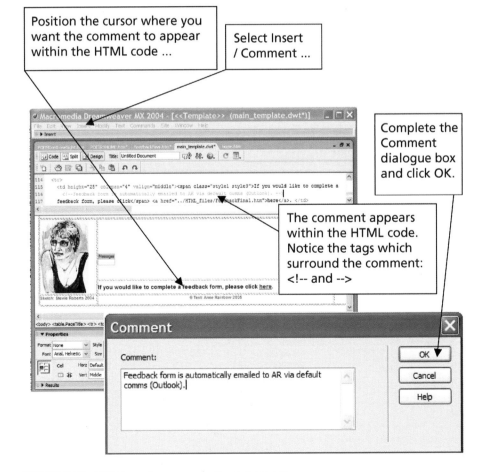

FIGURE 5.26 *HTML code example 3: comments*

comments and adding metatags. (See also Figure 4.3 page 129, for another example of HTML coding.)

Adding comments

It is helpful to add comments (Figure 5.26) to the code to explain how or why you have written something in a particular way. This makes maintenance of the website a bit easier because someone else who has to maintain the site may not be able to second-guess your thought processes; and if you are maintaining your own site, you may not be able to remember why you made certain decisions months or years later.

Metatags

Metatags (Figure 5.27) offer one way of informing

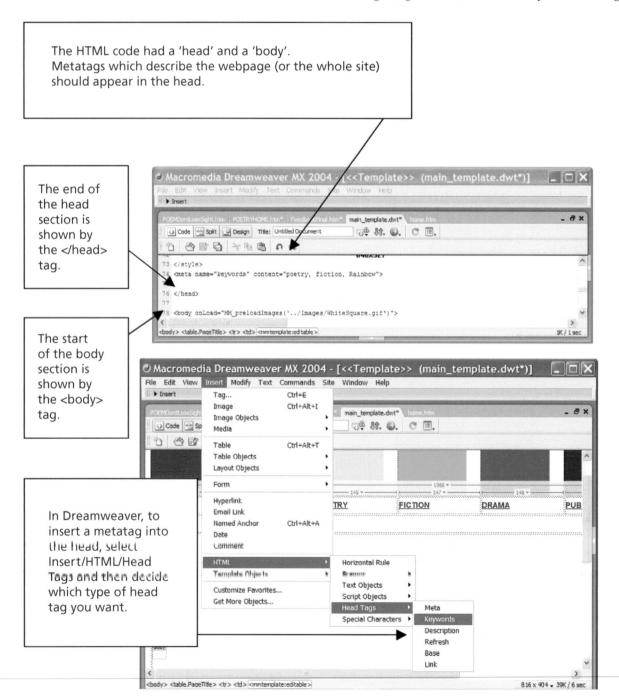

The HTML code had a 'head' and a 'body'. Metatags which describe the webpage (or the whole site) should appear in the head.

The end of the head section is shown by the </head> tag.

The start of the body section is shown by the <body> tag.

In Dreamweaver, to insert a metatag into the head, select Insert/HTML/Head Tags and then decide which type of head tag you want.

FIGURE 5.27 *HTML code example 4: metatags*

a search engine as to what information can be found on your website; it provides data about the data. For example, you may specify keywords that relate to a web page, so that when a potential

Key term

A *metatag* is a piece of code used to instruct the browser as to how to display the content of the web page.

URL stands for uniform resource locator. It is often the address of a file that holds the HTML code for a web page. However, it can also specify a file holding an image, or some other resource needed within a website such as a sound track or video sequence.

Assessment activity

1 Review your progress against your plan. You need to allow time to test and evaluate your website, so you might have to cut back on what you planned to complete.

2 Develop your design further so that it includes as many of the pages as you originally planned that you can complete in the available time.

3 Edit your HTML to incorporate comments so that it is easily maintained.

4 Incorporate metatags so that the keywords that may be used to search for your client's site are listed.

Assessment hints

✓ If you do need to cut back, check that you are meeting most of your client's needs.

✓✓ Keep in mind the intended audience.

✓✓✓ Check that your website shows you have a sound awareness of the purpose of the site.

Signposting for e-portfolio evidence

Continue to test your website as it develops. Save this work in your e-portfolio. It could contribute towards covering evidence (a), (b) and (c).

Knowledge check

1 What does WYSIWYG stand for?

2 Explain the use of drag and drop in building web pages.

3 Explain the differences between buttons, hotspots and rollovers.

4 What is a template?

5 Why is it important to choose meaningful titles for your web pages?

6 What is an anchor? How is it used as an aid to navigation?

7 What is an applet? Give examples.

8 How does an animation differ from an image?

9 What is a scrolling marquee?

10 What does HTML stand for?

11 Give three examples of what a URL may specify.

visitor makes a search, if their keyword matches yours, then the search engine will return your URL as a hit for the visitor.

5.6 Testing and user evaluation

When your website has been developed, you can start the final stages of the process: testing and user evaluation. It is important to test a website –

Think it over...

Discuss with others in your group how you might identify potential visitors to your clients' websites so that you might invite them to become involved in the testing of the sites.

and to obtain clearance from your client that he or she is happy with it – before it goes live. You also need to test it with likely visitors, to make sure that they can use it easily, finding what they want.

Testing

You can start testing your site as soon as the first web page has been created (Figure 5.28). As each new page is designed and produced and linked in with existing pages, you can check that it

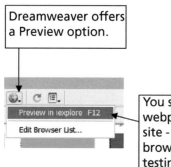

Dreamweaver offers a Preview option.

You should test your webpage - and the whole site - in more than one browser, but you can start testing with the one that is installed on your computer.

FIGURE 5.28 *Testing a web page*

looks right and can be accessed in the way you planned. Some of the testing can be done, therefore, before the site is uploaded, but some – such the testing of counters – has to be done when the site is online.

For your e-portfolio, you will have to supply evidence of testing. To earn maximum marks, you will need to test every aspect of the website – content, functionality and accessibility. All testing needs to be thorough and systematic, to ensure that all elements work as intended, that the client's requirements are met, and that the end user's experience of the website is a positive one.

Testing content

It is important that the website present accurate information to the visitor.

* Are there any spelling errors or grammatical mistakes? You should proofread all text and eliminate any such errors. (Do not rely on the computer's spellchecker to identify all errors, as it will not identify when a correctly spelt word is used incorrectly, for example beach instead of beech, or air instead of are.)

* Have you accurately entered the data supplied by your client? You should verify this by comparing one against the other.

The website should convey a clear message to visitors. Describe for yourself what you think the website's message is. Then ask yourself how effectively this is achieved.

* Is it done through the content alone – or does the design help to convey the message?

* Does the reputation of the site owner help to convey the message – and is this flagged by the use of logos?

The usefulness of a website is important to visitors. To convince visitors to return to a site, it needs to be useful to them. It has to provide answers to questions that the visitors might want to ask.

The site also needs to pass a usability test; this is a reflection of your design, for example how many mouse clicks it takes the visitor to find useful information, but also of functionality aspects, for example layout, presentation and navigational aids.

Testing functionality

In testing the functionality of your website, you are challenging yourself to answer each of these questions with a definite 'Yes':

* Is the layout and presentation of each page appropriate?

* Are you happy with the navigation of the site? Do the hyperlinks work? Do they lead to where a visitor might expect them to go? Are there no dead ends?

* Do any interactive elements, such as a form or a counter, work as intended?

If the answer to any of these questions is 'No', you need to improve your website.

Testing accessibility

The website will be viewed by lots of different visitors. Each may have a different configuration of computer, and may be using one of many different web browsers. Accessibility is a measure of how well your website is viewed, considering any special requirements of the person viewing it, and the software and hardware they are using. Users might be asked a series of questions:

* Does each web page display properly, regardless of which of the common browsers is being used?
* Is the web page unaffected by different monitor resolutions?
* Is the web page accessible to disabled users?

If the response to any question is 'No', then you should investigate further and try to amend your design so that it better fits the needs of visitors, and hence your client.

A test plan

It is important that your testing is systematic! Preparing a test plan will give you something to structure and guide testing so you don't accidentally overlook elements as you perform the test; it will also give you a framework for making notes on any problems or issues if they arise.

You could use your storyboard and/or your website structure flowchart as a basis for the testing. As you check each page shown in your storyboard, tick that page; as you check each link shown on your structure flowchart, tick the link.

If you find something that needs fixing, you might just make a note of it, and then make all the amendments at a later date. (This will generally be a more effective use of your time.) But if the problem prevents you from testing other pages, you may have to give that fix a higher priority and do it immediately.

Theory into practice

1 Follow the links from www.heinemann.co.uk and visit the W3C website to find out more about this organisation.

2 Explore the services offered by W3C, in particular the validation services.

Assessment activity

1 Write a test plan to show how you intend to test all aspects of your website.

2 Proofread each page of the site and eliminate any spelling or grammatical errors.

3 Work in pairs for this activity – it is difficult to find errors in your own work and to look at it objectively. Proofread your partner's web pages. Make recommendations for refinements to your partner's website design and point out any mistakes in the spelling or grammar. If your partner suggests changes, either to the wording or to some other aspect of your website design, note the recommendations and make any necessary refinements.

4 Test the functionality of your site to ensure that all links work correctly.

Assessment hint

✓ Be sure to carry out at least some basic testing of the site.

✓✓ Make sure the website works as intended.

✓✓✓ Comprehensively check all parts of the website to ensure full functionality.

Signposting for e-portfolio evidence

Document this process and save this work as evidence for your portfolio. It could contribute towards covering evidence (c) and (d).

You could make use web-based services such as those provided by the World Wide Web Consortium (W3C) to test web pages; these may help you to identify and repair barriers to accessibility.

User evaluation

Some sites include a feedback form asking visitors what they think about the site.

However, this is too late to make any major changes to the design of the site, so some user evaluation should happen before the site goes live.

In evaluating your website, you should focus on two main aspects:

* *Is the website fit for purpose?* Being fit for purpose means the site meets your client's requirements. To confirm whether this is so, you need to make sure you have analysed the requirements and made them clear in your documentation. Refer back to pages 175–180 to check.

* *Does the website meet the needs of the intended end users, i.e. the visitors to the website?* In your requirements analysis, you should have identified the target audience so you know what kind of visitor the website should attract, and what the visitor might expect. To confirm whether the website meets the end-user's needs, you need to do more testing.

You could evaluate the website on your own – but because you have been so involved in its design and implementation, it may be difficult for you to be objective in your evaluation. Instead, you should ask other people to give their honest opinion. During the development stage, you could incorporate a form into your website requesting comments, and/or include an e-mail link to yourself that visitors could use to send their comments. Then, when you are ready for comments, invite others to visit your site and to use these devices to send you their comments.

The more people you approach for an opinion, the better your web design may become. However, remember that different users will draw on different levels of experience in using computers and in dealing with the internet, and also that what suits one visitor may not suit another. So, take all suggestions on

Assessment activity

1 Devise a questionnaire to guide test visitors of your website and to obtain feedback from them. Include questions such as these:

* How useful did you find the site?

* How effective is the design of the site?

* Are you impressed with the content?

* Are you impressed with the presentation?

* Did you find it easy to navigate your way around the site?

* How usable is the site?

* Do you think the level of accessibility meets the needs of all types of visitor?

2 Identify a sample of people who fit the description of 'target audience' for your client's website. Ask them to explore the website and to complete your questionnaire. You may also ask friends and relatives to test your website and to answer the survey questions.

3 Analyse the feedback and make any last-minute changes to your website that are feasible within your time constraints.

Assessment hint

✓ Identify at least one sensible recommendation for improvement.

✓✓ Incorporate the feedback from users into your design and make changes that are recommended.

✓✓✓ Identify at least two suggestions, explaining how they will enhance the site.

Signposting for e-portfolio evidence

Save this work in your e-portfolio. It could contribute towards covering evidence (c) and (d).

Assessment activity

1 Arrange to deliver the website to your client. Explain that you consider the website development to be complete and that you are now requesting an evaluation – and acceptance – of what you have done.

2 Present your client with any accompanying documentation which may help in their evaluation, for example a copy of a statement of the intended purpose and target audience, plus a list of their original requirements and an indication as to how these have been met. You might also include a list of enhancements that came to light during testing, but that cannot be implemented at this stage.

3 Arrange to meet your client after a sensible time delay to discuss their findings. Make notes of the feedback given by your client.

4 Write a report to provide a detailed evaluation of your website, incorporating comments from your client as appropriate, and covering all aspects of your design.

Assessment hint

✓ Make at least two evaluative comments of how well the final site meets the client's requirements.

✓✓ Give a detailed evaluation of some of the key features of the site.

✓✓✓ Produce a detailed evaluation of the whole site.

📁 Signposting for e-portfolio evidence

Save this work in your e-portfolio. It could contribute towards covering evidence (d).

Knowledge check

1 Explain these terms: content, functionality, accessibility.

2 How can you ensure the accuracy of the content of your client's website? What two methods should you use?

3 Explain these terms: usefulness, usability.

4 What is the purpose of a test plan?

5 What is the W3C? How could it help you to improve your website?

6 In testing your client's website, what two main aspects should you focus on?

their merit and act only on suggestions that you feel will make a positive impact on your site. Also, there is a limit on the time you can afford to spend on enhancements; and a limit on how much a fee-paying client would be willing to spend.

Theory into practice

1 Follow the links from www.heinemann.co.uk and visit the Macromedia website. Macromedia offer 'everything you need for an online store' within an e-Commerce suite, and support for major payment gateways with their eCart software. Find out more about these features: how much they cost and how much memory they require.

2 Visit other sites that offer similar products and make comparisons.

5.7 Functionality

Functionality refers to what the website does or the options it offers the user. Some websites offer advanced features such as shopping baskets, customer personalisation, methods of payment, and invitations for customer feedback.

As time goes by and websites become

increasingly sophisticated, some of these features will become commonplace and others will be considered as 'advanced'. It is therefore important to keep abreast of technological developments in this area. If you keep up to date, you will be better placed to provide sensible advice to your client about appropriate ways of enhancing the functionality of their website.

This qualification does not require that you build advanced features in your website, but does require that consider them and, specifically, make recommendations as to how the site could be developed further to enable the client organisation to trade online.

E-commerce enhancements

This section looks at how a site might be enhanced to provide e-commerce functionality. You are not expected to carry out these enhancements within this unit. However, if you consider them to be advisable you may complete the enhancement as part of your work for Unit 2. This section considers the following possibilities for enhancement:

* online ordering/payment facility
* improving security
* personalised customer service
* customer feedback and evaluation
* database of product information linked to the website
* edit facility for the client.

Online ordering/payment facility

If the website is to be enhanced so that visitors can make purchases online, then there are some financial steps your client must take before you can build and achieve this functionality.

To buy a product online, the website visitor has to have some method of payment which is acceptable to your client. Payments by cash are not an option, and cheques would have to be

posted and cleared through your client's bank account before the goods could be despatched; most customers will not wait this long for delivery. So, most purchases on websites involve a credit card, and your client has to have set up a merchant account with the various credit card companies. Alternatively, your client could subscribe to an organisation such as PayPal which allows payments through all the major credit cards.

The website needs to provide a shopping basket (Figure 5.29) into which products that the visitors plan to buy are placed. To make purchasing as easy as possible, beside each product, there needs to be a button that says 'Add to Shopping Cart'. This leads the visitor to a web page that shows the items

> **Key term**
>
> The *shopping basket* concept is similar to that of the Recycle bin: its icon looks like its counterpart in the real world, and it serves the same purpose as a real shopping basket, i.e. you place the items you intend to buy inside the shopping basket and then, when you have finished shopping, you take it to the checkout to pay for your purchases.

FIGURE 5.29 *The shopping basket icon*

in the shopping basket already, plus this extra item. It should also show the individual cost of each item as well as the accumulated subtotal. The visitor may then return to shopping until such time as they decide they do not want to buy any more items and want to proceed to the checkout and complete the purchase of all items.

Once at the checkout, the visitor will need to complete a couple of forms, one giving all credit card details, and one specifying the destination address for the goods. The information requested by the

forms should be kept to a minimum; if you want to ask the visitor questions about what they think of the site, this is not the place to do it. They may decide to abandon the purchase and go elsewhere! You are more likely to obtain useful information from users by having a feedback form available elsewhere on the site, for example on the Contact Us page. Your client will already have a method of despatching goods to clients who order by phone or post, but may need to reconsider this system and to automate it so that despatch is triggered as soon as the visitor completes the transaction – even if that is at midnight on a Saturday evening.

An automated despatch system involves linking the contents of the order form completed by the visitor and feeding this data to a database of products.

Your client may also consider an automatic

e-mail confirmation to the visitor saying that the order has been placed. This can be set up within the website, so long as the visitor is asked to supply an e-mail address somewhere

on the order form.

Some websites offer an order tracking service and provide a unique order reference number and web link for this purpose. The visitor can then revisit the site at a later date, and see what progress has been made on shipping the goods.

Security

Security is an issue with online purchases. It is easy for someone who has obtained a credit card fraudulently to make a purchase online. If this happens, the credit card companies do not pay out, so the supplier doesn't receive payment for the goods they provided. So, it is important to build in checks to make sure that the visitor is indeed the card holder.

Personalised customer service

Visitors who return to the site may be saved time in completing the forms at the checkout if your client's site has offered to retain information about the visitor. This is achieved by asking the visitor to sign up or register in some way (where they have a user name and/or a password), and then placing a cookie on the visitor's computer, so that their password can be checked next time they visit your client's site.

Customer feedback and evaluation

To monitor their satisfaction (with the site and perhaps with the products/services being provided) and consider improvements to the site's functionality, your client may want feedback from visitors to the website:

* Some visitors may offer praise, for example on the speed of delivery. If such favourable comments are made available for other visitors to view, this can reassure other prospective purchasers.

* Visitors may have valuable comments on problems with the website, and your client may then decide to make changes accordingly.

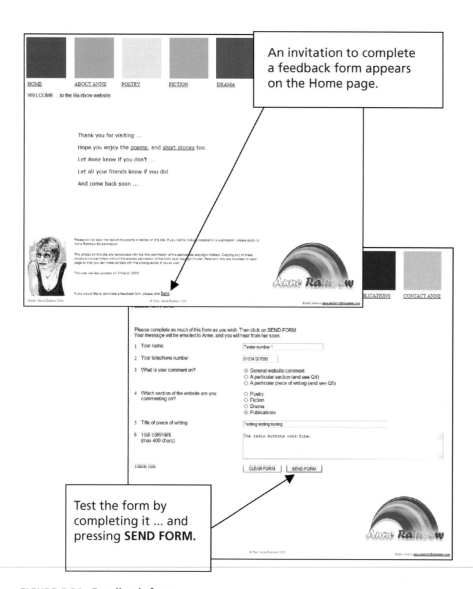

FIGURE 5.30 *Feedback form*

✳ Visitors may use this method to complain about the products or services they have bought.

How this feedback is obtained varies. To encourage immediate feedback, a form could be included on the site, inviting visitors to make

Theory into practice

1 Visit a website that sells online and look at the opportunities taken to obtain feedback, for example a form that the visitor can complete.

2 Check what cookies have been stored on your computer. See Unit 6 (page 214) to find out how to do this.

3 Consider including a user feedback form on your client's site. Where would you locate it? What information would you seek from the visitor?

comments (Figure 5.30). These comments can be sent direct to your client's e-mail address, where they can be responded to and appropriate action taken.

To obtain feedback after a sale, an e-mail could be sent automatically to each purchaser, say, one week after delivery was expected, asking for feedback about the process of purchasing online.

Holding product information in a database linked to a website

Your client's static brochure website presents details of the products (or services) on offer. Visitors can obtain information about the product, see a picture of it and find out its cost, but not buy it online.

Your client most probably has a database of products and uses this to control stock. It is possible to link the client's database to the website, so that the website has access to the most up-to-date information. The website is then called a dynamic website.

If the client also sets in place a mechanism for the ordering and payment of goods, a visitor can then place an order and the database be kept up to date for the next visitor to the site.

Edit facility for the client

Key term

The *webmaster* is the person who looks after a website on a day-to-day basis. He or she will make changes to the website – or supervise others who do the work – to improve the site and to fix any problems that arise.

The development of your client's website will have been completed using web authoring software, and it is unlikely that your client has the skills to use this software, or the time to learn how to use it.

It is quite likely, however, that your client will want to make changes to the website. Rather than pay a professional webmaster, the client may want the option to make small changes without your assistance.

You might, at an additional cost to the client, provide suitable training for your client so he or she can edit pages, or you could provide some facility that allows them to make alterations to the site independently. This may involve setting up a web-based application so that, for example, prices of products are taken from a database. The client can then maintain the database, and consequently the website is kept up to date.

Recommending enhancements

Before reviewing your own website to think about the recommendations that you might make, you should look back at the work you did for Unit 2. Revisit the transactional sites you studied and review the back-office processes that you considered.

In your report, you should list the additional features you would recommend and explain why you think they would enhance your site, rather than how you would achieve this change. You must also be able to advise on the impact that the changes you propose might have on personnel and practices within the organisation.

It would be easy to describe in general terms

Theory into practice

1 Visit a website that offers products for sale. Follow the route from product selection through to payment – but omit the last step which confirms the sale, unless you really do want to buy the product. Notice the information that is collected – and consider what similar information your client would need to collect.

2 Research more websites to look for enhancements that might suit your client's particular needs. Look in particular at sites of direct competitors.

Assessment activity

List some enhancements that you plan to recommend and explain how they would benefit your client in particular.

Assessment hint

✓ Identify at least three steps to enable the website to support e-commerce.

✓✓ Identify at least five steps to enable the website to support e-commerce, and offer alternatives for at least two of the steps.

✓✓✓ Consider how at least five steps might be implemented.

Knowledge check

1 What is meant by functionality?

2 Give three examples of extra features that may enhance a website.

3 What is meant by e-commerce?

4 What is a merchant account? Why is it needed?

5 What information would a visitor need to make use of an order tracking service?

6 Give examples of how feedback might be obtained from visitors to a website.

what features are used on a transactional website as given here, for example, allowing the visitor to select products, add them to a shopping basket and then, when they have finished shopping, to proceed to a checkout to pay (pages 198–199). However, the proposals for enhancements that you make to your client should be quite detailed and must relate directly to the client, their products/services, and the website that you have produced to promote these.

5.8 ICT skills

In producing your client's website, you will have used ICT skills.

* You will have used web authoring software to produce your web pages.

* You will have implemented your design ideas by applying colour schemes and styles.

* You may have included multimedia content and animations, and structured your data into tables where appropriate.

UNIT ASSESSMENT

1 Read back through this chapter to remind yourself of the skills you have developed since starting on this unit.

2 Check the contents of your portfolio to make sure that you have included evidence of all your ICT skills and all the documentation required.

UNIT 6

Technical support

Introduction

This unit builds on the practitioner skills learned in Unit 4, System design and installation, so you should complete Unit 4 before attempting this unit. This unit also has a practitioner focus. Ideally, you should gain real-life experiences of providing technical support. For example, you may spend time in a large technical support department, or you may shadow an IT technician at your centre.

What you need to learn

In completing this unit, you should achieve these learning outcomes:

* Be able to carry out first-line 'trouble-shooting' activities – diagnosing the problem and finding a solution
* Know how to use diagnostic tools and other fault-finding techniques
* Devise routine maintenance procedures to help prevent problems occurring
* Back-up systems to limit the damage in case of system failure
* Know how to implement hardware and software upgrades
* Understand the different methods of digital communication
* Support users who wish to use these technologies effectively.

Resource toolkit

To complete this unit, you need these essential resources:

* access to computer hardware, including a digital camera, scanner, tape recorder; access to computer software, including word processing software and presentation software; access to the Internet and web-based tools for collaborative working
* a wide range of information sources, such as books, weekly trade journals of the IT industry (for example *Computing* and *Computer Weekly*) and newspapers
* contacts working within the IT industry.

How you will be assessed

This unit is internally assessed. Page VII explains what this means.

There are four assessment objectives:

AO1 Install and test a hardware and a software upgrade for the system you installed in Unit 4 (assessment evidence a)

AO2 recommend routine maintenance procedures and trouble-shooting strategies for the system you installed in Unit 4 (assessment evidence b)

AO3 investigate web-based tools for collaborative working and demonstrate the setup and use of one of these tools (assessment evidence c)

AO4 describe the communication needs of a specified small business (SME) and make recommendations to meet these needs (assessment evidence d).

To demonstrate your coverage of the assessment objectives, you will produce an e-portfolio of evidence, showing what you have learnt and what you can do:

(a) You will provide evidence – a witness testimony and supporting evidence – of your successful installation and testing of a hardware and a software upgrade to the system that you installed for Unit 4.

(b) You will create an onscreen technical support manual recommending routine maintenance procedures, schedules, tracking procedures and trouble-shooting strategies for the system that you installed in Unit 4.

(c) You will give a presentation describing and evaluating the features of four different types of web-based tools for collaborative working; and a demonstration of the setup and use of one of them. The presentation should include screen shots that illustrate functions of the software. It will be delivered to an audience (not for someone to read onscreen) so the detail of your presentation will appear in your speaker notes/hand-outs, not on the slides themselves. The slides should be designed to convey key messages only.

(d) You will write a report addressing the communication requirements of a small business (SME) with justified recommendations for internet connectivity, security procedures, an internet access policy and e-mail.

How high can you aim?

Your e-portfolio will contain all the evidence on which your performance will be judged. So, the presentation of your e-portfolio is important. Aim to adopt a format that would be acceptable in industry. Some **Assessment activities** can be used towards your e-portfolio. These will contain **Assessment hints** on what you can do to pass (✓), gain a better mark (✓✓) or top marks (✓✓✓). For example, when you install and test the hardware and software upgrade, the amount of prompting you need and the amount of testing you do will determine the maximum number of marks that you earn. Your onscreen technical support manual for the system installed for Unit 4 also contributes to your final score and you will gain higher marks if your instructions are detailed and yet easy to use.

Your understanding of the key features of web-based tools for collaborative working will be measured by the quality of your presentation, and the quality and content of your report on the communication needs of a specified small to medium business enterprise (SME) which must be presented in simple, non-technical language will determine your mark. So, in working through this unit, remember that the maximum number of marks that you can earn – and hence your grade – will depend on the quality of your work, and what your manual, presentation and report say. Your actual mark is determined by the level of detail, the quality of your output, your mastery of software tools and the depth of your analysis and/or evaluation.

Ready to start?

This unit should take you about 60 hours to complete. Why not keep a log of your time? Devise a blank form that you could use to record the time that you spend on this course.

6.1 Routine maintenance

There is a saying: 'Prevention is better than cure' and, with computers, this is certainly true. To avoid disasters, a routine maintenance plan is vital.

✱ Preventive maintenance is conducted to prevent problems arising in the future due to neglect of the equipment, thus saving time in diagnosing and fixing faults. It can also extend the life of a PC.

✱ Routine maintenance is so called because it is scheduled to take place at regular intervals.

This section first considers what actions to include in a preventive maintenance schedule and how you might automatically schedule these. Specific routine maintenance tasks are then discussed:

✱ virus checking

✱ backing up

✱ restoring and archiving procedures

✱ file/storage management, such as removal of temporary files and cookies and defragmentation.

Preventive maintenance schedule

Like any machine, a PC needs some attention on a regular basis if only to keep it clean. Computers attract a lot of dust.

✱ If dust settles on the outside, it soon forms a grimy layer of dirt which is unsightly and attracts yet more dust.

✱ If dust settles on the inside, it blocks airways, preventing the cooling mechanism from working properly. Overheated components may then fail.

Just how regular the preventive maintenance tasks are performed depends on the task. It could be daily, weekly, monthly or annually, or just when necessary (Table 6.1).

FREQUENCY	MAINTENANCE TASK
Daily	• Virus scan of memory and your hard disk • Take backups of changed data files
Weekly	• Clean mouse (ball and rollers) and check for wear • Clean keyboard, checking for stuck keys • Clean monitor screen • Clean printer • Delete temporary files (disk clean) • Defrag hard disk and recover lost clusters
Monthly	• Clean outside of case • Take complete backup of data files
Annually	• Check motherboard: reseat chips if necessary • Clean adapter card contacts with contact cleaner and reseat
As required	• Clean floppy disk drive if it fails, using a proprietary disk drive cleaning kit to clean the read/write heads • Record and back up CMOS setup configuration • Keep written record of hardware and software configuration

TABLE 6.1 *Preventive maintenance schedule*

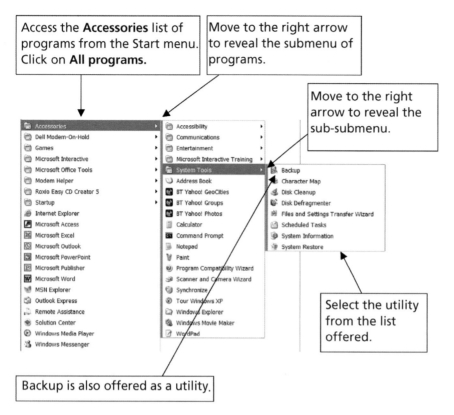

Access the **Accessories** list of programs from the Start menu. Click on **All programs.**

Move to the right arrow to reveal the submenu of programs.

Move to the right arrow to reveal the sub-submenu.

Select the utility from the list offered.

Backup is also offered as a utility.

FIGURE 6.1 *Disk cleanup and defragmentation utilities in System Tools*

Some hardware can – and needs to be – cleaned (for example casings, mouse rollers) but some hardware is sealed so your maintenance is restricted to software cleaning options, for example deleting temporary files from the hard disk.

Software maintenance involves the use of utilities like Disk Cleanup and Disk Defragmenter (Figure 6.1).

The frequency of tasks in the preventive maintenance schedule must be decided to suit the user:

✳ The frequency of backups depends on the volume of transactions and the importance of the material. Full backups may be required weekly or even daily.

✳ If the air in which the PC operates is dusty or smoky, even more frequent cleaning will be necessary.

Scheduling

To ensure that routine maintenance is completed regularly and on time, you should set up a schedule, and a tracking system to record when each task is done, and when it next needs to be done.

CASE STUDY

The support team of an SME arrange a schedule of backups direct from the servers. Backups are taken every day on a two-week cycle, and every Friday on an 8-week cycle, and monthly (Figure 6.2).

1 **Devise a way of presenting a schedule to your own SME.**

2 **Design a tracking system for their use.**

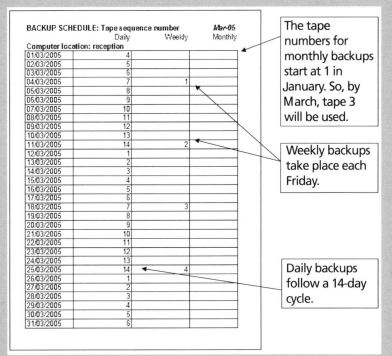

FIGURE 6.2 *Schedule of maintenance and tracking system*

Some tasks require your intervention:

* You may wish to clean your disk but need to individually select which files to delete permanently and which to retain. If need be, you might then go on to defragment your disk.

* You may wish to go online to your ISP, check your bulk e-mail inbox, delete any spam and

Key terms

ISP stands for internet service provider. Examples include btinternet, demon and yahoo.

Spam is unsolicited or junk mail, and it could carry a virus in an attachment.

mark for downloading the e-mails that you do wish to receive.

For the type of activity that involves decision-making on your part, you might set up a Task, for example in Microsoft Outlook® to remind you to perform the activity on a regular basis. When the task falls due, Outlook® reminds you and, if you are in the middle of something else, you have the option to press **Snooze**, so that you are reminded to complete the activity at a later time or date (Figure 6.3). Having completed the activity, you might make notes and adjust the timing for the next reminder.

If the task requires no intervention by you, the user, and needs to be done at the same time on a regular basis, an automatic scheduled task could

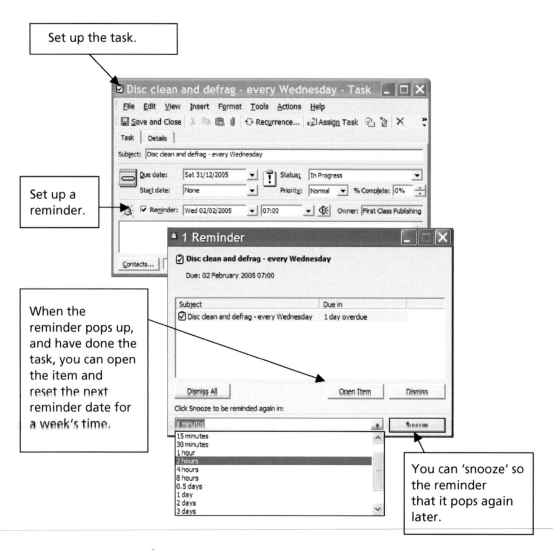

Set up the task.

Set up a reminder.

When the reminder pops up, and have done the task, you can open the item and reset the next reminder date for a week's time.

You can 'snooze' so the reminder that it pops again later.

FIGURE 6.3 *An Outlook® Task reminder with Snooze options*

be set up. Using **Scheduled Tasks** from the **Systems Tools** menu (Figure 6.4), you can set up a task to run daily, weekly, monthly, or at certain times (such as at system startup). This option makes sense for utilities like backups.

Utilities that need to be running all the time, such as anti-virus software, would best be started as soon as the computer is turned on, and so you should include the opening of this software in your Startup menu.

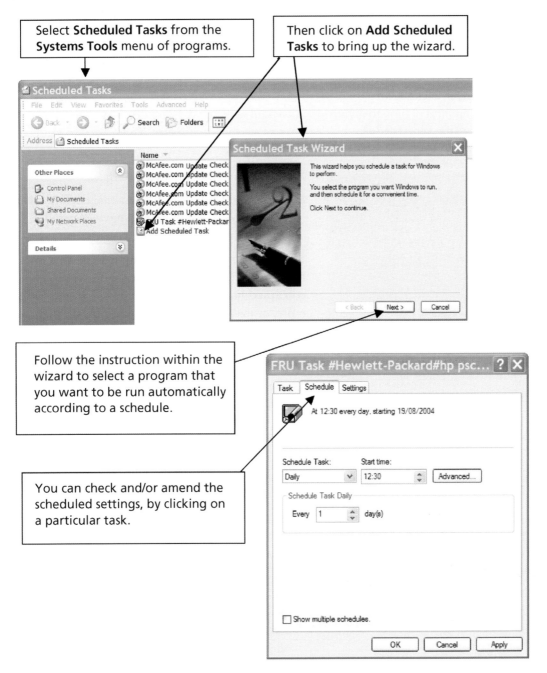

Select **Scheduled Tasks** from the **Systems Tools** menu of programs.

Then click on **Add Scheduled Tasks** to bring up the wizard.

Follow the instruction within the wizard to select a program that you want to be run automatically according to a schedule.

You can check and/or amend the scheduled settings, by clicking on a particular task.

FIGURE 6.4 *The Schedule Tasks wizard*

Virus-checker updates

Section 6.7 (page 250) considers viruses in some detail: how to identify them and the anti-virus software available to protect against viruses.

Whatever the source of a virus, and regardless of the anti-virus software installed, it is essential that you ensure your anti-virus software is as up to date as possible. You will need to go online to your anti-virus software provider and use their facilities to check your PC to see whether an update is necessary.

Some vendors offer to advise you automatically, and to download updates automatically, whenever you are online. You should accept such offers; it saves you having to remember to check for updates – and reduces the amount of time that your PC may be unprotected from the latest viruses.

Theory into practice

1 Check that your anti-virus software is as up to date as possible.

2 Using your anti-virus software menu, select the virus scan option. Perform an anti-virus check of your hard disk.

3 Set up your anti-virus software to run on startup, to check all incoming e-mails, and all files at the time of opening.

4 Set up a schedule to check for virus updates, or accept the anti-virus software vendor's offer of an automatic update option.

Backup, restore and archiving

Think it over...

In a small group, list the reasons for taking backups. Think of situations where you might need to restore data. Categorise these situations according to how you might try to prevent the disaster.

Backing up and restoring data

A backup is a copy of data taken at a particular time as a security measure. There are two kinds of backups:

* A full backup is a copy of all files.

* A partial backup – or incremental backup – is a copy only of those files that have changed since the previous backup.

The purpose of taking a backup is to be able to restore data should there be some disaster: a corrupted hard disk, a PC that just stops working, a fire, or even theft. The software needed to do a backup maybe provided as a utility (Figure 6.5) or you might buy a specialist package from a specialist vendor.

It is important that the process of taking backups is done in a systematic way, and that the saved data can be easily retrieved in the event of any disaster.

CASE STUDY

Diana's computer was once hit by a virus and suffered damage to her data, so she wisely installed anti virus software – and, even more wisely, started taking regular backups of her data. Recently, a file was corrupted and she needed to recover a backed up version of the file.

She pressed **Start** and selected **All Programs/Accessories/Systems Tools**

(Figure 6.5). She then selected **System Restore** and followed the on-screen instructions.

1 What Systems Tool should Diana have selected?

2 What does System Restore do?

3 Explain the effect of what Diana did.

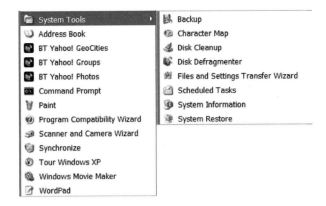

FIGURE 6.5 *System Tools*

✳ To minimise the amount of time taken during the backup process, you should choose a medium that has fast read/write times, such as another hard drive, a CD or a zip drive.

✳ To reduce the amount of data that has to be saved, incremental backups could be taken each day, with the full backup being done, say, weekly.

✳ The timing of the backup can be chosen so that the disruption to other work is minimised, i.e. scheduled for when little other work is being done, maybe late at night or at the weekends.

✳ To automate the backup procedure an automated scheduled task should be set up.

Theory into practice

For an organisation of your own choice, discuss their procedures for backing up data. Think about how their procedures are tailored to suit their workforce needs. Can you see any room for improvement of their procedures? Make notes.

Archiving

An archive is a store of out-of-date items. An item may be a data file but, in software such as Microsoft Outlook®, an item may be an individual e-mail message, an appointment, a task, a journal entry or a note.

In the same way that your hard disk will fill with data files, the folders within your e-mail

software gradually fills with items. As time passes, the oldest items are less likely to be referred to and, while you may not want to delete them, you could move them out of your current working area.

Archiving is the process of moving old files to a safe place, prior to their probable deletion at some later date. In Microsoft Outlook®, AutoArchive is an automated procedure which takes care of the archiving process for you.

Like any other scheduled task, AutoArchive can be set to run at schedules intervals, clearing out old and expired items from your e-mail and task folders, and your calendar and journal.

✳ An old item is one that is older than the archiving age you have specified, for example e-mails received over six months ago.

✳ An expired item is one that has passed its expiry date, for example an appointment that took place yesterday. Expiry dates are optional; you can set them up when you create an item, or at a later date. Once an item expires, however, it becomes unavailable.

Like other scheduled tasks, you can set up the system so you are reminded that archiving is due to be done (Figure 6.6).

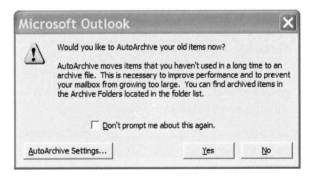

FIGURE 6.6 *Archiving reminder*

The archive file is a special type of data file. In Outlook, the first time AutoArchive runs, the archive file is created automatically in a location that depends on the operating system you're using. For Windows® 2000, it is stored in:

C:\Documents and Settings*yourusername*\Local Settings\Application Data\Microsoft\Outlook\ Archive.pst

Locating this data file may be hampered by the Local Settings folder being set as a hidden file. See Microsoft Windows Help for information about showing hidden folders.

After Outlook archives items for the first time, old items can be directly accessed from Archive Folders in the Outlook Folder List. Within the Archive Folders, Outlook maintains the existing folder structure.

* If there is a parent folder above the folder you chose to archive, the parent folder is created in the archive file, but other items within the parent folder are not archived. In this way, an identical folder structure exists between the archive file and the mailbox.

* Folders are left in place after being archived, even if they are empty.

* You work with the items in the same way you work with items in your main mailbox.

* If you decide you want archived items to be moved back into your main mailbox, you can import all the items from the archive file into their original folders or into other folders you specify, or you can manually move or copy individual items.

In Outlook, there are three levels of AutoArchive settings:

* Global settings, also called default settings, determine whether AutoArchive runs at all and what it does by default with the items in any Outlook folder (except Contacts, which is unaffected by AutoArchive).

* Per-folder settings override the default settings so you can decide an archiving policy for individual folders. If you don't specify AutoArchive settings for a folder, the default settings are automatically adopted.

* Items in your mailbox may also be subject to company retention policies. These policies take precedence over AutoArchive settings and may be set to encourage users to retain documents and items for only a fixed period of time.

Default settings and per-folder settings apply to the current mailbox only. If you want, you can also manually archive items.

You might also archive other material such as Word files that relate to projects that have now been completed. You could zip these files, to reduce the amount of space they take up, and store them in a separate folder.

File and storage management

If you continually create new files and don't delete old files, you will eventually run out of space on your storage medium. Your hard disk may have become so full that the files are being fragmented, thus slowing down the time it takes to save a file and to retrieve it. You may notice this when checking your computer's performance data; it may suggest that your system is slowing down (for more information about checking the computer's performance, refer to Unit 4, page 162).

The storage of temporary files can quickly fill your hard disk; these temporary files are set up automatically. For example, whenever you receive an e-mail attachment or surf the Internet they are set up, even if you don't formally save the item. And each time you visit a website that asks for personal data, such as your login name and password, you may be offered the opportunity for this data to be 'remembered' as a cookie, which is another type of temporary file. Some sites may set up special cookies known as spyware as soon as you visit them, even if you do not disclose data to them; they may be able to 'read' personal data on your system.

Deleting files

So, as your hard disk gradually fills with files, some tidying up is needed; you should rid your PC of any files that are no longer needed. First, decide which of your working files can be deleted. Select the file so that it is highlighted and right-click. Select **Delete** and the **Confirm File Delete** dialogue box will open (Figure 6.7). Don't be impatient that you have to confirm your intention to delete; it would be too easy to click on **Delete** when you meant to click on **Rename** or **Create Shortcut**.

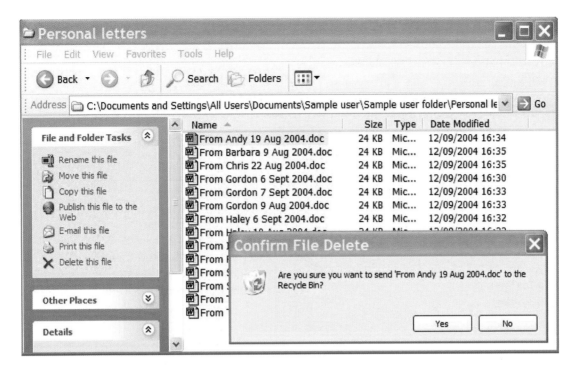

FIGURE 6.7 *Confirm File Delete*

Deleted files are not actually deleted from your hard disk; they are moved to the Recycle bin. They are still accessible to you and you can still restore them for a while. So, if you change your mind, select the file within the Recycle bin and choose the **Restore** option. The file will be put back in the folder you deleted it from. However, once you empty the Recycle bin – using an option within it, or by using Disk Cleanup – your deleted files will no longer be available to you.

Theory into practice

1 Using My Recent Documents on the Start menu, highlight a file and right-click. Delete the file.

2 Using My Computer, check that the file is no longer listed in its folder.

3 Go to the Recyle bin and click **Restore** to reinstate the file.

4 To confirm that the file has been restored, open an appropriate application and locate the file within its folder, using **File/Open**.

Disk cleanup

Once you have removed all the working files that you no longer need to retain – and moved them to the Recycle bin, you can delete the temporary files, including these deleted files, from your hard disk using the Disk Cleanup utility.

Disk Cleanup is supplied as a Systems Tool within the Accessories folder in Windows XP® (Figure 6.8). This allows you to permanently remove unwanted files and programs, thus freeing up space on your hard disk.

How to run Disk cleanup

1 Select **Start/All Programs/Accessories/System Tools/Disk Cleanup.** Wait while the utility searches your files to see what files might be deleted (Figure 6.8).

2 On the **Disk Cleanup** tab, mark the check boxes to indicate which files you agree to having deleted, and press **OK**.

– The **Temporary internet files** can safely be deleted. If you have set up bookmarks for your favourite websites, you can access them via the Favourites folder very quickly. The temporary files are only 'stills' of what the webpage looked like when you last visited

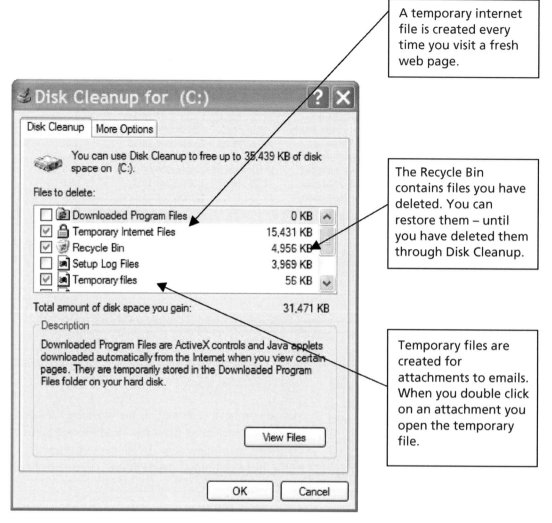

A temporary internet file is created every time you visit a fresh web page.

The Recycle Bin contains files you have deleted. You can restore them – until you have deleted them through Disk Cleanup.

Temporary files are created for attachments to emails. When you double click on an attachment you open the temporary file.

FIGURE 6.8 *Disk Cleanup*

it; it may have changed meanwhile, so you would want to see a fresh version anyway.

- The contents of the **Recycle Bin** can also be deleted, so long as you are sure there is nothing you might want to restore. To make absolutely sure, you could click on **View Files**.

- You may want to delete any cookies that have been set up on your computer. Note that if you delete cookies, you will need to supply information to the website next time you visit. This will result in the cookie being set up again! However, by selecting individual cookies to highlight them ready for deletion, you do have control over which cookies to retain and which to delete.

3 On the **Options** tab, decide also whether you need to remove any Windows components, or

programs. Any that you do not use could be uninstalled. There is also an option to free up more disk space by removing all but the most recent restore point.

Defragmentation

Performing the disk clean before you defragment your hard drive will free up as much space as possible. The gaps left by the deleted files may provide enough contiguous space for files that are currently held in separate clusters (i.e. fragmented), or for files that you save on the hard disk in the future. The defragmentation utility can then be used to 'squeeze' everything up in a more orderly fashion on your disk.

Fragmentation happens when files have to split up into sections and are saved in separate locations on the disk because there is no contiguous space available that is big enough to hold the entire file. Defragmentation tidies up the disk, making available clusters that are no longer needed (because files have been deleted) and collecting the separate elements of fragmented files together.

How to defragment a disk

1 Select **Start/All Programs/Accessories/System Tools/Disk Defragmenter**. Alternatively, access this utility through the Control Panel, within the Computer Management folder (Figure 6.9).

2 Click on the **Analyse** button. The utility will then estimate the disk usage after defragmentation and make a recommendation: either to defragment your disk, or not to, at this time.

3 If you are recommended to defragment your disk, click on the **Defragment** button. Defragmentation will take several minutes, so you are advised to leave the PC and spend the time doing something useful.

Knowledge check

1 Why is routine maintenance important?

2 Explain these terms: fragmentation, defragmentation.

3 What is a utility? Give two examples.

4 What does ISP stand for? Give three examples of ISPs.

5 What is the purpose of the Start Menu?

6 What is a backup? Describe two sorts of backup. What is the purpose of taking a backup?

7 What is an archive? Why should you archive files? Describe different AutoArchive settings.

8 What is a temporary file? When might one be created? Why might you delete temporary files?

9 What is the Recycle bin used for? For how long is it possible to retrieve files from it?

10 What is a cookie? Why might you decide not to delete a cookie?

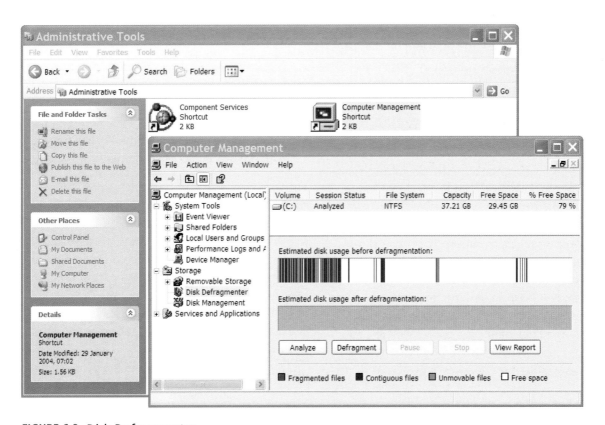

FIGURE 6.9 *Disk Defragmenter*

6.2 Troubleshooting strategies

In this section, you will learn how to predict potential problems. It will be important for you to invest time in gaining plenty of practical experience of carrying out routine maintenance and troubleshooting. This will provide you with the expertise that you can then share within the pages of your manual, a step-by-step instruction to help technical support staff to diagnose and solve particular problems in an ICT context.

Your manual should be designed, not as a self-help guide for an end-user, but for reference by an ICT technician. So, you should use correct technical terminology, and give sufficient detail for a suitably qualified technician. What follows is a step-by-step guide to troubleshooting, focusing on particular problems. Your manual should offer a similar level of guidance to the reader.

Problem-solving

A problem can be viewed as a puzzle that needs solving. If you recognise the puzzle, you may already know how to solve it, or be able to identify someone else who can tell you the solution.

If you don't recognise the puzzle, you will need to try various different ways of solving it, find out more information and keep thinking about the puzzle, until the solution dawns on you. You may feel as though you are in the middle of a maze and cannot find your way out. You may go down several blind alleys before you hit on the solution. This exploration may seem to be a waste of time but, if you make sure you note what you discover, whatever you learn in solving this problem may well help you when working on another problem at a later date.

Problem-solving strategies

When you are first faced with a problem, where do you begin? You need a strategy for problem-solving. Whatever problem you are faced with, it always helps to have a plan. There are some basic questions you will need to ask:

* What is the source of the problem?
* When did the problem start?
* What works? What does not work?
* Can the problem be recreated?
* Can the fault be isolated?

> **Think it over...**
>
> In a small group, brainstorm how you solve problems at the moment. Make notes.

What is the source of the problem?

Your first objective is to identify the source of the problem. This information may be hidden in the mind of the user, but he or she may be upset and/or may not be able to describe the problem in a technical manner. For users, the main problem is the failure of the PC to do what they want it to do, even though the actual problem may lie elsewhere.

* A user may complain that the printer is not working, when actually the problem lies with the printer driver.
* A user may complain that the CD drive is not working and you find that he or she has inserted the CD upside down.
* A user may complain that the PC has forgotten its password, so access is denied!

The user may also jump to conclusions and suggest things that are wrong with the PC, rather than just giving you the facts. So, you may need to calm the user down, and bring a reassuring tone to the conversation before you can begin to find out anything from them. As part of your problem-solving strategy, encourage the user to describe the problem as they see it, but ignore – or at least set aside – the interpretation given as to what is causing the problem.

If it turns out that the user is the problem, then you will need to use your communication skills to explain the correct procedures. Make sure that the user understands what happened and knows enough to prevent it happening again. Diplomacy and tact will be essentials tools!

When did the problem start?

The problem started at some point in time, with or without the user noticing. If this was at the same time as some change to the system, for example the addition of new hardware, then this suggests that the problem lies with the new hardware or its configuration. Finding out a date or time when things seemed to start going wrong can therefore help you to pinpoint possible causes. (If you are the user, you may find that talking to yourself – daft as it sounds – actually helps.)

What works? What does not work?

Thinking about the various symptoms that the user describes, you will try to match them with things that you already know about how PCs work. This may lead you to a conclusion as to what is going wrong and that can help you to solve the problem.

You do need to find out in great detail exactly what the PC is or is not doing. PCs involve a number of interconnected parts and so, sometimes, the real challenge is to identify what does work and then, by a process of elimination, discover what does not work.

Think it over...

With others in your group, discuss how a process of elimination can be used to isolate a problem.

Can the problem be recreated?

Taking the user back to a time when the PC was working will help them to think through the events that led up to the problem, in the right order and exactly as it happened. This may reveal vital clues, but it will be important to keep an open mind and to consider alternative sources of the problem. If you can recreate the problem, you could be half way to solving it.

Can the fault be isolated?

If the problem lies with the hardware, then the easy option is to replace the device. It may not be economical to repair a damaged component. Using your knowledge of PC equipment, you can check devices to see whether they are the source of the fault. You can also check the media, and how it is being used with the device to make sure this is not the cause of any problem. For example, if there seems to be a problem reading a CD-ROM, make sure the CD is the correct way up in the drive.

Theory into practice

1 Next time you meet a problem on your PC, go through the problem-solving strategy described, step by step. Ask a friend to watch how you tackle the problem – and solve it! – and to make notes. Afterwards, discuss your strategy.

2 Do the same for another friend – watch them solve a problem. Do not make suggestions to help them. Just make notes on their strategy. In discussing their strategy afterwards, make suggestions as to how they might reach a solution more quickly.

Initial checks

This section now looks at some common trouble spots:

* cabling and connections
* power supply voltage faults
* system setup problems that may cause system crashes.

Cabling and connections

Cabling is the wiring that connects the PC power supply to the power source at the socket. Cabling is also used to link the PC to the peripherals. At either end of a cable, there may be a connector; some cables are built in to the device.

Think it over...

Discuss with your group which devices are supplied with a built-in cable.

You should be able to recognise and correct common physical faults, for example a monitor cable being unplugged, the mouse and keyboard cables plugged in each other's sockets. Nowadays, the ports on a computer and the connectors are colour coded to help the technician connect things correctly. However, it is still possible to make mistakes, or to not make the connection firmly enough. With heavy or clumsy handling, it is also possible to damage a connector and/or a port so that it will not work at all.

So, what problems may relate to cabling? You could be using the wrong type of cable or the wrong length of cable.

✳ If the cable is too long, this can cause data corruption problems.

✳ For each peripheral device that you plan to attach, there may be a choice of cabling and connector that would work – you need to make sure you choose the correct one. Table 6.2 lists the most common types of cabling, and Figure 6.10 shows examples of each cable type. Table 6.3 then lists the various connectors and Figure 6.11 shows examples of these connectors.

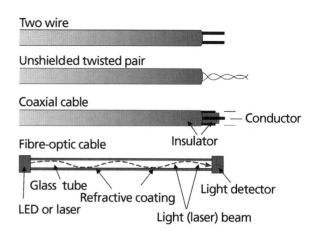

FIGURE 6.10 *Different types of cabling*

Problems may also arise if you use the wrong type of port for the connection. You may have to choose between a serial port and a parallel port, and configure the software accordingly.

✳ Serial cabling is circular in cross-section. It is connected to the PC at a serial port.

✳ Parallel cabling is a ribbon. It is connected to the PC at a parallel port.

The photograph on page 147 shows the rear of a computer and the various ports available.

CABLING	NOTES
Two-wire cabling	• The most basic form of electrical cabling • Has two copper wires separated by an insulator or dialetric • Tends to be used for low-speed transmissions, but if several of these cables are laid side by side, transmissions can suffer from interference called cross talk
UTP (unshielded twisted pair) cabling	• Pairs of insulated copper cable twisted together • Twisting reduces problems of cross talk and noise
Coaxial cable	• Similar to the cable used for TV aerials • Central copper conductor surrounded by a thick plastic sleeve • Plastic sleeve then surrounded by a braided metal shield and an outer plastic insulation
Fibre optic cable	• Does not use electrical currents to represent the data to be transmitted • Uses light impulses • Cable made of fine strands of glass, the light being internally refracted down the strands

TABLE 6.2 *Types of cabling*

CONNECTOR TYPE	NOTES
BNC	• Used with coaxial cables • BNC T often used to connect computers to LANs
DB9/DB25	• Used for the RS232 standard • Full standard has 25 lines but, in practice, only nine lines used
IEEE1394	• A high performance serial bus (HPSB), also known as i.Link, Lynx and FireWire • Faster than both the USB port and any parallel port
PS2/mini-DIN 6-pin	• Circular connectors (with 6 pins!) • May be used for a keyboard or a mouse
RJ-11	• Familiar plugs and sockets used for telephone connections
RJ-45	• Similar system to RJ-11; used in twisted pair LANs

TABLE 6.3 *Types of connector*

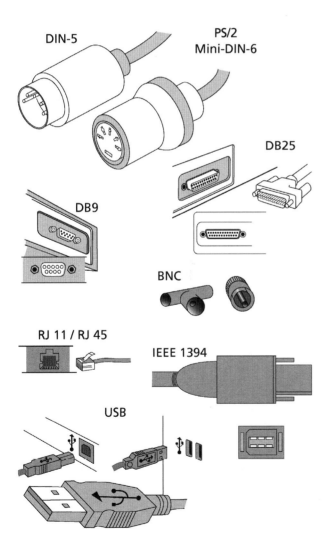

FIGURE 6.11 *Types of connector*

Having selected the correct port, you may fail to fit the connection firmly into the port, so that it is loose and not all pins make contact. If you move a PC, a loosely fitting connection may come adrift if any tension is put on the cable.

One or more pins could have been damaged. This can be avoided by careful handing, and taking care not to mis-orient the connection, i.e. trying not to put the connector into the socket the wrong way up.

It is important to use the correct cable orientation. Deciding which end goes where should not be a problem, but do make sure that at each end the cable is inserted the correct way up. Some connectors have an icon or some other mark to show which is the right way up, but with others the marking is not so obvious and you will need to take care not to force a connection. Notice also that some connectors are female (with holes) and others are male (with prongs).

Key terms

Cross talk is caused when electrical signals in one pair of wires creates a magnetic field, which then causes a signal to flow in another pair of wires.

RS323 is an American standard; the European equivalent is V.24. An RS323 port is a serial port.

Last, but not least, if everything else seems okay, it may be the wire within the cable that is damaged. Test for connectivity by using a multimeter (Figure 6.12), which measures the resistance in the cable.

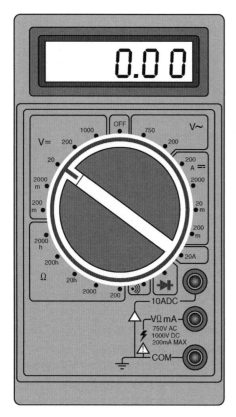

FIGURE 6.12 *A multimeter*

How to use a multimeter

1 Disconnect the cable at both ends.

2 Prepare the multimeter: to test ohms with an appropriate range.

3 Identify Pin 2 of the cable's connectors at each end (Figure 6.13).

If you cannot make a good connection at the female end, poke a wire segment (e.g. a paperclip) into the pin hole.

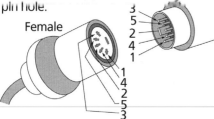

FIGURE 6.13 *Identify pin 2*

1 Touch one Pin 2 with the black probe, and the other Pin 2 with the red probe.

2 Check that the multimeter indicates continuity (by its reading, a beep or a buzzing noise, according to the model of multimeter).

3 If the multimedia does not indicate continuity, check all your connections.

4 If the connections are good and there is still no reading, then the cable is defective. Replace it.

Power supply voltage faults

If you experience an electrical shock from the case (other than ESD), there is a problem with the power supply unit (PSU), and one that can be dangerous. It is unlikely that you can fix it, so you should replace the PSU.

> ### Key term
>
> *ESD* stands for electrostatic discharge, an electrical shock caused when two objects (you and the PC) of uneven charge make contact. Electricity flows from high voltage to low voltage. So, if you are carrying a build-up of static electricity, you can give your PC a shock.

There are other situations which can also indicate problems with the PSU:

* After turning on the PC power, nothing happens.

* The power light is off.

* The fan is not blowing out air.

* When you power up, there is no beep or a continuous beep or a repeating short beep.

* The POST process reports an error in 020–029 range (refer to pages 223–225 for more information about the POST process).

* A parity error may be reported, indicating patchy power supply to a storage device or within the RAM.

In trying to locate the source of the problem, make these checks:

* Is there power to the wall socket?

* Is the power cord plugged in to the wall socket?

* Is the power cord plugged into the surge suppressor?
* Is the surge suppressor switched on and working?

If the power is available and plugged in, and the surge suppressor is working, then the fault lies with the power switch or the PSU. Either way: you may need to replace the PSU! Try using a replacement PSU to confirm that the old one is not functioning properly. If the original PSU is 'dead', then a replacement should solve the problem. However, problems can arise when a PSU begins to fail and starts to cause intermittent errors. These intermittent faults may lead you to think another component is at fault, for example:

* if a memory problem is reported, but cites a different address each time, it may be the PSU that is faulty rather than the memory
* if the PC reboots itself after a random amount of time, there could be a problem with the PSU.

Problems with the PSU fall into three groups:

* Physical failure means the PSU is not generating the right voltages on the right wires. This usually means the PC does not even boot up. You could check the voltages using a multimeter. A replacement PSU is usually the most cost-effective solution – and the safest option.
* Overloading can happen if you have too many devices configured with your PC. You will notice problems at startup when the disk drives use a lot of power to spin up to speed, or while working if you try to access the hard drive for example to save a file. If this is the problem then the replacement PSU will need a higher wattage than the previous one.

* Overheating is caused either by your blocking the passage of air, or – and it may seem strange – by not having the case closed. Like any air conditioning system, the cooling system in a PC relies on a clear airway, and one that directs air where it is needed, i.e. across those components that need the most cooling. So, if you leave the case open, the flow of air is not so cleverly directed and important components may overheat and, eventually, fail. Similarly, if some slots are not in use, the slot covers should be in place, so that gaps in the casing are restricted to those near the fan.

System setup

If your computer system is fully working, crashes should not happen at all. However, crashes are quite likely to happen after hardware or software upgrades. If you make any change to the configuration – either by replacing or upgrading hardware, or installing or uninstalling an application – and the system then crashes, it would be reasonable to assume that whatever you had done had caused the problem. If you take a system backup prior to making the change, it will be easy to undo your actions. Then, you should test the system to make sure that the fault does not lie elsewhere and that the timing – happening just after you had installed new hardware or software – was not just a coincidence.

Once you are sure that the fault lies with the change that you tried to make, you could try again, taking great care to make sure you do not introduce errors. Use the correct settings for software, and handle hardware gently. For example:

* an expansion board that has not been seated properly will not work
* memory chips have to be arranged in banks and have compatible speeds
* multiple storage devices need special settings so that the computer can recognise which is

first in line (called the master) and which follows (the slave drive).

If you think the hardware has been installed correctly, and the system still does not work, you may have a compatibility problem. The new hardware or software may clash with something already on your system.

✱ This may be an IRQ conflict: two devices trying to use the same system resource. You will need to check, through Device Manager (Figure 6.14), to see exactly which components are using which resources, and change the settings if necessary.

✱ It may be a program fault, as some software interacts badly with other applications. The software vendors should be aware of any

potential incompatibilities so your best source of information will be the vendors' websites.

You might also search the Microsoft Knowledge Base (Figure 6.15).

FIGURE 6.15 *Using Windows® help to search the Knowledge Base*

Sometimes, a system crashes for no apparent reason. Identifying exactly what is wrong will then involve the use of diagnostic tools.

Key term

IRQ stands for interrupt request. Peripheral devices gain attention from the CPU by 'interrupting' it. They place a flag to show they need processing time; the CPU notices the flag, deals with the IRQ and then resets the flag. Space is needed for this system resource, and each peripheral needs its own space. Clashes, i.e. two devices sharing the same IRQ space, can cause problems.

Theory into practice

1 Study the connections on your PC and identify examples of the different types, including male and female connectors.

2 Using the Internet, find out more about the standards RS323 and V.24.

3 On your PC, identify which cables carry serial communications and which provide parallel communications. Compare this with others in your group.

4 Use a multimeter to test for connectivity.

5 Research the Internet for more information about ESD. How can you guard against it?

6 On your PC, find out how to check the IRQ settings.

FIGURE 6.14 *Using the Device Manager to check use of system resources*

Diagnostic tools

Gaining experience of how a computer system should work, and what is most likely to go wrong, helps you to build up experience in troubleshooting. However, sometimes you need extra information to help you to pinpoint the cause of a fault. For this, you turn to diagnostic tools.

The BIOS and POST

The BIOS boots up the PC, i.e. it starts up a PC every time it is turned on. During the boot process, the BIOS checks the actual hardware configuration against the configuration data held on the CMOS chip.

The BIOS also tests the hardware to make sure everything is functioning as it should, running a POST during start-up boot sequence.

* Peripherals as specified in the configuration settings are confirmed as present and working properly, and all devices are tested for device speed and access mode.

* If there are problems at this early stage, the system will sound an error beep. The use of sound – available directly from a speaker on the motherboard – is necessary until the monitor is running properly.

* It then loads the device BIOS of the video adaptor into memory. From then on, communication can be onscreen – and instead of beeps, error codes can be displayed.

* Once all configuration setting checks are complete, the configuration is confirmed.

The POST ensures the integrity of the computer system. It ensures that the computer system – including all its peripherals – is ready for use. The POST can therefore prove to be the most important diagnostic tool available to you.

Once the POST process is complete, the BIOS checks the CMOS data to identify from which disk drive the operating system is to be loaded, for example drive A: (floppy drive) or drive C: (hard drive). It looks for the operating system's master boot record at cylinder 0, head 0, sector 0.

* If it finds the master boot record, the operating system is loaded and the code in the boot sector takes over from the BIOS.

* If the boot record is not where it was expected to be, the BIOS looks elsewhere, exhausting all disk drives before displaying the message 'No boot device available'.

The BIOS then handles the input and output of the computer, allowing the operating system to use particular features of hardware within the configuration. Figure 6.16 shows the information that CMOS holds about your configuration. This screen appears during the boot-up process.

If your BIOS is the most up-to-date version and is compatible for your PC, then you should

```
CPU Type        : AMD Athlon (TM)    Base Memory      : 640K
Co-Processor    : Installed          Extended Memory  : 130102MB
CPU Clock       : 1000MHz            Cache Memory     : 512K

Diskette Drive A : 1.44M, 3.5 in     Display Type     : SVGA
Diskette Drive B : None              Serial Port(s)   : 03F8
Pri Master Disk  : 40128MB           Parallel Ports   : 0378
Pri Slave Disk   : None
Sec Master Disk  : CDROM, Mode 4
Sec Slave Disk   : None


PCI device listing ...
Bus   Device   Func   Vendor   Device   Device Class         IRQ

0      7        1      1022     74B9     IDE Controller        14
0      7        1      1022     74BC     Serial Bus Controller 11
0      11       0      1037     9055     Network Controller    11
1      5        0      140E     662C     Display Controller    10
                                         ACPI Controller        9

Verifying DMI pool data .........
-
```

FIGURE 6.16 *On-screen display during boot-up*

experience no problems. However, if there is a problem, it is most likely to happen during the boot process.

Think it over...

Discuss situations which could result in your having to upgrade the BIOS.

If there are problems with your hardware that are detected during the POST, you will know because your PC will either beep or, when the screen driver has been loaded, a message will appear on your screen. If you hear beeps, the number of beeps indicates the problem. For example, continuous beeping may mean you have a PSU problem. Beep codes differ between different PCs so you will need to check the manufacturer's manual to interpret the codes.

Once the video has been checked, any error messages will appear on your screen. Figure 6.17 shows two examples: the first caused by the keyboard not being present; the second includes an error code and relates to a memory address error.

Having identified which device may be at fault, you might decide to disable that device. You could then test the system without the device; if it works, you have isolated the fault.

To disable a device, you will need to interrupt the BIOS POST and change the BIOS setting for the device. Figure 6.18 shows where you can find out how to interrupt the process; pressing a particular key during the POST process lets you enter the setup program.

Figure 6.19 shows the settings for a floppy drive. To disable the drive, toggle the entry for the floppy disk controller, i.e. click on it. Other devices can be disabled in the same way: change the setting from [Enabled] to [Disabled]. Similarly, you can enable a device by toggling the setting from [Disabled] to [Enabled].

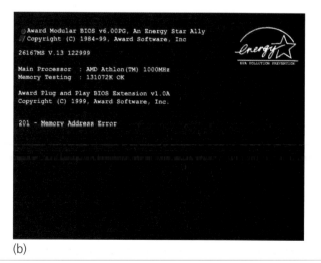

(a)   (b)

FIGURE 6.17 *Start-up error messages **(a)** when the keyboard is missing and **(b)** due to a memory address error*

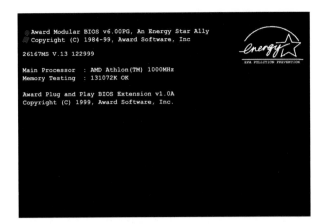

FIGURE 6.18 *Interrupting POST to enter the setup utility*

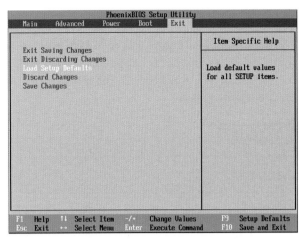

FIGURE 6.20 *BIOS setup utility*

```
                    PhoenixBIOS Setup Utility
        Advanced

            I/O Device Configuration              Item Specific Help

    Serial port A:          [Auto]          Configure serial port A
    Serial port B:          [Auto]          using options:
      Mode:                 [Normal]
    Parallel port:          [Auto]          [Disabled]
      Mode:                 [Bi-directional]   No configuration
    Floppy disk controller: [Enabled]
                                            [Enabled]
                                              User configuration

                                            [Auto]
                                              BIOS or OS chooses
                                              configuration

                                            (OS Controlled)
                                              Displayed when
                                              controlled by OS

    F1   Help   ↑↓  Select Item   -/+   Change Values     F9   Setup Defaults
    Esc  Exit   ↔   Select Menu   Enter Select ▶ Sub-Menu F10  Save and Exit
```

FIGURE 6.19 *The settings for a floppy drive*

If you make changes to the BIOS setup that causes the PC to stop responding, you will need to use the **Restore Defaults** command to erase your settings and go back to the original factory settings. You ought to have kept a note of settings that have been changed – settings that worked – since you obtained the computer system, and be able to return to where you were before you tried to make the latest changes to the BIOS. Figure 6.20 shows how to restore the defaults.

With each newly purchased computer system, the vendor will supply supporting utilities including diagnostic tools. You may also find free diagnostic software offered on the Internet, and there are also commercial alternatives available for sale.

Theory into practice

1 Restart your PC and note the key that is needed to interrupt the POST process.

2 Restart your PC and interrupt the POST process. Explore the menu system. Make a note of the CMOS settings for your PC.

3 Disable a device and exit setup, saving the settings. Then restart your PC and check that the device is no longer operational.

4 Restart your PC and enter setup. Enable the device. Restart your PC and check that the device is functioning again.

Think it over...

With others in your group, discuss any diagnostic software that you have used, apart from that supplied by the vendor of your system. Share your experiences.

Operating system utilities

The operating system offers many utilities. Disk Cleanup, Disk Defragmenter, Backup and Restore are discussed in section 6.1 (see pages 205–215). This section discusses other utilities that may help you to diagnose problems and find solutions, including Task Manager and System Restore.

Task Manager

The Task Manager (Figure 6.21) can give you some insight as to what is happening. To activate the Task Manager, right-click in the taskbar (or press **Ctrl-Alt-Delete**).

FIGURE 6.21 *Task Manager*

If an application hangs, i.e. the screen freezes, you could use the Task Manager to close down the application (Figure 6.22). You may then need to restart your computer before trying the component again.

Theory into practice

1 For an application of your choice, restore the default settings.

2 Experiment with using the Task Manager, for example to quit a program or to switch to another application.

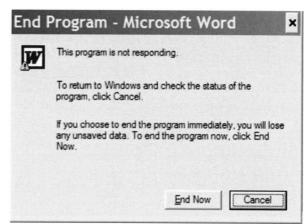

FIGURE 6.22 *Ending a program*

System Restore

If your operating system fails, there is little you can do, apart from restore the operating system. You will need an ERD (for older operating systems) and to use the Recovery Console (for more recent Windows-based operating systems). You will also rely on backups that you have taken, together with notes that you have made of settings to re-establish the system completely.

Think it over...

Within your group, share experiences of operating system failure, and how you overcame them.

Emergency repair disk: for Windows® 95 or Windows® 98

Ideally, you should create one or more of these emergency repair disks before anything goes wrong with the PC.

A startup disk is a bootable disk that includes the internal DOS commands (Table 6.4) and other useful command line utilities (Table 6.5) that will help you to troubleshoot when confronted with a PC that will not boot Windows®.

COMMAND	STANDS FOR	NOTES
CD	Change directory	In MS-DOS, what are now called folders, were referred to as directories, so the letter D appears in several DOS commands. CD changes the active directory to one that you specify. The prompt will then appear with a changed drive letter.
COPY	Copy	The COPY command allows you to COPY one or more files from one directory to another.
DEL	Delete	DEL deletes one or more files. The syntax allows wild card characters, so you can delete many files with the same extension with a single command.
DIR	Directory	
MD	Make directory	MD creates a new directory, i.e. a new folder.
RD	Remove directory	RD deletes a directory. The directory has to be empty before this command can be executed.
REN	Rename	REN renames a file.

TABLE 6.4 *Internal DOS commands*

UTILITY	NOTES
ATTRIB.EXE	Displays, and can be used to set and change, file attributes
EDIT.COM	A text editor that is not Windows-based
EXTRACT.EXE	Extracts files from compressed archives as on the startup disk
FDISK.EXE	The Fixed Disk Management partitioning utility, used to create and delete disk partitions
FORMAT	Formats both floppy and hard disks so that they can be written to
ScanDisk/Check disk	Checks the integrity of data on the disk and physically checks the surface of the disk

TABLE 6.5 *Windows based utilities*

A startup disk can only be made for the 9x versions. This is because later versions of Windows® (2000, XP) are based on Windows NT® rather than a command line operating system like DOS.

How to create an ERD

1 Place a blank floppy disk in your floppy drive.

2 Click on **Start** and go to the **Control Panel.**

3 Select **Add/Remove programs** and click on the **Startup Disk** tab.

4 Click on **Create Disk** and follow the prompts from there (Figure 6.23).

5 Label the disk 'Startup disk' and write the Windows version, the date and store this floppy disk somewhere safe.

The startup disk holds more files than could normally be held on a 1.44 Mb floppy diskette, so the files are compressed into an archive file.

When you use the disk to boot up, in Windows 98, you are given the option to start with or without CD-ROM support. If you opt for

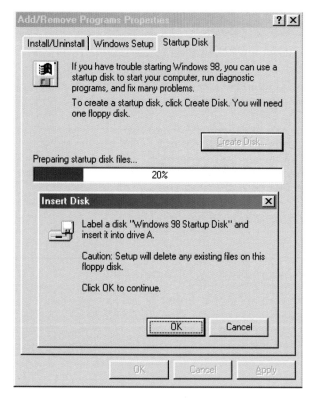

FIGURE 6.23 *Create disk sequence*

no CD support – or if you are in Windows® 95, and are not given the option – it will then create a RAM disk as drive D:, and it will extract the boot files from the archive on to that drive. This results in a renaming of the logical drives beyond D. You then need to manually correct the CONFIG.SYS and AUTOEXECT.BAT files. Since a Windows® 98 startup disk will work on a Windows® 95 PC, it makes sense to use this and take advantage of the CD-ROM support option. When the systems boots up, you are presented with command prompts, so you can start to troubleshoot straightaway.

Recovery Console: for Windows® 2000 and Windows XP®

For Windows® 2000 and Windows XP®, instead of needing an ERD, a Recovery Console is provided with the operating system.

Using the Recovery Console

1   The Recovery Console exists on the Windows® CD-ROM, so boot from that CD. It will start the Windows® Setup program.

2   Type R (for recovery) at the Welcome to Setup screen.

3   Type 1 to select the first Windows® installation of your PC.

4   Enter a password if asked.

You can install the Recovery Console on your hard disk, so it is more convenient to use. To do so, follow these steps.

1   While you are running Windows®, insert the Windows® 2000 CD in the CD drive. If it starts automatically, close it.

2   Click on **Start** and select **Run.**

3   Type D:i386\winnt32/cmdcons and click **OK.** (This assumes your CD is in drive D:. Amend the drive letter if necessary.)

4   Confirm by clicking on **Yes.**

5   After the installation is confirmed, click OK.

Having the Recovery Console on the hard disk makes the PC act in dual-booting mode. Each time you boot, you will see a menu and one of the options is Recovery Console.

Key term

Systems that have more than one operating system installed start up in *dual-booting mode* and give the user the option as to which operating system is to be loaded and run.

Once you are in the Recovery Console, you will see a prompt. Typing HELP (and pressing **Return**) will give you a list of available commands. These are the same ones as for Windows® 9x (Tables 6.4 and 6.5) plus some more as listed in Table 6.6.

Theory into practice

1   Create an emergency repair disk for a PC running under Windows® 9x.

2   On a Windows® 2000 PC, install the Recovery Console. Check that the menu appears when you start up.

3   Experiment with Windows® Recovery Console commands.

UTILITY	NOTES
BATCH	Executes batch commands in a given text file
DISABLE	Disables a given Windows® 2000 service or driver; see ENABLE below
DISKPART	Similar to FDISK, it manages hard disk partitions
ENABLE	Enables a given Windows® 2000 service or driver; see DISABLE above
FIXBOOT	Writes a boot sector on the disk
FIXMBR	Repairs the master boot record
LISTSYC	Lists all drivers, service and start up types that are available

TABLE 6.6 *Windows® Recovery Console commands*

Think it over...

Share your experiences of creating the startup disk and using the Recovery Console commands with your group.

Think it over...

Discuss with your group what other boot-up modes you have used.

Safe mode

In safe mode (Figure 6.24), the PC boots up as normal, except it does not load drivers for non-essential devices. It also uses a generic VGA display, i.e. needing the simplest of display drivers, rather than using the driver that you will have installed for your video card.

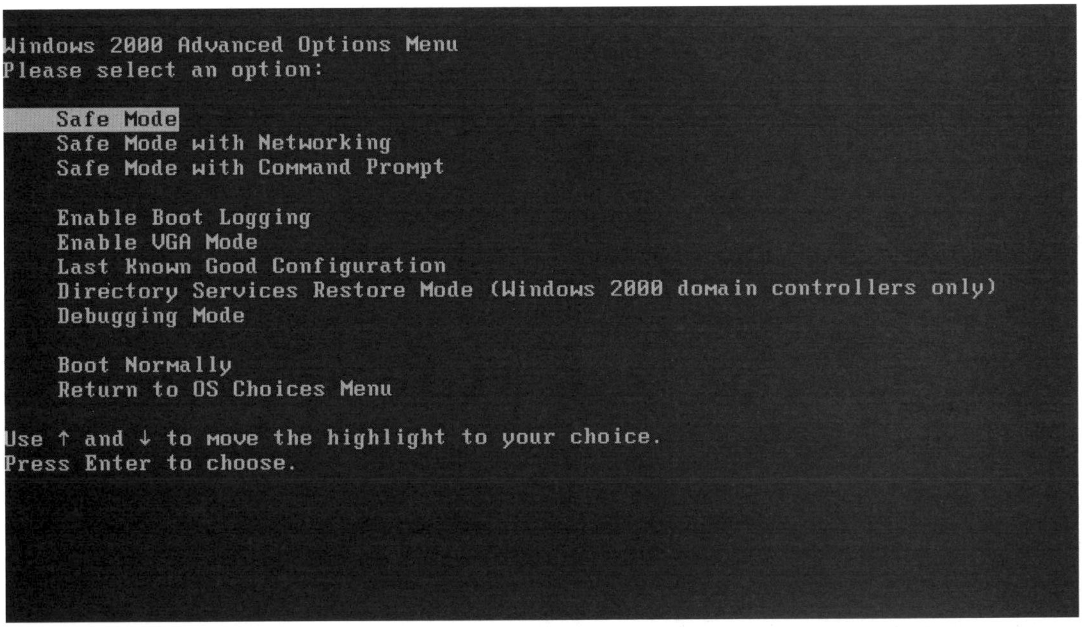

Alternative boot-up modes

Dual-booting is one of many modes that can be adopted when starting up a computer system.

```
Windows 2000 Advanced Options Menu
Please select an option:

   Safe Mode
   Safe Mode with Networking
   Safe Mode with Command Prompt

   Enable Boot Logging
   Enable VGA Mode
   Last Known Good Configuration
   Directory Services Restore Mode (Windows 2000 domain controllers only)
   Debugging Mode

   Boot Normally
   Return to OS Choices Menu

Use ↑ and ↓ to move the highlight to your choice.
Press Enter to choose.
```

FIGURE 6.24 *Safe mode*

Booting up in safe mode avoids any startup problems that may be due to device conflicts. For example, if you installed new hardware or software and it prevented Windows from starting, safe mode would allow you to uninstall the offending hardware and/or software and undo the damage done. You then have a working PC again, although you have not managed to install the new device or the new software.

Once you have done this you should restart the PC normally before using any applications. It is unlikely that applications will enjoy much functionality in safe mode, and you will want the display to return to the normal standard. Also, you should study carefully any documentation for the new hardware, visit the vendor's website and, maybe, download a fix, before you attempt the installation again.

Theory into practice

1 Disconnect one device from your computer system and start up. Check that it reports the device as missing.

2 Restart in safe mode. Disable the device.

3 Restart and check that no missing device is reported.

4 Turn off the computer, reconnect the device.

5 Restart, interrupting the boot and enable the device. Check that everything now works.

Manufacturers' manuals and websites

Manufacturers produce the hardware and software, so they should be the best sources of technical information about their products and services. Some will be supplied as printed materials and some will be supplied online.

* Manufacturer's documentation should be available for all hardware. This can be referred to if a component fails and you need to replace it. Manufacturer's documentation for software

may be provided in various forms, according to who might read it.

* Printed manuals may be produced to provide detailed specifications for a piece of hardware or a software package. Because they contain so much detail, manuals may only suit the most technical reader.

* Printed procedure guides and notes tend to provide a more user-friendly source of help for non-technical users.

* Most manufacturers put as much information as possible on their website. This cuts down the number of queries they might have to handle, and reduces the need for costly hardcopy manuals and guides. It also enables them to provide up-to-date information.

* Manufacturers will include FAQs (frequently asked questions) on their website. This again reduces the number of queries that might need to be handled. Many of the most common problems can be solved this way.

* Manufacturers supply hardware compatibility lists (HCLs) so, before buying extra components to upgrade your PC, you can check that they will work on your PC configuration.

* Manufacturers also make recommendations as to the minimum requirements needed before their software will run successfully on a particular PC.

Theory into practice

1 In a small group, look at a selection of printed manuals. Check how the information is presented. Decide on three advantages of having information available in this form compared with online provision.

2 The SpaceBall is an input device which offers a user the ability to manipulate 3D objects on the screen with simultaneous control of all six degrees of freedom. Using a browser such as Google, search for information on Microsoft's HCLs to find out what versions of Microsoft Windows® support this product, and any special requirements, for example hard disk space.

Assessment activity

Use the information you have learned in sections 6.1 and 6.2 to create an onscreen technical support manual describing the routine maintenance procedures, schedules, tracking procedures and troubleshooting strategies you would recommend for the system you installed in Unit 4.

Assessment hint

✓ Manual contains brief instructions for maintenance and troubleshooting.

✓✓ Manual contains clearly presented detailed instructions.

✓✓✓ Manual contains complete and easy-to-follow instructions that enable someone else to maintain the system.

 ### Signposting for e-portfolio evidence

Save this work in your e-portfolio. It could contribute towards covering evidence (b).

Knowledge check

1 What is cross talk? How can it be avoided?

2 What is the European equivalent to the American RS323 standard for serial communication?

3 Give examples of what a multimeter might be used to test.

4 What is ESD? How can it be avoided?

5 What is a power surge? How can you protect against a power surge?

6 What is meant by overloading the PSU? How can this problem be fixed?

7 How might a PSU suffer from overheating? Why is this to be avoided?

8 What is meant by a compatibility problem?

9 What is CMOS?

10 Describe, briefly, the POST process.

11 What is an ERD used for? What system is used on more modern operating systems?

12 What is dual-booting?

13 Under what circumstances might you boot up in safe mode?

14 What are FAQs?

6.3 Upgrades

This section covers advising on and implementing simple hardware and software upgrades required by either the user (to fix problems or to improve functionality or performance) or by the manufacturer.

Hardware upgrades

This section considers installing particular devices: floppy drives, IDE devices such as a hard disk, SCSI devices such as CD drives and DVD drives and additional RAM.

Key term

SCSI stands for small computer systems interface. An expansion card, installed on the motherboard, allows the PC to support more peripheral devices than the IDE channel. The SCSI then copes with the systems resources such as IRQs for the devices that are attached in this way.

Installing/replacing a floppy drive

A floppy disk drive is attached to the motherboard by a data cable and to the PSU by a power cord.

✱ The data cable could be attached to an adaptor card or it could be connected directly to the motherboard. It is a 34-pin two-connector flat

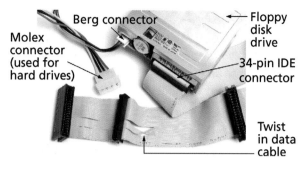

Molex connector (used for hard drives)

Berg connector

Floppy disk drive

34-pin IDE connector

Twist in data cable

Floppy drive connections

ribbon cable with a coloured stripe down one edge. This is to help you to connect the cable the right way around. There is also a twist in the ribbon. The drive attached behind the twist is recognised as logical drive A, and is therefore the default drive when you boot up your PC.

✳ The power cord is a four-pronged cable that is inserted into the back of the drive.

Key term

The disk drives are given names: A, B, and so on. Because a hard disk can be physically partitioned into more than one drive, say, C and D, these are called *logical drives* (as opposed to the physical drives). By default logical drive A is assigned to the floppy disk drive.

You may need to replace a floppy drive, or just install a new one. Installing an extra one should be straightforward: you just need a spare slot, a power cable and a data cable, and the fixing screws. If you don't have a spare power cable, you can use a Y-splitter so that both floppy drives work from the same power cable.

Key term

A *Y-splitter* is a connector that allows you to run two cables together so that they only need one power source.

Before removing a floppy drive – even one that does not appear to be working – you need to make sure that you can boot the computer from another floppy drive, or from the hard disk. Otherwise, if things don't work after the

replacement, you will be faced with a dilemma:

✳ Was it not working before you started working on it?

✳ Did you do something to stop it working?

To avoid this situation, check that you know the condition of the PC before attempting to replace a floppy disk drive.

How to remove a floppy disk drive

1 Turn off the computer and open the case.

2 Before you disconnect the data cable, notice its orientation: the coloured edge shows pin 1 and this is matched with pin 1 on the circuit board. Notice also the position of the twist in the data cable: this determines which drive is (logical) drive A and which is (logical) drive B. Disconnect the data cable from the motherboard.

3 Disconnect the power cable from the PSU. Be careful not to apply too much pressure when disconnecting the power cable; you might damage the board.

4 Undo the fixing screws that hold the floppy drive in its bay. Be sure not to remove any other screws, and keep the ones that you do remove safe.

5 Check whether you need to slide the drive out of its bay, or whether you have to lift a catch to release it.

How to add a replacement floppy drive, or to install a new one

1 You may need to remove a cover by reaching inside the PC and pushing the cover out.

2 Slide the floppy disk drive into the bay, until the front of it lines up with the front of the computer case.

3 The screw holes on the side rails of the case should also line up with those on the drive. Use the fixing screws to hold the drive in place.

4 Connect the drive to the motherboard using the data cable. Be careful with the orientation; match pin 1 on the board with the coloured edge of the ribbon. Check also the position of

the twist; this determines the setting for drive A/drive B.

5 Connect the drive to the PSU using the power cord.

6 Turn on the PC and test the drive. If it works, turn off the PC and replace the casing. If the PC does not work, turn the PC off before checking all the connections.

Installing IDE/EIDE devices

Key terms

IDE stands for integrated drive electronics. This means the device has some intelligence in a built-in controller, rather than a separate chip as part of the motherboard chipset. This means drive technology can progress without changes having to be made to the chipsets.

EIDE means enhanced IDE – a more sophisticated version of IDE, so-called at one time because it supported a particular new technology. Nowadays, all such devices are EIDE and are often just called IDE.

If you want to have a hard drive and a CD drive, you could attach both as IDE devices.

✳ The hard drive may be connected to the primary channel or IDE1 connector on the motherboard using an IDE 40-pin 80-conductor ribbon data cable. This is similar to the CD cable (see below) – and is easily mistaken for it – but each conductor has a ground wire and hence there are 80 instead of 40 conductors. If you use the wrong cable, the hard drive will not work properly.

✳ A CD drive – or another hard drive – can then be attached to the secondary channel or IDE2 connector on the motherboard using an IDE 40-pin 40-conductor ribbon data cable. The CD drive is also attached via an audio cable. Audio cables are usually notched to help you to plug them in the correct way. (If you connect it the wrong way around, you may hear no sound when you power up.)

How to install a hard drive

Installing a hard drive is similar to installing a floppy drive (see above) except the cover does not need to be removed.

1 Set the jumpers (Figure 6.25). If you are installing a second drive, you will need to check the settings for the first drive; they will need changing for example from 'single' to 'master'.

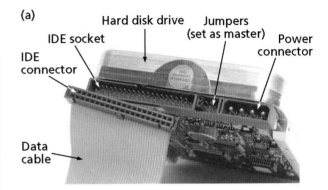

FIGURE 6.25 *Master/slave settings on a hard drive*

2 Put the drive into the bay. You may need to screw the drive into place, or there may be mounting rails that fasten to the side of the drive so that you can click the drive into place.

3 Connect the drive to the motherboard using the ribbon cable. You need to select the correct cable: 40-wire or 80-wire, depending on the specification of the hard drive. They are the same width and both fit into the same connector. The cable has two ends: one for the motherboard and one for the drive. There is also a connector midway which you might need to use for another device. However, if you are installing a second IDE device, and the second IDE connector is available on the motherboard, use that – you may achieve better performance if the two devices are not sharing a cable. The end that is furthest from the midway connection belongs in the motherboard. Be sure to orient the cable correctly: the red stripe along the edge of the cable indicates wire 1, and this needs to match pin 1 on the connector. The connector may have a '1' or a small triangle to show which end is pin 1.

4 Connect the drive to the PSU. (This is more straightforward.) Select a free connector from the PSU and plug it into the drive. The orientation should not be a problem: the connector is rounded on the top edge so it will only fit one way.

Your BIOS should automatically update itself when you next switch on the PC. Having installed a hard disk, though, you may decide to partition it, and you will need to format the hard disk.

Installing SCSI devices

The requirements for the SCSI card will be available with documentation supplied with it, but you can also look on the Internet for this information. SCSI devices may be internal devices or external SCSI devices. Internal SCSI devices, such as disk drives, are connected to the SCSI expansion board from inside the PC. The internal SCSI connector can be one of two types according to the device type:

* The SCSI A cable looks very much like the IDE ribbon cable but has 10 more wires (50 instead of 40).

* The SCSI P cable has 68 wires and a D connector, except that the two rows of pins each have 34 pins, so it is not the traditional arrangement of pins that you will see.

When you install two disk drives on the same IDE bus, you have to identify one as the master and the other as the slave. Similarly, if you install a chain of devices on a SCSI, each device needs to be identified. Otherwise, it will not be clear which data belongs to which device. This involves making the jumper block settings – or moving a thumb wheel or counter – to assign a unique identifier to each device in the chain. If you use jumpers, you may see three pairs of pins, each pair of pins labelled with the numbers 1, 2 and 4 (each one being a power of 2: 2^0, 2^1 and 2^2). Figure 6.26 shows how to set the jumpers to assign each of the numbers from 1 to 7 to any one device in the chain. Note that if you intend to boot up from a SCSI hard drive, this device will need to be assigned the identifier '1'. The board takes the identifier '0' and the operating system will

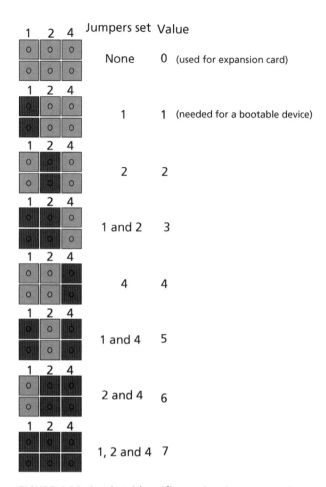

FIGURE 6.26 *Setting identifiers using jumper settings*

expect the next device to have the relevant information for booting up.

The final device in the chain needs a special setting so that the PC knows that there is nothing beyond it. The device is terminated by setting yet another jumper:

* When the jumper straddles the pins, the device is the terminating device.

* If the jumper does not straddle the pins, there is at least one more device beyond this one in the chain

Having physically installed a SCSI device, when you turn on the PC, it should recognise the new hardware and have already configured it. There are a couple of 'extras' to remember though.

First, the CD-ROM installation lets you prepare a CD-ROM or CD-RW drive for use, but only allows you to read from it. To enable you to write to a

CD-RW, you need to install a CD writing application, such as Adaptec's Easy CD Creator, which is usually supplied with the drive, or could be bought separately. This software provides a wizard to guide the user through the writing process.

Second, if you install a DVD drive – or some combination drive that allows you to read/write to CD-ROMs as well as reading DVDs – you need also to have an MPEG decoder. Material on the DVD – sound and pictures – is compressed and has to be decompressed before you can view it. The MPEG decoder may mean another expansion board to install, or it may be done using software. If you do have a separate MPEG decoder board, this too has to be connected to the DVD drive.

How to install an internal SCSI device, for example CD-ROM drive

1 Set the jumpers to assign a unique identifier to each device, and to identify the terminating device.

2 To install (or remove) an internal SCSI device, such as a CD drive, the cover needs to be removed. Slide the CD drive in from the front of the case and push it into place until the screw holes line up and it is flush with the front of the case. Don't screw it into place just yet. Wait until you are sure it is working.

3 Connect the CD-ROM drive to the SCSI card using the CD cable.

4 For a CD-ROM drive, if you intend to listen the audio CDs, you need also to connect the drive to the sound system. An audio cable should run from the CD-ROM drive to the sound card on your motherboard – or direct to the motherboard, if there is a built-in sound support on the motherboard. You will need to check the documentation to make sure you are using the correct cables.

5 Connect the CD drive to the PSU unit.

Adding additional RAM

In adding (or removing) RAM, your objective may be to increase (or decrease) the capacity of your PC. You need to decide which type of memory to add/remove: SRAM and/or DRAM.

You also need to take into account the memory access time, i.e. the time it takes for data to be made available. You may want the fastest possible time, but this will be limited by your PC's capability of adding faster memory. Avoid mixing memory access speeds within a single PC; do this by filling each memory bank with the same type, speed and technology of memory.

If you must mix speeds, put the slowest memory in the first bank. Then, if auto-detection is being used to determine the access speed, the slowest speed (in the first bank) will be applied to all banks. (If you put the faster speed in the first banks, other memories may be accessed at too fast a rate, with disastrous results.)

There will be a maximum amount of RAM that can be supported by the motherboard; this information will be in the manual for the motherboard, or you could find it using the Internet. So, before adding extra memory, you need to find out how much memory is installed already. Turn the PC off and then on; this will put it through its POST diagnostic routine and this displays the amount of RAM installed.

Alternatively, open the case, and identify the RAM chips. Each RAM chip should display a manufacturer's name, its type, capacity and speed. Adding up the capacity of each will give you the total RAM for your PC.

There are three main types of packaging for memory chips: DIP, SIMM and DIMM.

Key terms

DIP stands for dual inline packaging; the pins are arranged in two rows either side of the chip.

SIMM stands for single in-line memory module; the SIMM package is a mini-expansion board. The edge connector has either 30 or 72 pins, and its capacity ranges from 1MB to 16MB.

DIMM stands for double inline memory module (twice the size of a SIMM).

* The pins on either side of the DIP chip need to be inserted into holes on the motherboard, arranged in banks. The width of the bus determines the number of DIP chips that are needed to make a bank. You must fill one bank before you start the next bank. The pass-through mounting allows a direct connection to the circuitry beneath the DIP socket.

Align the pins with the holes   BIOS chip

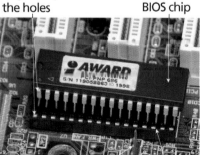

Notice the jumpers here   Socket for BIOS

Inserting a DIP chip

* The Pentium processor uses a 64-bit path to memory and SIMMs are 32-bit, so you need to install them in pairs. You must fill each SIMM bank before moving on to the next.

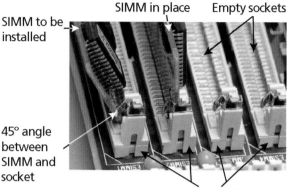

SIMM in place   Empty sockets
SIMM to be installed
45° angle between SIMM and socket
SIMMS are installed in pairs

Installing a SIMM

* A DIMM can be installed into any available memory slot.

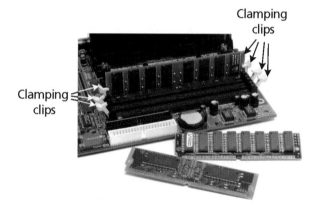

Clamping clips
Clamping clips

Installing a DIMM

Theory into practice

1 Examine the insides of a PC to identify various hardware components: floppy drive, hard drive, CD drive. Check the connections.

2 Look to see what memory chips have been installed. What types of memory, and how much of it have been installed? Compare this with the information provided by the system (going through the Control Panel).

Software upgrades

Evaluating existing software provision

When investigating the current software provision, ask yourself these questions:

* What operating system is installed for each computer?

* What applications have been installed on each computer?

* Which particular components of applications have been installed? What components, if any, of those applications have *not* been installed?

* Which versions of each application have been installed?

* What licence arrangements have been made?

* What utilities – including virus checkers, e-mail, internet access – have been provided for the users? What protection is in place against viruses and hackers?

* What facilities are available for using e-mail and internet browsers?

The answers to these questions will help you determine what sort of software upgrade is appropriate. This section considers two main types of software upgrade: upgrading to a new operating system, and updating applications using manufacturer updates such as service releases.

Upgrading to a new operating system

To upgrade a PC from one Windows® operating system to another, such as Windows® 2000, first it is important to check that the upgrade is possible. For example, it is not possible to upgrade from Windows® 3.x or Windows® Me to Windows® 2000. The documentation with Windows® 2000 spells out what can and cannot be done by way of an upgrade. The documentation is supplied on the CD and includes tools to help you to check for compatibility. So, either you will be able to upgrade your system, or you will have prepared it for a clean start.

When you are ready to start, you will need to run the appropriate setup utility. As with most things on a PC, there is more than one way of accessing the setup program:

* From the command line for DOS or Windows® 9x, type: EXECUTE WINNT.EXE.

* From the Start Run dialogue box in Windows® 9x or Windows NT®, type: EXECUTE WINNT32.EXE.

* For a system that can be upgraded, placing the CD-ROM in the drive should automatically load and run the setup program.

There are then three basic stages of installation:

1 During setup loading, the installation files and SETUPLDR are copied from the CD to the hard drive. This either creates or modifies the BOOT.INI file.

   SETUPLDR loads NTDETECT.COM and NTBOOTDD.SYS and does some initial checking of hardware, loads the device driver for the hard disk controller and passes control to the kernel. Depending on how this stage started, the end-user licence agreement (EULA) and the product ID dialogue are displayed at this point (Figure 6.27).

2 During text-mode setup, the screen goes blue. The operating system makes an inventory of the systems hardware (motherboard, CPU and hard drives), creates the Registry, detects PnP devices, partitions and formats the hard disk,

FIGURE 6.27 *Setup loading*

and then creates the files systems (or converts any existing system NTFS file system).

3 In the GUI-mode setup, the Setup wizard appears on the screen. This detects and configures devices found on the PC and creates Setup log files in the installation directory on the hard drive.

When asked if you want to run a System Compatibility report, select **Yes**. This will reveal any incompatibility problems with hardware and/or device drivers. If any device drivers are missing, you will need to load them.

The final stage is to create a start-up disk. The onscreen instructions will guide you through this stage.

Theory into practice

1 Install Windows® 2000 – or another operating system – as directed by your teacher. Make brief notes on the process.

2 Make a start-up disk.

Installing manufacturer updates

Microsoft release upgrades to their software regularly to fix errors that are found in their software, and to improve security against hackers. These are called service releases, each one being numbered so that it is clear how up to date your software is at any given time (Figure 6.28).

The Microsoft® website homepage leads to the Update service.

There is an option to check what updates you might need, and then to install them, if you so wish.

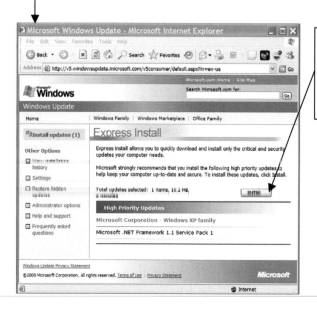

FIGURE 6.28 *Microsoft Service Packs*

6.4 Internet connectivity

The Internet is one huge network. For those who are connected to it, it provides access to information and a wide variety of services. As with any other client–server network, you can identify two categories of computer on the Internet:

✱ The Internet clients – the end-users – enjoy access to the Internet to send and receive e-mails, and surf the web.

✱ The Internet server provides its clients with an access point, from where the clients can tap into the Internet. Some ISPs also retain e-mail messages for their clients, rather than the client downloading them using communications software like Microsoft Outlook®.

Connection methods

There are a number of methods of connecting to the Internet. You need to know about each of these and be aware of their advantages and limitations. This knowledge, along with information you will obtain about a client's existing computer system, their requirements and their budget, will help you to make informed decisions to meet the client's communication needs.

To access the Internet, you need some form of communications software. E-mails can be received and sent using a communications package such a Microsoft Outlook®. Section 6.5 (page 242) focuses on e-mails and the software you would choose. Then, to surf the Internet you need a browser.

To send data files from one computer to another via a telephone or a wireless link, you need also need some additional hardware – a modem. The modem may be internal (housed within the processor case of the computer) or external (Figure 6.29).

The Internet client computer can then be connected to the ISP computer using a telephone line in a number of ways:

* A cable link may be available, for example through a television cable service. This is only available as a residential service, but does provide good transfer speeds, for example from 512 KBps to 2 MBps.

* The modem, internal or external, may be linked to a telephone line, and a dial-up connection made each time the client wants to access the Internet. This system is available wherever there are phone links, but it does tie up the phone line and is slow (56 KBps).

* The client may have a broadband connection. The broadband supplier may provide a special (external) modem which allows data transfer at the same time as voice conversations – or a connection may be via a mobile phone, using Bluetooth technology. The external modem may be connected via a USB port. Broadband connections offer a much faster service – and it is possible to use the one telephone line for broadband and 'normal' telephone conversations at the same time.

* With ISDN phone lines, the data transfer speed is much faster, for example from 64 KBps to 200 KBps.

Communication may be by satellite rather than by telephone line – or part of the 'journey' may be by telephone line, part by satellite.

* In a one-way satellite system, the satellite is used for downloading only, and the satellite dish can be used to receive TV signals. A modem is needed and dial-up networking (DUN) achieves 56 KBps for uploading and 512 KBps for downloading.

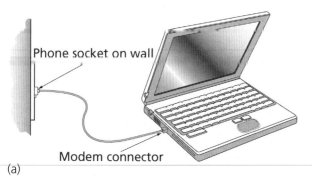
(a)

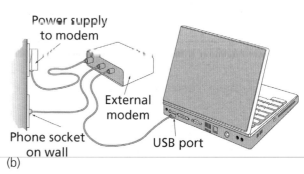
(b)

FIGURE 6.29 *Modem options: (a) internal and (b) external connections to a telephone line*

✱ A two-way satellite service requires a special two-way satellite dish, but this does improve the speeds of transfer, for example from 512 KBps to 1.5 MBps.

There are also options to have special T1 or T3 lines connected from the phone company to an organisation, and these provide very fast speeds, for example from 1.5 MBps to 44 MBps. These are expensive and would suit larger organisations that have many employees all requiring internet access. Such large organisations are most likely to set aside at least one computer to act as a web server for the other client computers on the organisation's network.

For the very largest organisations, fibre optic technology offers an expensive but very fast internet connection: 155 MBps.

Setting up a system for Internet access

For Windows® systems, there are two main types of communications link: those that require dial-up networking (DUN) and those that don't. Those that do not require DUN tend to be supplied with their own setup software. So, the cable, DSL (digital subscriber line) or satellite service provider will supply a CD-ROM and/or specific instructions for setting up the service. You may be supplied with a 'box' which acts as a modem and is to be connected to a USB port. You will have to consult the provider's instructions and follow them carefully.

To access the Internet using DUN (Figure 6.30), you would probably use a modem (internal or external) and a telephone line.

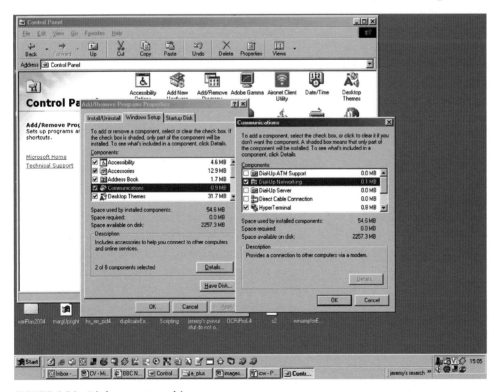

FIGURE 6.30 *Dial-up networking*

Standard modems are operating systems neutral (i.e. independent of the OS) and need a generic device driver. The Windows® modem is an internal PnP device that needs a special device driver as supplied with the Windows® operating system.

An ISP provides a host computer to which users can connect by dialling in. This host computer manages all communications, storing e-mails, web pages and files for its subscribers. The host computer is connected to the Internet and this allows the subscribers to communicate with other computers and hence other users who subscribe to other ISPs.

Note that not all outgoing connections are made to the Internet. It is possible, instead, to connect to a corporate server. For example, you may be working from a laptop and need to access data on the company network. Having dialled up, you can then log on to the corporate LAN and gain access to the WAN.

Key term

LAN stands for local area network.
WAN stands for wide area network.

Theory into practice

1 Methods of connection – and choosing the most effective – depend on a user's needs and what is currently available. Research the Internet to find out what methods of connection are available, and at what cost.

2 ISPs are in direct competition with each other, so they vary the services they offer, and the prices they charge in a constant battle to win subscribers. Research the Internet to find out what ISPs are currently offering, and at what cost.

3 Compare your findings with others in your group. Who found the best deals?

Knowledge check

1 Distinguish between one-way and two-way satellite systems.

2 List the different methods of connecting to the Internet and the advantages and limitations of each.

3 Distinguish between Internet clients and the Internet server.

4 What is an ISP? What is its role?

5 What hardware is needed to give a PC access to the Internet?

6 What is a modem? What does it do? Where might it be housed?

7 What is broadband? How might this connection be achieved?

8 What is DUN?

9 Explain these terms: PnP, LAN, WAN.

6.5 E-mail

E-mails are used to communicate electronically. The body of an e-mail message is best used for brief, informal messages. Although it is possible to write a long letter using e-mail, the formatting features are limited (or may not be acceptable to the recipient). Instead, if you want to communicate a more complex structure of information (such as a business letter, diagram or table), you should prepare it using the most appropriate software, save it in a document and then send as a file attached to an e-mail message.

Spam and filtering

E-mail was once seen as a boon: a quick and easy way to communicate. Nowadays, the downside is beginning to be realised. E-mail traffic is increasing and many users have to cope with e-mail overload:

✳ Some users complain that downloading e-mails takes too long; and when they open their inbox, it is full of spam.

✳ Some users return from holiday to find an inbox with hundreds of e-mails, and then have problems working out what to look at first. Some employees receive nearly all their work correspondence via e-mails and have a similar problem in that they receive too many e-mails to process in a day, and need to be selective about which ones to read and which ones to action first.

These two issues – spam and e-mail overload – can be addressed by filtering e-mails. Most e-mail software providers include filtering features to cut down on spam. Yahoo, for instance, put any mail that might be spam into a Bulk Mail folder (Figure 6.31).

Even if your e-mails are normally downloaded into an Outlook inbox, this bulk mail is not downloaded until you look at it and confirm that it is not spam. So, you should aim to do this regularly – say, once a week – just in case there is a bulk mailing that you do want to receive, for example from a club that you belong to, which needs to send legitimate bulk mailings to all members, or a notice from your bank to say a statement is ready to download.

Bulk mailing does have its advantages for those sending e-mails. See page 245 for more information on bulk e-mailing.

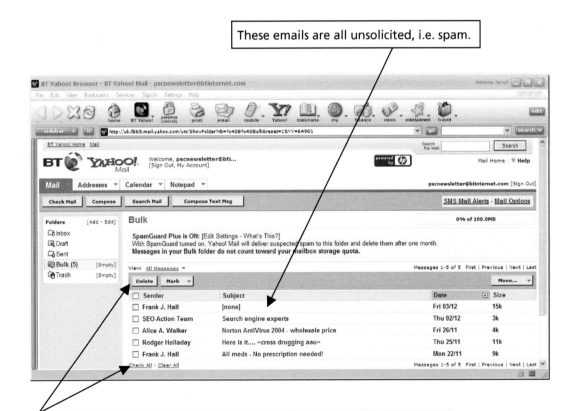

These emails are all unsolicited, i.e. spam.

It takes two seconds to Check All and then Delete all spam emails. This is preferable to letting these emails go straight to your inbox, waiting for these emails to download – and reduces the risk of virus attack.

FIGURE 6.31 *Bulk inbox in Yahoo*

You may also want to filter the mail so that you can identify the most important e-mails and process them first. Or, if incoming e-mails are from different clients, or colleagues working for the same organisation, it is possible to have separate inboxes, one per client or maybe one per project. Then, by setting up rules, incoming mail can be automatically redirected (Figure 6.32) from the main inbox into specific inboxes, according to the sender (and/or the content).

As mail arrives, the user can therefore prioritise the e-mails – simply by opening the inboxes of the most important colleagues and

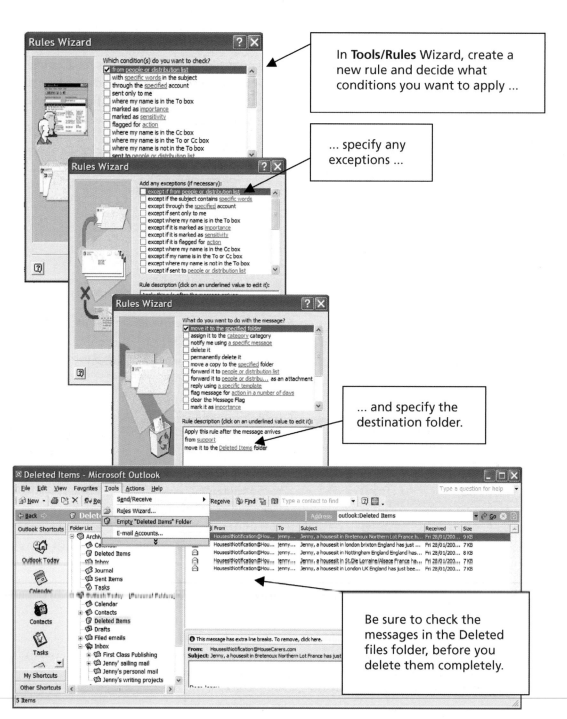

In **Tools/Rules** Wizard, create a new rule and decide what conditions you want to apply ...

... specify any exceptions ...

... and specify the destination folder.

Be sure to check the messages in the Deleted files folder, before you delete them completely.

FIGURE 6.32 *Using the Outlook® Rules Wizard*

clients before looking at those of contacts whose e-mails that may not be so urgent.

Users can set up their own spam filter, for example, by setting up a rule that sends unwanted mail straight to the Deleted files folder. For example, if you are being bombarded with e-mails offering you a degree, you could automatically transfer e-mails which have the word 'degree' into the Deleted Items folder. However, before you permanently delete the e-mails in the Deleted folders, you should glance through them to make sure there is nothing of interest to you.

Theory into practice

1 Check what ISPs such as Hotmail offer as protection against spam.

2 Check that filtering options are available on the e-mail software you are using.

3 Compare your findings with others in your group.

Automatic features

Communications software offers a number of automatic features.

* You can assign a flag to an e-mail to show its level of importance: low, medium of high. This may appear as an exclamation mark beside the e-mail entry in the inbox.

* Digital signatures offer a level of protection for the receiver of an e-mail; it confirms who sent it. Refer to Section 6.7 (pages 250–258) for more detail about this feature.

* Out of office responses can be set up by an e-mail account holder, so that incoming e-mails can be replied to, instantly on receipt, whenever the receiver is away (for example at a conference or on holiday) so that the sender of the original message knows the recipient will not be able to respond immediately. The message can include details of when the person will return, and who should be contacted instead, with contact numbers. Using

this feature can reduce the number of e-mails that await you on your return (if people wait until you come back before continuing to send messages), but more importantly, it provides the senders with timely feedback. They are not left wondering why you have not replied.

Theory into practice

1 Find out how to attach a high level of importance to an outgoing e-mail.

2 Find out how to filter all highly important e-mails into a separate inbox, using filtering techniques.

3 Find out what facilities your e-mail software provider offers for digital signatures.

4 Find out what software setup is needed to allow individual users to create out-of-office responses to incoming e-mails.

E-mail address book distribution lists

Setting up a distribution group (Figure 6.33) to include all the people to whom an e-mail needs to be sent, can save time if this group often have to be sent an e-mail.

Theory into practice

1 Set up a distribution list to send an e-mail to all the others in your group. Include yourself on the list.

2 Send an e-mail to your distribution list. Check whether the e-mails went straight to an inbox, or were trapped by some filtering option.

Restrictions on use

E-mail attachments can be of any type. For example, if you need to prepare some material for a project planning meeting, you could produce a schedule using spreadsheet software, a map explaining how to reach the meeting using graphics software, and a covering letter

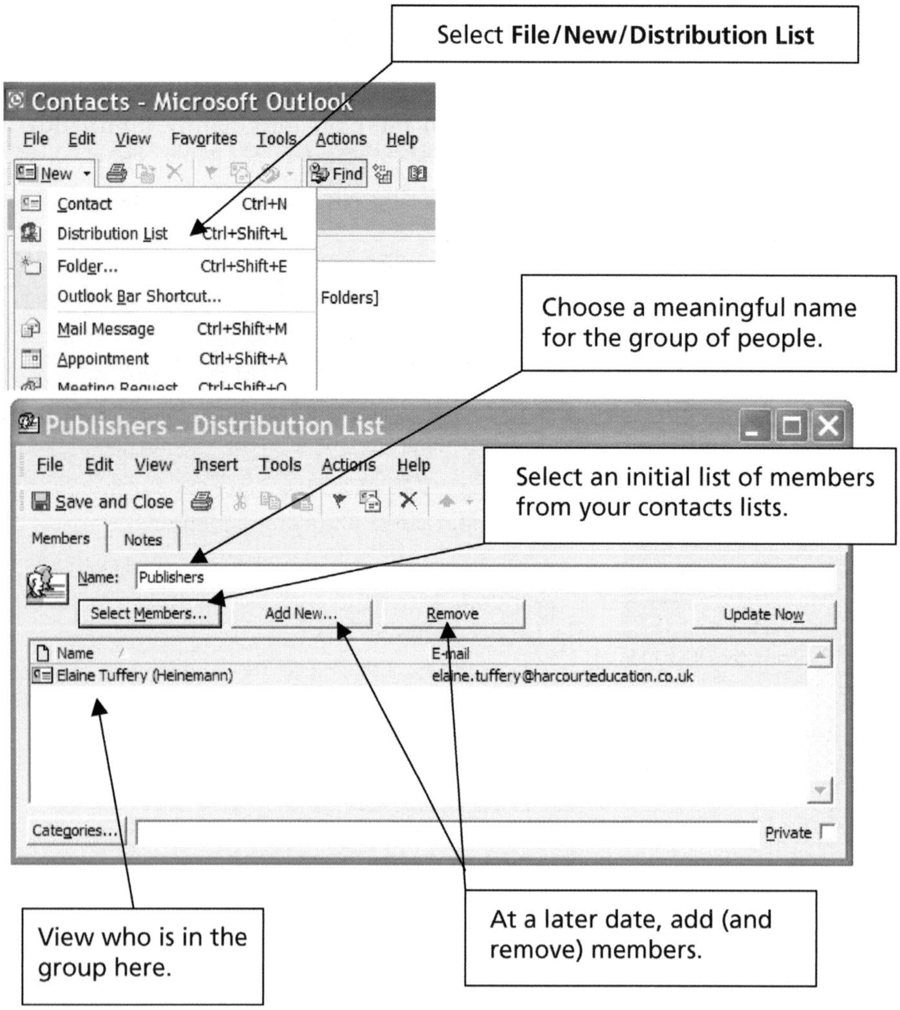

Select **File/New/Distribution List**

Choose a meaningful name for the group of people.

Select an initial list of members from your contacts lists.

View who is in the group here.

At a later date, add (and remove) members.

FIGURE 6.33 *Setting up a distribution list in Outlook®*

including the agenda using word-processing software. All three can be saved separately and then attached to a single e-mail, and addressed and sent to all those who are invited to attend the meeting.

However, e-mails with attachments take longer to upload and download. Some ISPs put a limit of the size of the inbox and/or the attachment for any single e-mail. Zipping a file before attaching it reduces the size of the attached file, and so reduces the upload/download time (Figure 6.34).

Key term

Zipping a file involves using *compression* techniques to reduce the size of the file, without losing any data within the file.

Theory into practice

1 For one ISP, find out what restrictions apply to various grades of subscription, in terms of size of inbox, number of e-mails that can be sent/received, size of attachment and traffic during a given period.

2 Compare this with the restrictions set out by a competing ISP.

3 Decide which provide the best service, and then compare notes with others in your group.

Virus checking

E-mails offer viruses a route into your computer system. Files can arrive at a PC as attachments to

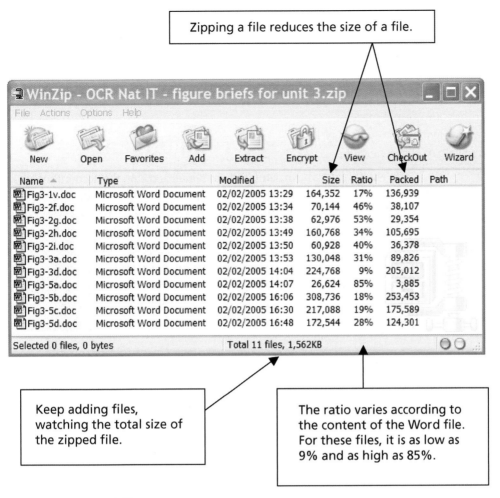

Zipping a file reduces the size of a file.

Keep adding files, watching the total size of the zipped file.

The ratio varies according to the content of the Word file. For these files, it is as low as 9% and as high as 85%.

FIGURE 6.34 *Zipped files*

e-mails. If the file was sent from a PC that was infected, the receiving PC can become infected as soon as the attached file is opened. You should therefore avoid opening e-mails from people and e-mail addresses you do not recognise. You should also be wary of e-mails from people you do know – in case the e-mail is generated by a worm. Virus protection software can protect your computer system from virus attack through e-mail attachments. Refer to pages 251–254 for more information about anti-virus software.

Think it over...

Discuss why you should never open an attachment unless you are absolutely sure that the source is reliable and/or you have used a virus check on the attachment.

Allow/disallow HTML e-mails

HTML e-mails pose a particular threat because the HTML code may include malicious code. However, you can disable HTML, or enable them if you are happy to take the risk.

Theory into practice

1 Find out how to enable or disable HTML using your e-mail software.

2 Carry out some research to discover what proportion of companies insist on HTML being disabled in incoming e-mails.

Web-based mail

There are two main ways of accessing e-mails.

* Using web-based e-mail, you can access your e-mails through the Internet. This is particularly useful when away from your normal place of work, and the only access available to you may be through an Internet café or someone else's PC. However, it is relatively slow, and you have to be online while processing your e-mails. You may also face restrictions such as not being able to access attached files.

* You can have your e-mails downloaded into software that is resident on your PC, such as Microsoft Outlook. You only need to be online for as long as you are receiving or sending e-mails and can work offline otherwise (which is more economical, unless you have broadband access). However, unless you filter your e-mails in some way, anything that is sent to you will be downloaded, and this can take a long time, potentially slowing down your computer.

Legal requirements

In setting up an e-mail account, the accountholder has to agree to abide by a code of conduct in the nature of e-mails. Account holders are also bound by the Computer Misuse Act and other legislation such as the Obscene Publications Act. To ensure that employess do not abuse the privilege of using the Internet, employers may impose legal restrictions on employees regarding Internet activity. Employees who break these rules may face dismissal.

Theory into practice

1 Explore the features available on your communications software. Work through any tutorials supplied (Figure 6.35) so that you are fully conversant with the various formats of e-mails and how these impact on the features available and the security issues.

FIGURE 6.35 Microsoft Outlook™ tutorials

2 Consider the suitability of e-mail software for office-based staff, those who sometimes need to be able to access e-mail at home, as well as mobile workers who need to access e-mail on the move.

3 Find out what code of conduct applies to e-mail account holders for one ISP.

6.6 Collaborative working

Some web-based tools – such as group e-mail, instant messaging, web conferencing and videoconferencing – allow employees in different physical locations to work together, to share information, and to contribute to shared documents despite the distance between them. This technology can have positive effects on productivity:

* Time that might have been spent travel to a common venue for a meeting is available for other, more important, activities.

* Costs of travel, hiring meeting rooms, subsistence and overnight accommodation are reduced.

* Discussions can happen in real time, when you want them to, rather than being spread over a series of e-mails or letters.

Group e-mail helps people to work collaboratively because people whose e-mail addresses are included in a distribution discussion list can join in a discussion, by choosing the 'Reply to All' option when sending a reply.

Instant messaging, for example, using Yahoo (Figure 6.36) or Messenger via Windows allows two or more people who are online at the same time to have a text-based conversation in real time.

Web conferencing is an extension of instant messaging. The participants view a web-based presentation but can interact using audio links. So, it is possible to have an ongoing negotiation or

FIGURE 6.36 *Instant messaging*

debate. Some software vendors offer courses via web conferencing (Figure 6.37).

Video conferencing goes one more step further than web conferencing. Requiring a webcam at

FIGURE 6.37 *Macromedia conferences*

both ends of the 'conversation', or at all the venues involved, it means everyone who is participating can see what is happening at the other venues. Some distance education courses include video and/or web conferencing as part of their teaching and tutorial services.

Theory into practice

1 Identify examples of web-based tools being used within local organisations.

2 For instant messaging, identify the hardware and software needed. Specify what the communicators need to do to set up the link between them, prior to any conversation.

3 Focusing on web conferencing, research the Internet for companies that offer training in this way. What hardware and software do you need to take part in one of these conferences?

4 Identify the hardware and software needed to set up a video conference. Compare these costs with those of travel and subsistence for one full-day meeting of three people, currently located in three different countries, for example England, Bulgaria and New Zealand. (Don't forget to take into account time zone differences.)

5 Set up and use at least one of the web-based tools for collaborative working.

Assessment activity

1 Prepare a presentation describing and evaluating the features of four different types of web-based tools for collaborative working; and a demonstration of the setup and use of one of them. Include screen shots that illustrate functions of the software.

2 Deliver your presentation to an audience. Make sure the slides convey key messages only, and that your speaker notes/hand-outs fully explain the main features and benefits of this way of working, and mention any limitations.

 Signposting for e-portfolio evidence

Save this work in your e-portfolio. It could contribute towards covering evidence (c).

Knowledge check

1 Explain the difference between bulk e-mail and group e-mail.

2 What is the benefit of instant messaging over e-mailing?

3 What is the difference between web conferencing and video conferencing?

6.7 Internet security and legal issues

Employee use of a company's Internet connection to undertake non-work related activities is a waste of the company's resources (the time and money wasted during such activities, as well as bandwidth being used). There could also be serious legal repercussions if, in conducting such activities, the employee doesn't follow the company's directives and introduces viruses or other harmful entities.

Lack of security awareness among users within an organisation can result in virus infections which damage data files and may bring down a computer system for a time, or the release of sensitive data to those outside the organisation.

Educating each employee in methods that will minimise such risks is therefore important. Some organisations extend this to insisting that all employees follow an internet access code of practice, and contracts of employment include a clause demanding adherence. Dismissal is then used as a threat to anyone who disregards the stated internet access policy. This may seem extremely harsh, but it needs to be remembered that a slip by a single individual could result in disaster for an entire organisation.

Theory into practice

1 Collect and study the Internet access codes of a number of organisations. Note any common points.

2 Draft a proposal for a suitable Internet security environment. Compare your proposal with others in your group. Discuss any differences between your proposals.

3 Explain why an organisation should have an Internet access policy and what it should cover.

You will need to be able to advise clients on potential threats and recommend adequate internet security measures, including: virus protection software, hackers and firewalls, spyware, data mining, e-mail address protection, denial of service attacks and digital security certificates.

Virus protection software

The Computer Misuse Act (1990) defines electronic vandalism and makes it a criminal activity to write viruses that can cause damage to software and data, and disrupt the operation of a computer system. The Act also covers hacking through a firewall and theft of data. See Units 1 and 2 for more information on legislation (pages 10–11, 21–2 and page 63, respectively).

Key term

Hacking is the unauthorised access to a computer system. See page 254–255 for more details.

Types of virus

The least offensive form of a virus (see Unit 4, page 137) is the impostor virus. An e-mail will warn you of a virus and suggest that you check whether you have a particular file somewhere on your hard disk. When you check, you find that indeed you do have this file. You set about deleting the offending file as per instructions given in the e-mail, only to find that it was a hoax. Apart from the waste of time, and the stress involved in thinking you have a virus, you may delete an important file and reduce the functionality of your PC software.

Think it over...

Within your group, share experiences of Imposter virus attacks.

Other forms of virus can positively damage your PC data.

* A boot sector virus plants itself in the boot sector of every bootable floppy disk or hard disk. This guarantees that it will run each time you boot up. These viruses spread from disk to disk, and hence from PC to PC if you take a floppy disk from one PC to another.

* File viruses are infected program files with extensions of .exe or .com; the program is run when the file is opened, and then causes whatever damage it was designed to do.

* Macro viruses hide within the macro of applications such as Microsoft Word® and Excel®. Such viruses spread from one open document or spreadsheet to another.

* BIOS viruses are the most harmful; they attack the flash BIOS, overwriting the system BIOS and making the PC unbootable.

Other forms of virus are trojans and worms.

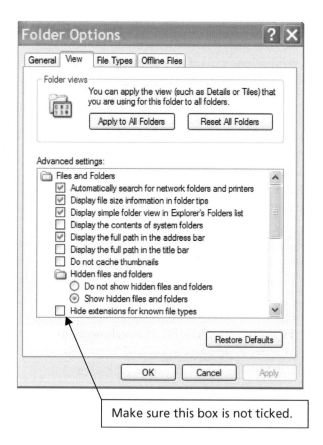

Make sure this box is not ticked.

FIGURE 6.38 *Hiding file extensions*

for which you want to check the file extensions.

2 On the menu bar, select **Tools** and then, from the drop down menu, select **Folder options**.

3 Click on the **View** tab and make sure that the item that reads 'Hide extensions for known file types' is unchecked (Figure 6.38).

How viruses infect a PC

Viruses show themselves in various ways (Figure 6.39).

Viruses can be introduced to a PC by one of three sources.

＊ If you save data onto a floppy disk from one PC that is infected with a virus, and then read that floppy on a second PC, the virus can infect the second PC. This can happen when a file is opened from the floppy, or when you boot from the floppy disk. It is advisable, therefore, to check a floppy disk for viruses before introducing it to your computer system.

Some viruses hide by using a double file extension. A file may be called harmlessfun.jpg.vbs. The 'vbs' part shows that it is a Visual Basic program – and a potential virus. However, if you have opted to hide file extensions, this virus program will show in a folder listing as harmlessfun.jpg – and look just like a JPEG image file to you.

How to display file extensions

1 From My Computer or using Windows Explorer®, select the folder containing the files

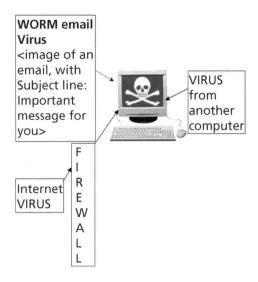

FIGURE 6.39 *Symptoms of a virus attack*

* Files can arrive at a PC as attachments to e-mails. Refer to pages 251–252 for more information about how this might happen.

* Viruses may infect a PC during access to the Internet. A firewall may protect the computer from such attack (see page 255 for more information about firewalls).

Because viruses are programs, they can only infect programs. However, having done so, they can wipe or corrupt files on your hard disk and/or make your PC crash and/or become inoperable.

> ### ✳ REMEMBER
>
> If you accidentally leave a floppy disk in the drive and boot up, you will get an error message at start up. Do not remove the disk and press any key as suggested. If the floppy disk has a virus it has already infected your PC and has transferred itself to the memory. Instead, remove the floppy disk and press the reset button – this dumps the memory (losing the virus infection) and starts to reboot again.

How to combat viruses

Almost at the same rate as virus writers invent new viruses, anti-virus software vendors produce updated versions of their software. Anti-virus software attempts to trace viruses by looking for the virus signature. This sequence of characters can be recognised by the anti-software vendors, having analysed the virus code. To prevent discovery, however, virus writers adopt cloaking techniques:

* Polymorphing: Just as cells in a diseased body mutate, this type of virus is designed to change its appearance, size and signature each time it infects another PC, thus making it harder for anti-virus software to recognise it.

* Stealth viruses: Hide the damage they cause so that it looks like nothing is wrong with your computer system, until the computer crashes without warning.

* Directory viruses: Corrupt a directory entry so that it points to itself instead of to the file the virus is actually replacing.

Anti-virus programs

The only defence against viruses is to subscribe to a reliable anti-virus software vendor's virus protection service (Figure 6.40). Regular scanning of the PC is recommended, as is immediate update of virus software as soon as a new one is released.
There are a variety of products available:

* Virus scanner software is the most common form of anti-virus software. The scan is initiated by the user.

* Startup virus scanner software runs each time the PC is booted up. It checks only for boot sector viruses.

* Memory-resident virus scanner software stays in the memory and checks incoming e-mails and browser documents. In this way, it automatically checks the environment in which your PC operates.

* A behaviour-based detector is a form of memory-resident virus scanner software that watches for behaviour that would indicate the presence of a virus.

Anti-virus software vendors maintain a database of information about viruses: their profiles and signatures. A profile includes the barest details of a virus such as its name, when it was first discovered and what effect it has. The virus signature is unique string of bits, or the binary pattern, of a virus. It is like a fingerprint in that it can be used to detect and identify specific viruses.

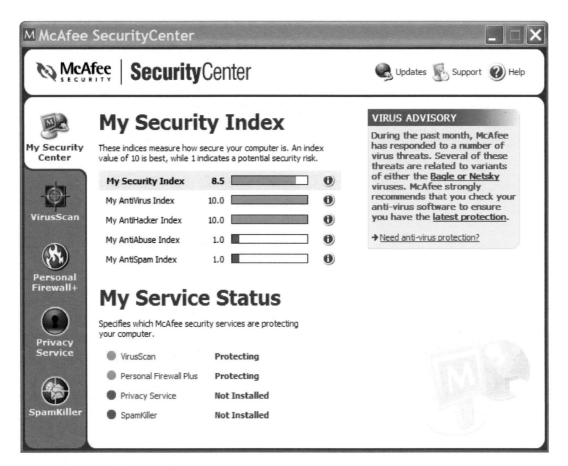

FIGURE 6.40 *McAfee Security Center*

Users who subscribe to an online anti-virus protection service may have this database – called a DAT file – downloaded to their PC automatically each time an update is released. Other users may receive an e-mail telling them that an update is available.

You will be asked to identify which parts of your PC you want checked. You might want to check only a floppy disk, or a CD, from which you intend to read files. You should, however, on a regular basis, check your hard disk too.

Installing a firewall, having the most up-to-date DAT file, scanning regularly and avoiding opening e-mails that look like they may contain viruses is all that PC users can do to protect themselves.

If a virus is detected

If the software detects a virus, a pop-up screen informs the user and may offer options: to quarantine the file (i.e. move it somewhere it can do no harm), to repair the file (i.e. delete the virus but retain the file) or to delete the file. If possible, your anti-virus software will attempt to solve the virus problem for you by cleaning the infected area. When this is not possible and the file has to be deleted, if it is important, for example, an important systems file, you may need to reinstate it – from your backup files. See pages 210–211 for details on backing up.

Anti-virus software vendors may include the option to create a rescue disk. This is a bootable disk that also contains anti-virus software. If your system fails due to a virus and will not boot, this rescue disk should solve the problem. Write-protecting the disk, for example by physically removing a notch and/or slipping a notch across, will prevent it becoming infected with a virus.

Hackers and firewalls

A hacker is a person who tries (successfully or otherwise) to gain unauthorised access to a

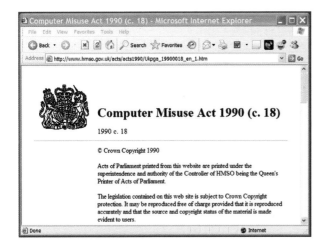

FIGURE 6.41 *Computer Misuse Act*

computer system, to beat an organisation's security system or break through its firewall.

A firewall is a program that builds a protective barrier around one or more computers, so that when they are connected to a network, only authorised programs can access data on that computer system. This should prevent hackers from accessing the system.

The Computer Misuse Act (1990) is aimed mainly at computer hackers and virus writers. The Act makes hacking into a system a criminal offence, punishable by imprisonment and/or a fine, even if it is not done maliciously (Figure 6.41).

Theory into practice

1 Research the Internet to find out the offences introduced by the Computer Misuse Act (1990).

2 What length of sentence may be given to a hacker who gains unauthorised access to a computer system, with the intention of transferring money from your bank account to their own?

3 Download a firewall, and experiment with it to check how it works.

Spyware

Spyware is any application that tracks your behaviour in accessing websites without your knowledge or consent. There are a number of ways spyware can work.

* The application may incorporate a keylogger which records your every keystroke. This may include your password or other sensitive data such as a bank account number.

* Toolbars that you download to make browsing easier – such as those offered by Google and Yahoo – have the capability to record all your activity through that toolbar, and to send this record back to the toolbar supplier.

* Driveby downloads are programs that may be downloaded to your computer, maybe while you are downloading something else, often without your knowledge or consent. For example, these can be initiated during a visit to a web page, or by opening an HTML e-mail message.

* When you visit a website, the website software may be written so as to leave a tracking cookie on your computer. These cookies do not pose a security threat. If you have a firewall, your computer may reject attempts to leave a cookie on your computer, but you may need to grant access for some software; otherwise, you cannot access online help pages, and updates automatically.

Anti-spy software can identify spyware and list them. Figure 6.42 lists the tracking cookies found during a scan; note the option to remove them. However, next time you visit the same websites, the cookies will reappear, so you might as well leave some of them where they are, especially if there are websites you visit frequently and you don't want them to lose the personal data you have previously given.

Theory into practice

1 Research the Internet to find out more about spyware.

2 What software is available – and how much does it cost – to protect a computer against spyware?

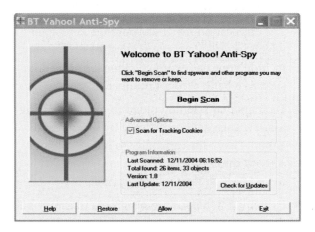
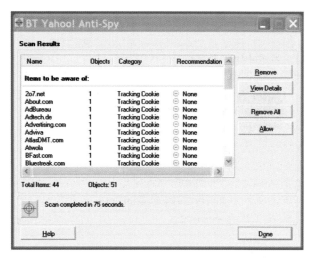

FIGURE 6.42 *Spyware*

Data mining

Data mining is the analysis of data in a database using tools that look for trends or anomalies in the data without knowing what the data actually means. The term originates from marketing and it involves finding underlying structures and relationships in large amounts of data, so as to help make marketing decisions, as described here.

* Since the introduction of Reward cards at superstores, retailers may look for possibilities for cross-selling by analysing patterns of products frequently purchased together.

* Response modelling involves predicting which customers are likely to purchase based on their purchase history. This can be used to target direct mail more accurately and hence more cost-effectively.

* Segmentation and profiling involves understanding customer segments, i.e. groups of customers who share the same characteristics, such as income bracket. By profiling archetypal customers, i.e. identifying typical types of customers, and by matching incomes and other data, such as age, to purchases made, supermarkets can more carefully target their marketing.

These are all valid and legal examples of data mining in a marketing context. Apart from the marketing applications of mass mailing/telemarketing, data mining has proved useful in medical diagnosis and computer intrusion detection. It can also be used to detect fraud, for example observing a pattern of spending on a credit card that is different from the usual pattern may indicate that the card has been stolen or the details used fraudulently.

Data mining is a bit like gold mining: sifting through lots of ore to find the occasional valuable nugget of gold. With the growth of internet usage and e-commerce, it has become very easy to collect data on web users. Data mining of website logs can provide information on who has visited a site, what they have purchased, and can provide a huge database of information to use for marketing purposes. It can also be used to measure website usage, the success of sales efforts and customer profiling.

Think it over...

With others in your group, discuss in what ways data mining is a potential threat.

Theory into practice

1 Search the Internet for articles on data warehousing.

2 Find out about these categories of data mining: case-based reasoning, neural networks, data visualisation and fuzzy query analysis.

E-mail address protection

Some spammers scan the entire web for e-mail addresses to add to their lists. These spam robots can recognise e-mail addresses because the address follows a standard format, including an '@' symbol separating the two parts of the e-mail address. So, because it is so easy to spot a string of characters like myusername@mydomain.co.uk, one method of cloaking or disguising your e-mail address is to replace every character with its ASCII equivalent code.

The e-mail address then translates into a series of codes, each one starting with &# (to show it is a hexadecimal character) and each one ending with a semi-colon. However, this cloaking method is straightforward and recognisable and spammers might scan for it too. So, an even better cloaking device is to convert random characters in your address. However, this is more complicated and you would need special coding to make this happen.

Theory into practice

1 Find out the ASCII code for the characters A to Z.

2 Convert your e-mail address into a string of ASCII characters.

3 Use this 'address' to send yourself an e-mail. Does it work?

4 Research the Internet to investigate the availability of a cloaking service for e-mail address protection.

Denial of service attacks

To create a denial of service attack, a webserver is flooded with false requests for information which ultimately crash the site, thereby preventing it from providing its usual webservice.

There may be legitimate hits on a server that have the same effect: the Inland Revenue's website experienced difficulties close to the deadline for online tax returns to be filed at the end of January 2005. Because the volume of hits was too high, the system slowed down to the point where it was unusable – causing much frustration to the taxpayers who were hoping to file their returns electronically.

Theory into practice

1 Research the Internet to find out how and why denial of service attacks happen.

2 Find out the meaning of the terms: authentication request, sniffer filter.

Digital security certificates

As a security measure for internet e-mail messages, it is possible to obtain a digital ID – or digital security certificate – from an external certifying authority, such as VeriSign. This has to be set up for use on your communications software. Each user on the system then needs a special password, called a token. This allows them to send digitally signed messages. Digitally signed messages give some level of security that the e-mail is from the person it says it is from. This is important if an e-mail is used to confirm the agreement of a contract, for example to purchase a product or service.

If you do not have a digital ID and want to make a purchase over the Internet, you normally have to provide an e-mail address. A confirmation is then sent to the e-mail address given – and the recipient of that confirmation then has the option to deny they placed the order. Similarly, if you subscribe to a service, you may receive an e-mail asking you to confirm that you actually did subscribe. This is to prevent automatic subscription generated maliciously to increase the amount of e-mail traffic to the point of slowing done the service for everyone.

To send encrypted messages, you also need the recipient's digital ID.

Signposting for e-portfolio evidence

Save this work in your e-portfolio. It could contribute towards covering evidence (d).

6.8 ICT skills

In supporting your client, you will have used a range of ICT skills.

* You will have implemented hardware and software upgrades.

* You will have employed troubleshooting techniques.

* You will have used system maintenance utilities.

* You will have received and sent e-mails and used other e-mailing features.

* You will have set up and used web-based collaborative software tools.

UNIT ASSESSMENT

1 Read back through this chapter to remind yourself of the skills you have developed since starting on this unit.

2 Check the contents of your portfolio to make sure that you have included evidence of all your ICT skills and all the documentation required.

GLOSSARY

Analogue
A physical form of information; radio waves for your FM radio are analogue.

Anchor
Labels a particular position on a web page, so that you can then jump to that position from elsewhere on the same page or from another page within the website.

Animation
A sequence of stills which, when run together, form a moving picture.

Applet
Short for application and describes a very short program, i.e. a piece of code, written for use on the world wide web.

ASCII
American Standard Code for Information Interchange. Each letter and character has a unique ASCII code in the range 0 to 127; for example, the letter M is 77.

ATX
AT is an old IBM computer that became the standard for computer cases and power supplies; ATX is an extension of the AT standard.

Audio cable
Cable with three wires which runs from the CD-ROM drive to the sound card, enabling the PC to play audio CDs through the sound card and out through speakers.

Automatically processed
Processed by computer or other technology.

Banner
An image link used to advertise a sponsor of a web site.

Bar code
An internationally recognised, machine-readable symbol widely used in a number of applications where items need to be recognised, such as supermarkets, stock control and asset management.

Bespoke
Something made for individual use or to meet individual requirements, such as a custom-made computer system.

BIOS
'Basic input output systems'; it is a computer chip which controls the computer startup process.

Bit
'Binary digit'. A bit is either on or off and is represented by '1' or '0'.

Bitmap
An image that stores each pixel (image element) as a two-dimensional grid.

Blog
(A shortened form of 'weblog') a web page that serves as a publicly accessible personal journal for an individual.

Bookmark
Add a wesbites URL (uniform resource locator) to a list of favourite sites which can then be revisited quickly, by clicking on the bookmark.

Boot sector
A sector on the disk set aside to hold programs that control the loading up of other programs, from which the system is booted up.

Broadband
A term for a higher speed internet connection for the home or small office user. The connection speed varies from 128 kbps to more than 3 Mbps, depending on the service provider. The speed is constantly increasing as technology improves; soon home internet access will be of a comparable speed to the speed of the average corporate network ten years ago.

Broadcast
A network message that is sent to everyone on the stem that is listening.

Browser
A program which lets you view web pages on the internet.

Button
A feature that looks like a button and – when you click the mouse while the cursor is positioned on it – some event happens.

Byte
8 bits = 1 byte.

Chat rooms
A method of communication provided by the internet. Users key in messages about some topic of interest which are displayed in real time on the PCs of all the users who are currently in the same chat room.

CMOS
Complementary metal-oxide semiconductor, an essential hardware part of the motherboard, which holds the BIOS, an essential software part of the motherboard.

Comma separated values (CSV)
A text file which can be used to store database records. Each field on the file is separated by a comma, and each record is separated by a carriage return. CSV files are sometimes used to transfer data between systems since they can be easily exported and imported.

Command
An instruction given to the central processor by a computer program (set of instructions).

Configure
Customise the computer system for a specific purpose.

Cookie
A text file that a web server can store on a user's hard disk when they view a page from that server.

CPU
Central processing unit, the technical term for the processor that runs the computer.

Credit card
A card allowing purchases which are added to a monthly account. A monthly statement lists all transactions, some or all of the outstanding balance must be paid.

Cross talk
Caused when electrical signals in one pair of wires create a magnetic field, which then causes a signal to flow in another pair of wires.

CRT (cathode ray tube)
The type of monitor that uses the same technology as a TV.

Data controllers
Those who control the contents, and use of, a collection of personal data. They can be any type of company or organisation, large or small, within the public or private sector.

Data subjects
The individuals to whom the personal data relates.

Debit card
A card issued by a bank allowing a person to make payments from a bank account to anyone

who can accept the card. The payments are taken more or less immediately from your bank account.

Defragmentation
Tidies up the disk, making available clusters that are no longer needed (because files have been deleted) and collecting the separate elements of fragmented files together.

Digital
This signifies the data of the computer systems as binary 0s and 1s, or as ON/OFF electrical pulses.

DIMM
Double inline memory module.

DIP
Dual inline packaging; where pins are arranged in two rows either side of the chip.

DOS
Disk Operating System.

Drag and drop
Select an object (an image or some highlighted text) by clicking on it. Then, without releasing the mouse button, drag the object using the mouse and place in the required position on the web page, where it is dropped by releasing the mouse button.

DRAM
Dynamic RAM; the cheaper RAM, but one that does need frequent refreshing – i.e. rewriting – of the data.

Dual-booting systems
Have more than one operating system installed and give the user the option as to which operating system is to be loaded and run.

DUN (dial-up networking)
An option for connecting to the internet.

E-books
Digital books designed to be viewed onscreen. E-books can contain animated video clips and audio files, animated diagrams, 360-degree stills and photographs that can be zoomed into, etc.

EIDE
Enhanced IDE – a more sophisticated version of IDE, so-called at one time because it supported a particular new technology.

Electronic Data Interchange (EDI)
A method used by businesses to transfer documents electronically over the Internet or other network.

Enclosure connector
A cable from the case to the motherboard for the reset button and various lights.

Encryption key
A secret numerical code applied to a message so it is transmitted or stored in indecipherable characters. The message can only be read after it has been reconstructed through the use of a 'matching key'.

Encryption software
Software which scrambles message transmissions.

ERD (emergency repair diskette)
A rescue disk or a startup disk, created during or after installation using RDISK.EXE.

ESD
Electrostatic discharge, an electrical shock caused when two objects (you and the PC) of uneven charge make contact. Electricity flows from high voltage to low voltage so, if you are carrying a build-up of static electricity, you can give your PC a shock.

Exposure to risk
An estimate of how likely it is that an event will take place. The estimation is based on a number of factors. Insurance companies, for example, estimate how exposed to risk a person or organisation is when they calculate premiums.

Feasibility study
An investigation when trying to resolve a problem within a given system. The feasibility study provides a stepped approach to collecting, analysing and reporting systems information.

Fibre optic technology
A light beam travels down a thin glass tube with a refractive coating at the speed of light, does not suffer from noise or other disadvantages of the cheaper cabling options.

File transfer protocol (FTP)
The set of rules used for exchanging files over the Internet.

Firewall
Hardware or software that filters incoming internet traffic. It prevents applications from accessing data on the PC it protects.

Flash BIOS
A rewritable type of BIOS you can change using special software, rather than having to change the whole chip. However, it is vulnerable to attack by a virus which can also overwrite the chip, making it unusable.

Flash
An application used to develop animations and interactive applications for websites.

Fragmentation
When files have to split up into sections and are saved in separate locations on the disk because there is no contiguous space available that is big enough to hold the entire file.

Functionality
The general quality of something being useful, useable or having a use. Specifically in ICT it is a feature or element within an operating system which improves the use of the application, device or operating system.

Gantt chart
A project plan which displays a time line, with tasks allocated a time span, to show how the interaction of tasks can affect the completion date of the project.

Global gateway
A gateway that can be accessed, at any time, anywhere (providing you have the necessary

hardware and software) and by anyone. It is an international network of information and resources that is not restricted by geographical or cultural boundaries.

GUI (graphical user interface)
What the user sees in order to be able to use the computer system.

Hacking
Unauthorised access to a computer system.

Hit counter
Records the number of visitors to a website to date.

Hotlink
Text or an image which, when clicked on, takes you to another page within a website or to another website altogether.

Hotspot
Similar to a button except the link is text which normally appears in a different colour, to distinguish it from other text that is not a hotspot.

HTML
The abbreviation for hypertext markup language, which is the code used to create all web pages.

IDE (integrated drive electronics)
The current standard technology for transmitting data from a hard drive which can support up to two drives per cable. Most computers have two IDE cables so they can support four devices.

Intellectual property (IP)
A person or organisation's ideas, inventions or 'creativity' (for example, the work of writers or artists).

Intellectual property rights (IPR)
Protect a person or orgaisation's 'property' under the Copyright, Designs and Patents Act.

IRQ (interrupt request)
Peripheral devices gain attention from the CPU by placing a flag to show they need processing time; the CPU notices the flag, deals with the IRQ and then resets the flag.

ISDN
Integrated digital subscriber network.

ISP (internet service provider)
Includes btinternet, Demon and Yahoo!.

Iterative
An approach which involves revisiting a design as many times as necessary to produce the desired effect.

JPG
(Pronounced jay-peg) the term for the image format devised by the Joint Photographic Engineers Group. (The E was dropped for historical operating system reasons.)

Jumper
A small switch used to configure the hardware.

Kernel
The innermost area of the system.

Keylogger
Software which records every keystroke made.

Knowledge worker
Anyone whose job involves the development or use of knowledge, including anyone in ICT fields.

LAN
Local area network.

Landline
A fixed telephone connection at home or work, a connection that travels over terrestrial circuits.

LDAP (lightweight directory access protocol)
Technology not (yet) as widely used as OLE. It allows a system to share common 'directory' information with other systems, independent of its technology.

Linux
A free and open source operating system developed by Linus Torvald that can be installed on your computer. Because of the open source movement, there are many versions of Linux available and they all interact with each other.

Master
The storage device which is in control; in a computer the hard drive used to start the operating system.

Mbps (megabits per second)
A measurement which indicates how quickly data is transferred on a normal Ethernet network system.

Metatag
A piece of code used to instruct the browser as to how to display the content of the web page.

Modelling tools and techniques
Tools which can, for example, help perform advanced calculations, add rules to given sets of data, forecast and predict values for a given point in time.

Modem
An abbreviation for modulation/demodulation; a device which converts the signal that the computer creates into one that can be sent along the telephone line (this is called modulation), and then back again at the receiving end (called demodulation).

Motherboard
The body of the computer, supporting all the components that run in the computer system.

MPEG (pronounced em-peg)
The digital moving image format developed by the Movie Players Engineers Group.

Multimedia
Computer technology which integrates images (video, graphics, text) and sound to produce interactive and entertaining products.

Multi-user games
Designed to be played by a number of users, usually in real-time.

OLE (object linking and embedding)
A technology that enables, for example, a Microsoft Excel® spreadsheet to be imported into a Microsoft Word® document, or for a Word® document to be recognised by other applications. OLE is a standard feature of Microsoft applications. Other operating systems use OpenDoc to enable applications to 'see' each other.

One-to-many relationship
A relationship that can exist between records on two different tables. The 'one' end of the relationship table has individual records which can be related to many records on the other table, for example, in a doctors' surgery database each doctor on the Doctor table can be related to many patients on a Patient table.

Open source software
Software which anyone is free to use or adapt, on the understanding that they do not re-sell.

PDF (portable data format)
Documents in PDF format always retain their pagination and layout when you download them. This is not true of other formats, such as the .doc files created in Microsoft Word.

Personal data
Information about living, identifiable individuals. Personal data does not have to be particularly sensitive information and can be as little as name and address.

PnP (Plug 'n' Play)
A configuration standard which allows the BIOS and your operating system to recognise and automatically configure a peripheral as soon as you plug it into your computer.

Power surge (or power spike)
Can be caused by an anomaly in the electrical supply grid, for example a lightning strike. This results in a very large voltage for a very short period of time.

Private sector organisations
Organisations owned by individuals or shareholders. They range from self-employed people to large multinational corporations such as Ford, Sony and Tesco.

Prototype
An initial version of a website, showing the navigational links that are proposed and the overall design (use of colour and images to create a theme).

PDSU (power supply unit)
Provides electrical energy to the computer from the power source at the socket. It converts the incoming supply into one suited to each component, and also houses a fan used to cool the PC.

Public sector organisations
Organisations funded by the public through taxes providing services to the public. They are controlled by the government and are accountable to them and the public. Examples include schools, libraries, local councils, the police and the armed forces.

RAM
Random access memory; a type of memory that is lost when power is removed – also called volatile memory.

Real time
Refers to events that take place more or less immediately.

Registry key
A unique reference to a device or driver in the operating system.

Relational database
A database which uses a system of tables and links (called relationships) to store and manage large quantities of data.

Resolution
The number of pixels (image units) per image; the resolution offered by an average digital camera is 1024 × 768.

Rollover

An area on screen which, when the cursor is moved across it, something happens, like the area changes colour.

RS323

An American standard; the European equivalent is V.24. An RS323 port is a serial port.

RSI

An injury caused by a repetitive action in a limited range of movement (for example playing tennis or the guitar). In terms of computer use it can arise from poor typing technique and posture when typing.

RTF (rich text format)

A text format available for transfer of data independent of the system.

Screen grab (or screen shot)

An image created from the screen display.

Scrolling marquee

A message that moves across the screen, repeatedly.

SCSI (small computer serial interface)

A standard device used for higher speed systems, such as file and web servers. Some systems can support up to 15 hard drives.

SCSI (small computer systems interface)

An expansion card, installed on the motherboard, allows the PC to support more peripheral devices than the IDE channel. The SCSI then copes with the systems resources such as IRQs for the devices that are attached in this way.

Secure connection

A connection used to protect information (such as credit card numbers and personal information) as it is transmitted from the customer to a website. The data sent is encrypted so no one else can read it.

Semi-conductor

The electrically sensitive material used to make a central processor.

Serial ATA (or SATA)

Serial advanced technology attachment, a high speed technology now used for the transfer of hard drive data. Most newer, larger hard drives use SATA connections.

Service level agreement

A legal agreement that defines response time; level and method of technical support; whether you will get new for old, in the case of a fault; and the terms and duration of any repair warranty.

Service pack

An update to an operating system.

Shareware

Software that can be obtained and downloaded free of charge.

Shopping basket

An icon which serves the same purpose as a real shopping basket, i.e. you place the items you intend to buy inside the shopping basket and then, when you have finished shopping, you take it to the checkout to pay for your purchases.

SIMM (single in-line memory module)

A mini-expansion board. The edge connector has either 30 or 72 pins, and its capacity ranges from 1Mb to 16Mb.

Single user games

Games played individually.

Slave

Any additional storage device which resides in your computer system.

SME (small to medium business enterprise)

An organisation with a workforce of 5–25 employees.

Source code

The original programming code used in the development of a web page or an application.

Spam
Unsolicited or junk mail, which could carry a virus in an attachment.

Spyware
The name often given to advertising-supported software. This is normally used by shareware authors to get information on your computer habits and activities.

SRAM (static RAM)
A memory type in which the transistors do not need frequent refreshing to 'remember' the data it holds.

Stock control
The methods an organisation uses to track and record the stock it has.

Stock
The goods that a company has in storage which, in the case of a commercial organisation, is waiting to be sold.

Storyboard
A panel or a series of panels of rough sketches that can outline a sequence of events or activities in a story, normally associated with a plot or film production. A storyboard can be used in the initial stages of developing an e-book where rough ideas and designs can be sketched to form the basis of each page.

Structure chart
A geographical representation of the overall structure of a product, similar to an online site map.

Style sheet
Default styles used to format a document. They can be altered to a preferred style.

Surge suppressor
Protects a PC against problems with the external supply by taking the hit from any power surge.

Synchronise
Two devices ensure that they are holding the same common data.

Systems model
A model which defines the start of the system (its evolution), the mechanics of the system (how it works, etc.) and the completion of the system (what happens next).

Template
A master document that can be used again and again which contains basic information that can be changed for the particular circumstances.

TFT (thin film transistor)
The technology used in new flat panel and note-book computer displays.

Toolbar
The list of icons you will see at the top, bottom, left or possibly right hand side of any application.

Transaction
An agreement to provide goods or services in exchange for payment.

Transactional website
A site where visitors can complete some kind of transaction, such as ordering and paying for goods or services. Other types include sites provided by banks, where customers can check their account balance, transfer money and pay bills.

Transistor
A micro-circuit switch, like the one which turns on your light, but at a considerably smaller level.

Trojan
A virus which infiltrates a PC by pretending to be a file or program that would normally be found on a PC. It is designed to allow others unauthorised access to your computer. It can cause problems and, because it is 'disguised', it can be difficult to track down.

UHF (ultra high frequency)
A method of describing the way the television signal is carried.

URL (uniform resource locator)

Often the address of a file that holds the HTML code for a web page. However, it can also specify a file holding an image, or some other resource needed within a website such as a sound track or video sequence.

Utility

A useful program, often supplied with a PC, or you may purchase it from a specialised vendor. Utilities do things like rid the memory of unneeded temporary files and tidy up how files are stored within the hard disk.

Vector

A numerical store of information about an image, it holds only two coordinates for each shape. Although vectors take very little time to download, you need additional software to view them (e.g. Flash Player).

Video conferencing

A communication technique using audio and video links to allow remote groups of people to have a 'virtual' meeting.

Virtual Learning Environment (VLE)

An environment that has been set-up to promote online learning based on flexibility and choice.

Virus

A file which will inflict some form of damage to your computer system; like a medical virus, it can self-replicate, infiltrating your computer from another infected computer.

Visual basic extension

Data that can be linked to a variety of other computer, software and operating systems.

W3C

A forum for information, commerce, communication and collective understanding. It develops material – such as specifications, guidelines, software and tools – to lead the Web to its full potential.

WAN

Wide area network.

Web authoring software

Software which helps the user create web pages and links to other sites, and enables the transfer of the website to the WWW.

Web server

A computer which runs software that responds to requests to display web pages.

Webmaster

The person who looks after a website on a day-to-day basis. He or she will make changes to the website – or supervise others who do the work – to improve the site and to fix any problems that arise.

Wireless

A radio-based communication system which can reach up to 100 metres.

Worm

A malicious program that can move itself from computer to computer via e-mail or the internet.

Y-splitter

A connector that allows you to run two cables together so that they only need one power source.

ZIF (zero insertion force)

A no-strain connector for a processor on a motherboard.

Zip

A program which uses compression techniques to reduce the size of a file, without losing any data within the file.

INDEX

Windows
  checking system   164
  computer management   166
  control panel   138
  displaying file extensions   252
  e–mails   244, 246
    tutorial   248
  emergency repair disk
          226–8
  operating system   125
    management   138–9
    security   137
    support   139
    system tune–up   166
  operating systems   135
  Outlook Rules Wizard   244
  Recovery Console   228–9
  system restore   226–9
  Task Manager   226
  upgrading   237–9
  utilities   225–9
  see also Microsoft
wireless technologies   3, 5–6

networks (WLAN)   5, 6, 144, 149
wizards   70–2, 76, 106, 111
word processing   108–10
  checking documents   109–10
  importing data   108
word processing software
          128
  OpenOffice.org   134
  Word   128, 130
working
  flexible locations   7
  standard ways of   ix–xviii
  styles   19
workstation layout   19, 152
  ergonomic   149, 150–1
worms   137, 251, 252

x-drive   17

Y-splitter   232

ZIF connector 155
zip files   246, 247